BEYOND PRESERVATION

IN THE SERIES *Urban Life, Landscape and Policy,*
EDITED BY ZANE L. MILLER, DAVID STRADLING, AND LARRY BENNETT

ALSO IN THIS SERIES

William Issel, *For Both Cross and Flag: Catholic Action, Anti-Catholicism, and National Security Politics in World War II San Francisco*

Lisa Hoffman, *Patriotic Professionalism in Urban China: Fostering Talent*

John D. Fairfield, *The Public and Its Possibilities: Triumphs and Tragedies in the American City*

BEYOND PRESERVATION

Using Public History to Revitalize Inner Cities

Andrew Hurley

TEMPLE UNIVERSITY PRESS PHILADELPHIA

Temple University Press
www.temple.edu/tempress

Copyright © 2010 by Temple University
All rights reserved
Published 2010

Portions of this book originally appeared in Tim Baumann, Andrew Hurley,
and Lori Allen, "Economic Stability and Social Identity: Historic Preservation
in Old North St. Louis," *Historical Archaeology* 42 (Winter 2008): 70–87, and in
Andrew Hurley, "Narrating the Urban Waterfront: The Role of Public History
in Community Revitalization," *Public Historian* 28 (Fall 2006): 19–50; © 2006 by
the Regents of the University of California and the National Council on Public
History. Reprinted with permission.

Library of Congress Cataloging-in-Publication Data

Hurley, Andrew, 1961–
    Beyond preservation : using public history to revitalize inner cities / Andrew
Hurley.
        p. cm. — (Urban life, landscape and policy)
    Includes bibliographical references and index.
    ISBN 978-1-4399-0228-8 (cloth : alk. paper) — ISBN 978-1-4399-0229-5
(pbk. : alk. paper)
    1. Urban renewal—United States.   2. Historic preservation—United States.
3. Public history—United States.   4. Community development—United States.
I. Title.
    HT175.H87 2010
    307.3'4160973—dc22   2009047690

Printed in the United States of America

100711-P

For Kathryn, the love of my life

Contents

Preface

This book aims to make historic preservation a more effective instrument for revitalizing inner-city neighborhoods through the strategic use of public history. Across the United States, historic preservation has become a catalyst for urban regeneration. Entrepreneurs, urban pioneers, and veteran city dwellers have refurbished thousands of dilapidated properties and put them to productive use as shops, restaurants, nightclubs, museums, and private residences. As a result, inner cities—once disparaged as zones of poverty, crime, and decay—have been rebranded as historic districts. While these preservation initiatives, often supported by government tax incentives and rigid architectural controls, deserve credit for bringing people back to the city, raising property values, and generating tourist revenue, they have been less successful in creating stable and harmonious communities. Historic preservation has enormous potential for enriching the urban experience. At its best, it not only invigorates local economies but strengthens communities by nurturing a deeper attachment to place, greater levels of social cohesion, and a collective agenda for local development. At its worst, however, it operates as a mechanism of capitalistic opportunism and aggravates social tensions by pricing the poor out of their own neighborhoods.

The central argument of this book is that inner-city communities can best turn preserved landscapes into assets by subjecting them to public interpretation at the grass roots. Bereft of interpretation, recycled buildings lose their capacity to anchor people in the flow of time and to expose relationships between the past and present. Only when associated with stories and imbued with meaning do yesterday's material remains acquire the capacity to articulate shared values and visions. Only through careful analysis of previous uses and functions can communities build intelligently on what previous generations left behind. Only by acknowledging the full array of social forces that contributed over time to the uniqueness of urban places can city dwellers cultivate an inclusive sense of belonging and ownership that translates into collective stewardship. Yet buildings cannot speak for themselves. For all the inspiration, money, and sweat that have gone into salvaging aged structures and putting them to productive use, "we have not quite figured out," in the words of Rebecca Conard, "how to utilize historic buildings, structures, sites, and objects to communicate effectively the complex process of cultural layering on the landscape"[1] Fortunately, many of the tools we need are at our disposal because of developments in the fields of public history and archaeology. By adopting these best practices and more carefully aligning historical narratives with locally derived agendas for change, historic preservation can engage urban populations as self-conscious agents in the reproduction and revitalization of urban places.

Beyond Preservation is written from an "in-the-trenches" perspective of a participant-observer. Since 2000, I have had the good fortune to work on a variety of community-based history projects under the auspices of the Public Policy Research Center at the University of Missouri–St. Louis. As part of its mission to produce and disseminate methodologically sound research for broader civic purposes, the Research Center links a variety of local nonprofit organizations and government agencies to university faculty with relevant expertise. Hoping to take advantage of new state laws that offered generous tax credits for property rehabilitation in historic districts, several inner-city neighborhood organizations approached the Research Center for assistance in identifying and publicizing their historical attributes. In response to these requests, an archaeologist colleague, Timothy Baumann, and I established the Community History Research and Design Services (CHRDS) unit of the Public Policy Research Center in 2003. Through our activities in CHRDS, we developed and refined a model for involving residents in historical research that complemented preservation and community planning goals.

In crafting local-history projects, we drew heavily on the experiences and insights of others engaged in similar work in different parts of the country. This book documents many of the projects that influenced and inspired our efforts in St. Louis and serves as a catalogue of innovative practices in the fields of public history and, to a lesser extent, public archaeology. Just as CHRDS profited from lessons learned elsewhere, those with like-minded goals may benefit by reading about our strategies, mistakes, and accomplishments. In this capacity, *Beyond Preservation* contributes to an ongoing dialogue among professionals and scholars in the fields of historic preservation, public history, public archaeology, and urban history. Although several professional organizations do an excellent job of circulating information within these respective fields through newsletters, journals, conferences, and Web sites, there are surprisingly few channels of communications that cut across them.

This book was originally conceived as a collaborative venture between me and Timothy Baumann. Jointly, we developed and organized several CHRDS projects that blended archaeology and history. The germ of this book was an article we coauthored on a community-history project in a North St. Louis neighborhood. It appeared in the Spring 2008 issue of *Historical Archaeology*, and portions of that article appear in different parts of this book. Unfortunately, a change in job venues and responsibilities prevented Tim from continuing the collaboration through the writing of the full manuscript. As a result, the sections about archaeology are more abbreviated than originally intended. Nonetheless, this book begins to puncture the long-standing communication firewall separating the related but distinct fields of public archaeology and public history.

Although the approach outlined in this book can be adapted readily to many kinds of places, it applies most directly to inner-city neighborhoods in the United States. CHRDS has concentrated its activities in the core areas of a major metropolis; hence the prescriptions offered in this book spring from inner-city settings. Personal experience aside, there are good reasons why such environments merit special attention. In recent years, preservationists have focused their efforts and scored their biggest victories in downtown districts and their surrounding neighborhoods. Thus, the inner city represents fertile terrain for expanding on recent successes and further broadening the scope of preservation. Moreover, the continued revival of the urban core remains vital to the sustainability of metropolitan regions. For too many years, cities have bled investment and population to the greenfields of suburbia. The result has been an environmentally destructive and socially fragmenting pattern of metropolitan development, commonly referred to as sprawl. Although it would be foolish to argue that inner-city environments have any more inherent historic value than their suburban counterparts, their preservation and regeneration offer greater possibilities for managing natural resources efficiently and integrating diverse urban constituencies and cultures more tightly within a cohesive whole.

Advocating interpretive frameworks that speak directly to the issues confronting inner-city neighborhoods and seeking to build on preservation methods already operating in these places requires some understanding of the dynamics that gave rise to current conditions and practices. Hence, this book is as much urban history as it is prescriptive analysis; the approaches recommended herein are placed directly in the broader context of urban developments over the past half-century. Thus, the opening chapter traces the evolution of historic preservation as an urban revitalization strategy, with particular emphasis on the period after World War II. During these years, preservation gained currency as an alternative to urban renewal, and its effectiveness became increasingly measured according to economic criteria. What was sacrificed, however, was preservation's capacity to facilitate a constructive dialogue between past and present and unify people around a shared civic vision. As a result, neighborhood rehabilitation caused considerable social disruption and conflict. Chapter 2 expands the historical perspective by describing how a more democratic brand of public history and public archaeology emerged from the intellectual ferment and social revolutions of the 1960s and 1970s. Some of the most exciting projects constructed in this mold sought to strengthen people's attachment to place by employing the built environment as the primary vehicle for communicating history to present-day audiences. Thus far, however, there have been few attempts to use public history in the pursuit of specific community-development goals.

Chapter 3 documents an initiative on the north side of St. Louis that sought to revitalize a distressed neighborhood by merging historic preservation with cutting-edge practices in public archaeology and history. Under the auspices of a U. S. Housing and Urban Development Community Outreach Partnership Center grant, faculty, staff, and students from the University of Missouri–St. Louis collaborated with a neighborhood organization to develop a series of programs that attracted fresh investment, established a sense of neighborhood identity, and stabilized the population without sacrificing its social diversity. The project was unusual in granting primary authority over research design and interpretation to local residents rather than professionally trained scholars. A consideration of the project's accomplishments and shortcomings introduces readers to some of the issues confronting public historians who seek collaboration with inner-city communities in preservation-based revitalization projects.

Chapters 4, 5, and 6 address selected challenges and opportunities associated with the public interpretation of historic urban landscapes. These chapters draw on projects in other parts of the country in addition to several in St. Louis. Chapter 4 explores the challenge of aligning public-history-based preservation initiatives with community planning efforts. Chapter 5 argues for a more comprehensive approach to landscape preservation by considering the role of the natural environment in historical development and community revitalization. Chapter 6 considers some of the difficulties associated with reaching consensus in historical interpretation across the professional, ethnic, racial, and class divides that commonly characterize university-community partnerships.

The book concludes with some suggestions for developing public-history projects that contribute to economic revitalization through historic preservation and social stabilization. If not exactly a road map, as no two cities or even neighborhoods warrant the same approach, Chapter 7 offers some general principles and techniques worthy of consideration.

Understandably, some readers may be wary of a book written from such a subjective stance. I recognize the inevitable conflict between the goal of critical analysis and my personal investment in a particular brand of historic preservation. To guard against this bias, I have attempted to ground my argumentation in a wider literature and—wherever possible—note the limitations as well as the benefits of the strategies endorsed here. At the same time, I make no apologies for measuring public history and preservation endeavors against a model of grassroots preservation activity that I have played some role in shaping. I will leave it to readers to judge my dexterity in performing this balancing act.

It should come as no surprise that in writing a book about collaborative projects I have relied heavily on the assistance and support of others. It is a great pleasure to be able to thank them here. The University of Missouri–St. Louis has provided a supportive environment for conducting work that often falls beyond the orbit of acceptable scholarly activity. Alan Artibise and Mark Tranel, directors of the University's Public Policy Research Center, graciously provided CHRDS with resources and an institutional home. Kay Gasen and Lynn Josse were of invaluable help in cultivating constructive relationships with community partners and generating publicity for CHRDS activities through a variety of conferences and symposiums. Through the generosity of the Research Center and other external funding sources, I have had the good fortune to work with some wonderful graduate research assistants, including Chris Hanks, Ryan Flahive, Dan Goodman, Loren McLane, Justin McKnight, Justin Watkins, Elizabeth Perkins, and Raymond Perkins. Benjamin Israel deserves special mention for doggedly tracking down information about innovative public-history and preservation initiatives across the nation. Jay Rounds, director of the University's Museum Studies program, helped keep me abreast of community-engagement initiatives in the world of museums.

Beyond the University of Missouri–St. Louis, many friends and professional colleagues made important contributions. I gained a wealth of insights about urban development and public-history practices through casual conversations with Joseph Heathcott, Mark Tebeau, Andre Odendaal, Eric Sandweiss, Sylvia Washington, Chris Wilson, and Marci Reaven. Patricia Cleary, Laura Lyon, Caleb Carter, and Ellen Thomasson helped me procure photographs for this book. Two journals, *The Public Historian* and *Historical Archaeology*, published earlier versions of portions of this manuscript.

Elsewhere in this preface I mentioned my partnership with Tim Baumann, cofounder of CHRDS, now at Indiana University, but I cannot overstate his contribution to this book. Not only did he do as much as anyone to shepherd the various community projects we initiated in St. Louis, but he was instrumental in crafting the approach to public history described in this book. I deeply regret that we were unable to carry through on our original intention to write this book together.

The editors and staff at Temple University Press have been a joy to work with. I thank Mick Gusinde-Duffy for helping me make some critical editorial decisions and for guiding the manuscript through the review and production process smoothly. Series editors David Stradling, Zane Miller, and Larry Bennett made the usually difficult decision of choosing a publisher an easy one by displaying extraordinary enthusiasm and confidence in this project as it neared its final stages. Along with two external readers, Max Page and the anonymous Reader B, David and Zane also read through the entire manuscript and offered sound editorial criticism.

This book surely would not have been written were it not for all the dedicated citizens of St. Louis who agreed to embark on public-history projects in conjunction with the University of Missouri–St. Louis. Without question, my best education in public history came from my conversations and interactions with neighborhood residents and community representatives in the City of St. Louis. To thank each of them by name would consume dozens of pages, but at the risk of excluding and perhaps offending many who donated significant time and energy, I would like to publicly acknowledge the following community volunteers: Carole Gates, Susan Tschetter, Gloria Bratkowski, Johnnie Owens, Alvin Willis, Pamela Talley, Mattie Divine, Ernestine Isaiah, Geraldine Finch, Jackie Jaekels, William Perry, Linda Coleman, Kenneth and Clara Coleman, Columbus Edwards, Shirley Leflore, Thomasina Clarke, Sylvia Bennett, Andra Lee, Sheryl Robnett, and Glenn Haley. In addition, the staff members of several community organizations were indispensible to the work described in this book, and so I owe a debt of gratitude to Doug Eller of Grace Hill Settlement House, Sean Thomas and Diane Roche of the Old North St. Louis Restoration Group, Irving Blue and Ralph

Martinez of the Forest Park Southeast Development Corporation, and Vikki Love and Almetta Jordan of the Scott Joplin House State Historical Site.

I have saved my most heartfelt acknowledgement for last. My wife, Kathryn Hurley, has added to this project in so many ways. This book has benefited directly from her exquisite editorial guidance and her fine cartographic skills. Her companionship, patience, encouragement, and wise counsel were no less instrumental in bringing this book to fruition. Writing it certainly would have been a much lonelier process without her, and I will remain forever grateful for her willingness to share my exhilaration and frustrations throughout this roller-coaster endeavor. It is with great delight and love that I dedicate this book to her.

1

Preservation in the Inner City

American cities hit rock bottom in the early 1970s. Affluent white families had fled en masse to the suburbs, leaving behind racial minorities and the poor. Manufacturers had abandoned the city as well, depriving urban populations of what had long been the major source of decent-paying jobs and tax revenue. Strapped for cash, municipal governments slashed basic services and still came perilously close to bankruptcy. Crime rates soared while property values plummeted. It was the era of urban crisis, and the future of the city looked bleak. Nowhere was the demise of urban America more visible than in the older residential areas surrounding central business districts. Here, weed-strewn lots, crumbling buildings, broken windows, and graffiti-covered walls presented overwhelming and unmistakable evidence of decay, despair, and obsolescence.

Despite these stark signs of decline, inner cities did not spiral into oblivion. Thirty years later, in one city after another, the same neighborhoods that appeared on the verge of total collapse were held up as proof of a vibrant "back-to-the-city" movement. In Savannah, St. Paul, Denver, Pittsburgh, Seattle, Portland, and St. Louis, the story was much the same: new investment and new residents poured into the districts on the edge of downtown, spurring the rehabilitation of century-old homes, stores, and warehouses. The inner city had become the historic core; its aged infrastructure, once its greatest liability, had become its strongest asset. Cities enjoyed a new lease on life by virtue of what made them most distinctive—their rich history.

The comeback of urban America, particularly the resurgence of the historic core, is often attributed to the historic-preservation movement. The basic principle of historic preservation—that it is better to save old buildings than to tear them down—certainly contributed to the urban renaissance by allowing older areas to showcase their history. In an age of globalization where landscapes have become increasingly standardized, those areas that have managed to stand out from the homogenized mainstream have gained a decisive edge in the competition for people's attention and interest. By helping to cultivate a unique "sense of place," historic preservation has made the urban core an attractive site for tourism, residential living, and fresh investment.

Historic preservation has not been an unmitigated success, however. In particular, it has fallen short in fostering stable and strong communities. The economic vitality attributed to successful preservation campaigns in and around downtown has not always translated into a sense of belonging or purpose for people who live and work there. Likewise, the manipulation of history for profit has not always fortified the social connections that alert people to their shared responsibilities. Indeed, in some places, historic preservation has inflamed existing social tensions, thereby destabilizing communities.

It would be a mistake, however, to invoke these adverse consequences in a blanket indictment of historic preservation or to conclude that the strategy is incapable of improving urban social relations. In philosophy and practice, historic preservation has evolved considerably over the past two centuries. As an explicit revitalization strategy it can be traced to the decades after World War II, when it emerged as an alternative to urban renewal and the wanton destruction of the physical environment. In the midst of urban crisis, the allure of preservation was based on its promise to restore what urban renewal could not: the economic viability of cities. Thus, in recent years, preservation initiatives have been assessed primarily in terms of their economic impact. Yet historic preservation as a practice boasts a much longer history with varied roots and traditions that speak to other dimensions of the urban condition, including the formation of community identities and the strengthening of social relations. As the most widely employed means of delivering history through the urban landscape, historic preservation stands poised to make a much greater contribution to the amelioration of urban woes than ever before. For it to do so, however, requires us to reevaluate its strengths and weakness within a broad historical and social context.

Preservation Becomes a Revitalization Strategy

The earliest preservation campaigns in the United States had little to do with saving urban neighborhoods. Early in the nineteenth century, guardians of the nation's heritage thought in terms of individual buildings rather than entire districts. The most heralded triumphs in the years before the Civil War involved the protection of rural estates such as Mount Vernon, George Washington's homestead, and the Hermitage, Andrew Jackson's birthplace. The urban preservation movement picked up momentum after 1870 when rapid development within eastern-seaboard cities threatened many prominent buildings from the colonial era. Still, the focus remained on solitary structures, especially those that perpetuated the memory of Revolutionary War heroes and their struggle for liberty. Having let John Hancock's home slip through their fingers, Bostonians marshaled their forces more effectively when urban development imperiled the Old Statehouse, the Old South Meetinghouse, and the Bullfinch State House. Philadelphians rallied to the defense of Betsy Ross's home even though many scholars disputed her claim to fame—sewing the first American flag—and there were no records documenting her occupation of the house in question. Anyplace that George Washington slept, ate, or burped became a structure worth saving during the late nineteenth and early twentieth centuries. New York City was typical in this regard; its early preservation triumphs included the Morris-Jumel Mansion, where Washington was headquartered for part of the Revolutionary War, and Fraunces Tavern, the site of George Washington's farewell address to his officers in 1784.[1]

Williamsburg, Virginia is often cited as the first example of district-wide preservation. As the colonial capital of Virginia from 1699 to the end of the American Revolution, Williamsburg was an important and thriving town. But when the capital was moved to Richmond, Williamsburg stagnated and many of its historic buildings fell into disrepair. However dilapidated, many of the town's original buildings were still standing in the 1920s when the local minister, Reverend William Goodwin, launched a campaign to return Williamsburg to its colonial-era glory. In 1926 Goodwin scored a coup when he convinced oil magnate John D. Rockefeller, Jr., to bankroll the project. With nearly 80 million dollars at their disposal, archaeologists, architects, and historians set about restoring existing buildings and reconstructing replicas of those that had been demolished. Although Goodwin, Rockefeller, and their allies wanted tourists to visit their restored colonial town, they did not conceive the enterprise primarily as a moneymaking venture. Rather they saw its value as educational, important for "the lesson it teaches of the patriotism, high purpose, and unselfish devotion of our forefathers to the common good," as Rockefeller explained.[2] The ambitious mission and vast scope of Colonial Williamsburg certainly excited the imagination of America's preservationists, but few communities had the resources to undertake anything on that scale.

If Williamsburg provided inspiration for comprehensive urban preservation, it was Charleston, South Carolina that developed a more workable model, one that did not require a rich benefactor like Rockefeller. Like Williamsburg, Charleston boasted a glorious colonial past. Carolina's thriving plantation economy, based on oppressive slave labor, generated tremendous wealth during the eighteenth century, much of which was funneled into Charleston, the region's primary port city. There, planters and merchants built lavish homes in the then fashionable Georgian, Federal, and Classical Revival styles. Charleston's prosperity extended into the antebellum years, but it too lapsed into a long period of economic decline. There was an upside to poverty, however; Charlestonians simply could not afford to replace their old buildings with newer ones. By the time a legitimate threat appeared in the 1920s in the form of oil companies looking to place gasoline filling stations on properties occupied by aging homes and northern antique collectors eager to strip antebellum mansions of their grillwork and paneling, local citizens had fallen in love with their architectural relics. Indeed, they had become the cornerstone of civic identity. The tactic they devised to save their cherished landmarks—historic zoning—was revolutionary. A 1931 ordinance subjected modifications to building exteriors within a prescribed historic district to review by a board of local citizens. Charleston's Board of Architectural Review then made a recommendation as to whether the proposed modification violated the integrity of the historic landscape.[3]

Although Charleston's ordinance did not invest its review board with anything more than "advisory" power, subsequent adopters of the Charleston approach gave their arbitration panels stronger police powers. A major turning point was the 1954 U. S. Supreme Court ruling in *Berman v. Parker*, which held that local governments had the right to demolish blighted properties for the sake of improving neighborhood appearance. On the face of it, the decision seemed detrimental to preservation since it made it easier for public authorities to tear down old buildings that stood in the way of urban-renewal projects. Yet by establishing the principle that local zoning could be based on aesthetic considerations alone, the high court allowed preservationists to turn the logic on its head and defend the safeguarding of historic structures on the basis of their contribution to neighborhood beautification. Across the country, cities seized on this legal justification to arm architectural review boards with greater powers of enforcement.[4]

While preservationists' tactics and tools evolved considerably between the 1870s and the 1930s, their motivations remained fairly consistent. From Boston to Charleston preservationists cast themselves as defenders of their city's heritage—indeed, the nation's heritage—against the incursions of an amoral real estate market. Preservationists did not dispute that land occupied by old churches, meetinghouses, and mansions might be put to more productive economic use. That was not the issue. What was at stake was something much more valuable, the tangible reminders of history. Indeed, it was unrestrained economic growth that threatened America's material connection to the past. Preservation thus pitted history against the market.

To fully appreciate the early preservationist perspective, it is important to understand how it served an elitist social and cultural agenda. The leading preservationists of the late nineteenth century represented old wealth. Their status, however, derived less from their fortunes, which in many cases were dwindling, than from their lineage. Many were direct descendants of Revolutionary War heroes and aristocratic antebellum planters. In saving historic buildings associated with the feats and prestige of their grandparents and great-grandparents, they hoped to assert a cultural authority that was under assault from a rising capitalist class. By the turn of the twentieth century, the crusade to save historic structures gained greater urgency and a broader middle-class constituency—doctors, lawyers, ministers, professionals—as millions of foreigners filled America's cities with their "uncivilized" and potentially undemocratic traditions. By trumpeting a colonial or even early-nineteenth-century past, preservation legitimized the superiority of Anglo-Saxon culture and became an instrument of social reform. A cityscape defined by highly visible historic landmarks provided an antidote to the disorder of unrestrained capitalism and its social underside: slums, corruption, congestion, ugliness, and unsanitary conditions. Conveying powerful messages about cultural authority and the proper direction of future development, it was decidedly didactic. Preservation thus placed history in the service of a larger civic goal: the perpetuation of an urban social order controlled by an Anglo elite.[5]

Only a few cities went against the grain and pursued preservation strictly for economic reasons. Yet in so doing, they pioneered an alternative model that eventually gained traction as an antidote to late-twentieth-century urban woes. Santa Fe, New Mexico was the first. With its economy in the doldrums in 1912, the city devised a plan to promote tourism through the widespread adoption of a distinctive and exotic architectural style. Harkening back to a

Figure 1-1. *San Francisco Street, Santa Fe, New Mexico.* In the early twentieth century, Santa Fe became the first city in the United States to promote a uniform architectural aesthetic for the purposes of reviving a moribund economy. The ubiquity of adobe facades continues to give the city a distinctive appearance and sense of identity. *(Courtesy of the author.)*

Spanish and Native American past, new buildings presented a homogenous adobe stucco appearance. Although city planners failed to secure legislation that would enforce conformity to specific architectural standards until 1957, the idea enjoyed such overwhelming community support that most builders adopted it willingly. What became known as "Santa Fe style" proved instrumental in making the city a tourist mecca (see Figure 1-1). In this variant of preservation, aesthetics trumped historical authenticity. Unlike preservation campaigns in other cities, Santa Fe's experiment had more to do with the design of new structures than the condition of old structures. What was being preserved was an architectural tradition.[6]

Although Santa Fe introduced the concept of showcasing a distinctive architecture style to attract tourists, New Orleans became the more widely emulated model. New Orleans followed Charleston as the second city in the nation to create a local historic district. In 1936, a state referendum authorized the city to review all modifications to building exteriors within the area of the original French colonial settlement, known as the Vieux Carré. In the many years since the Louisiana Purchase, the importance of the Vieux Carré had been eclipsed by the adjacent central business district. Yet as the era of French and Spanish control receded into the remote past, the original French Quarter—with its unique architectural style characterized by shuttered windows, courtyards, and iron balconies—became an object of local admiration, especially among the artists and writers who came to inhabit the area shortly after World War I. With the active support of several women's clubs, they spearheaded a campaign to save the district from rail development and industrial encroachment. As visitors flocked to New Orleans over the next several decades in ever-greater numbers, the economic impact of preservation became apparent. Largely because of the exotic atmosphere of the French Quarter, New Orleans ranked as one of the nation's leading tourist destinations by the 1960s. Other cities looking to replicate its success aspired to assemble comparable packages of waterfront amenities, public markets, and street festivals bound within an identifiable and memorable preserved landscape.[7]

During the 1950s, preservationists in the College Hill section of Providence, Rhode Island and the Georgetown district of Washington, DC demonstrated that preservation could also be used to boost residential property values and turn slums into middle class havens. As in many other cases, the preservation campaign in the College Hill neighborhood grew out of an imminent threat. In 1951, Brown University embarked on a plan to expand its facilities into the surrounding neighborhood, which required the demolition of many old, dilapidated homes. In response, a group of local citizens formed the Providence Preservation Society, not simply with the mission of saving precious colonial homes but of bringing economic stability to "an old and graceful section of the city." This revitalization objective proved popular with city officials at a time when Providence was suffering from a declining tax base and few prospects for new investment. The idea of transforming College Hill into a middle-class neighborhood had already occurred to city planners, who advocated the demolition of old homes and the construction of new ones. Preservationists offered a different route to the same end: the rehabilitation of existing homes. Through the intervention of private real estate companies funded by stock sales, buyers purchased homes that possessed desirable architectural features, fixed them up, and resold them to affluent families. The results of this "planned gentrification" exceeded expectations as restored homes doubled in value.[8]

Early in the twentieth century, the Georgetown district of Washington, DC was renowned for its ramshackle alley houses that provided cheap lodging for a poor African American population. An influx of government workers

Figure 1-2. *Georgetown Homes, Washington, DC.* Georgetown's transition from a socially mixed neighborhood to an elite residential enclave resulted from the preservation of its Federal-style homes in the 1950s. *(Courtesy of the author.)*

during the New Deal era diversified the neighborhood's social mix somewhat, but as late as the 1940s Georgetown rents were sufficiently low to make it a magnet for struggling artists and bohemian types. With Congressional passage of the Old Georgetown Act in 1950, however, the character of the neighborhood began to change rather dramatically. Aimed at stemming further commercial development and the incursion of multifamily dwelling units, the Act authorized a review process for any new construction as well as for most exterior modifications on existing buildings. Through these regulatory mechanisms, Georgetown cultivated a uniform architectural aesthetic consistent with its antebellum Federal-style homes (see Figure 1-2). The most notable consequence was a dramatic surge in property values and rents that turned the district into a picturesque enclave for affluent white people.[9] The upgrading of College Hill and Georgetown were heralded in the press, and both areas established important precedents for an approach to preservation that relied on enhancing the economic value of old buildings rather than on removing them from the real estate market.

Despite these successful and nationally lauded examples of economically driven preservation, the National Historic Preservation Act of 1966 was not conceived as either an economic development or an urban revitalization program. A direct response to the excesses of urban renewal and the threat it posed to buildings with historic value, it aimed to halt the destruction of America's architectural heritage. That the law would eventually become an instrument for resolving the nation's urban crisis could not have been anticipated by its creators; its profound contribution to the late-twentieth-century urban renaissance was the product of largely unforeseen social, cultural, and economic currents operating in conjunction with subsequent policy directives. Of particular importance to the fate of inner-city neighborhoods was the creation of the National Register of Historic Places. Properties receiving national registry designation were guaranteed at least a review process if any project relying on federal funds threatened their integrity. Reflecting the trend away from targeting isolated landmarks, the law provided for the inclusion of districts on the national register. Districts might be as small as a block or as large as an entire neighborhood. To qualify for historic-district status, the area in question had to meet certain standards. First, the buildings within the district had to exhibit or represent some unifying feature. A neighborhood unable to define its historic significance coherently was unlikely to secure approval from the state historic-preservation offices that were charged with administering the program. Second, the nominated district had to meet the law's criteria for historic significance. Accordingly, there were several grounds on which a neighborhood might stake its claim: by virtue of association with important events or individuals, by expressing distinctive types of architecture, or by serving as repositories for important information in prehistory or history. Although the register was a national one in the sense that it accumulated entries from across the United States, successful classification did not require demonstration of national importance; local or regional importance was considered sufficient. Under these provisions, hundreds if not thousands of urban neighborhoods might reasonably claim eligibility. Still, historical significance stood at the core of the nomination process; the potential for urban regeneration was considered irrelevant.

Even if the 1966 law was first and foremost an attempt to nourish a historical consciousness, its authors were by no means oblivious to its potential for improving urban life and reviving urban economies. It is doubtful that the law would have been passed at all had not urban renewal been severely discredited as a revitalization strategy. The basic premise behind urban renewal, as most people came to understand the term, was that by offering a fresh slate for redevelopment at rock-bottom prices, local governments would lure private investors and middle-class residents back to the inner city.[10] The acceleration of population and capital flight to the suburbs in the years immediately following World War II convinced urban planners and politicians that drastic action was necessary; cities would have to be remade from the ground up. That meant tearing down grimy tenement districts and replacing them with gleaming apartment towers surrounded by ample green space. It also required easing traffic congestion in and out of the central business district with high-speed, limited-access freeways.[11]

Drawing up plans to improve the appeal and efficiency of cities was a relatively painless enterprise, but their implementation was far beyond the budgetary capacity of most cities. The breakthrough came with a series of laws that made federal resources available for urban reconstruction. Under the provisions of the Housing Act of 1949, cities could establish local redevelopment agencies with the authority to acquire blighted properties, demolish all structures on them, and then sell them to private developers at discount prices. Federal funds covered most of the write-down cost, that is, the gap between the cost of acquiring and clearing the land and income received when the property was sold at below-market rates. Congressional passage of the 1956 Interstate Highway Act seven years later provided cities with a similar windfall. By shifting the financial burden of road building to the federal government, cities could now construct wheel-and-spoke highway systems that connected a series of circumferential beltways with radial arteries emanating from the central business district.[12]

Eventually, these policies contributed to the revitalization of America's downtown districts. Most of the hotels, convention centers, office towers, and luxury apartments funded by renewal mechanisms sprouted on recently cleared land in or near central business districts. Highways made downtown districts more accessible and provided direct connections to the more remote high-tech industries and research institutions that increasingly drove the metropolitan economy. Although the recovery period took longer than many expected and major retail functions were lost permanently to the suburbs, downtowns nonetheless emerged from the postwar era in decent shape.[13]

These same policies, however, had disastrous consequences for the older residential areas fringing the central core. Through the mechanism of Title I of the Housing Act, urban redevelopment obliterated entire neighborhoods. Between 1949 and 1967, 383,000 dwelling units surrendered to the wrecking ball and more than 600,000 residents were displaced from their homes. African Americans constituted 80 percent of these refugees, a statistic that led many critics of the federal program to label urban renewal "Negro Removal."[14] Because one of the ostensible goals of the Housing Act was to guarantee "a decent home and suitable living environment" for every American family, the federal government assumed the responsibility for providing shelter for at least a portion of those displaced from cleared districts. Yet between passage of the law and 1955, the federal government funded only 200,000 public housing units, not nearly enough to compensate for all of those whose homes were destroyed and far less than the 800,000 units originally planned.[15] Adding insult to injury, new highways slashed through those residential districts spared by redevelopment, gobbling up acres of occupied homes and active businesses and fragmenting once-cohesive neighborhoods. In the rare instances when citizens voiced their disapproval, city governments plowed ahead anyway, dismissing criticism as shortsighted and selfish.[16] Although the 1954 amendments to the Housing Act gave a nod in the direction of community involvement by making "citizen participation" a prerequisite for receiving urban-renewal funds, the advisory boards pulled together by city governments did little more than ratify the decisions already made by local planning agencies.[17]

As the destructive impact of urban surgery became apparent, public opinion shifted dramatically, leading ultimately to a rejection of the "demolish and rebuild" philosophy. Jane Jacobs, an architectural critic, fired the first penetrating blow to federal urban-renewal policies with the publication of her best seller *The Death and Life of Great American Cities* in 1961. Where planners and politicians looked at old inner-city neighborhoods and saw urban blight, Jacobs saw visual appeal, pedestrian-friendly streetscapes, lively social interaction, and the incubation of entrepreneurial skill. In tearing down vast expanses of the historic core, urban renewal sucked the social and economic life out of cities.[18] A year later, the sociologist Herbert Gans corroborated the Jacobs thesis by documenting in *The Urban Villagers* the destruction of Boston's vibrant West End neighborhood at the hands of federal renewal policy.[19] Charles Abrams offered a slightly different but equally damning critique with the publication of *The City is the Frontier* in 1965. In this empirical assessment of urban renewal from an economic perspective, Abrams concluded that federal policy stimulated very little in the way of new investment.[20] Jacobs, Gans, and Abrams assailed urban renewal from the left, but the right was no less critical. According to Columbia University professor Martin Anderson, urban renewal was nothing less than a "fiasco," and its goal of providing decent housing for every American family would have been better achieved by leaving the real estate market to its own devices.[21] These important works articulated what many city dwellers and urban observers could see for themselves amid the vacant lots and drab, dangerous housing projects that stood where interesting, if perhaps gritty, neighborhoods once thrived: urban renewal had not lived up to its promise. For the first time in decades, the time was ripe for trying something new.

That something new was a concept called "adaptive reuse." In the past, if a building had outlived its function, the prevailing wisdom held that it should be torn down and replaced with a more appropriate structure. Preservation offered an alternative: repair and repurpose the original building. Usually this meant keeping the façade intact but reconfiguring the interior so that, for example, an old church might become a bookstore, an old warehouse might be converted into condominiums, or an old mansion might be retrofitted for use as a restaurant. Adaptive reuse aligned preservation with economic development because it allowed, and even encouraged, rehabilitation for profit-making ventures. For cities, it offered a way to attract new investment, stimulate job creation, and increase tax revenue.

While the National Historic Preservation Act never mentioned adaptive reuse as a goal, its rhetoric and provisions were consistent with the doctrine. The passage stating that "the historical and cultural foundations of the Nation should be preserved as a living part of our community life" bespoke a departure from traditional preservation practices. The implication was that historic landmarks should not stand apart from their host societies as relics of a bygone age but rather should serve the ordinary needs of present-day populations.[22] Accordingly, Congress posed no obstacle to owners who wanted to refashion old buildings for new uses. The law triggered a review process for any building listed on the national register slated for demolition with the use of federal funds. Yet the question of how a historic building was to function was left entirely up to the owner. If Congressional support for adaptive reuse was implicit in the 1966 law, it became explicit in subsequent federal legislation. In 1976, Congress passed the Tax Reform Act, which allowed investors to recover depreciation expenses on income-generating structures certified as important to a historic district. At the same time, the law discouraged the destruction of such structures by forbidding developers from claiming the costs of demolition as a deductible business expense. Two years later, Congress sweetened the bait by establishing a tax credit program for developers who rehabilitated historic properties. Finally, the Economic Recovery Tax Act of 1981 expanded the tax credit program by loosening the criteria for qualified buildings and by increasing the actual credit to 25 percent of the total cost of rehabilitation. With these generous financial incentives encoded in federal tax rules, adaptive reuse became an inviting business proposition. Not surprisingly, the new laws won over many urban real estate developers to the cause of preservation.[23]

Indeed, the lure of financial gain provided the primary impetus for the surge of inner-city historic-property rehabilitation that followed in the wake of these laws. No doubt, the federal policies, especially the revised tax code, inspired the phenomenal explosion of historic districts. Within twenty-five years of the passage of the National Historic Preservation Act, more than 8,000 districts, most of them in towns or cities, had secured a listing on the national register. Within these districts, the rehabilitation of historic properties proceeded swiftly and extensively once Congress revised the tax code in 1976. Over the next ten years, 17,000 projects qualified for federal tax incentives, accounting for $11 billion dollars worth of new investment, much of it in urban historic districts.[24]

The enthusiasm for inner-city preservation should not be ascribed solely to favorable legislation, however. Larger economic, cultural, and demographic factors were at work. As noted earlier, preservation in the urban core flourished because it complemented the function of the postrenewal downtown. A modest rise in downtown office construction in the 1970s enlarged the market for inner-city housing, especially among well-paid corporate managers and urban professionals who chose not to orient their lives around children. The postwar suburbs were designed for nuclear families. For childless households, however, the allure of suburban living diminished considerably. After 1960, a number of cultural and demographic factors conspired against the nuclear family. Young people were moving away from home at an earlier age but getting married later in life. Also contributing to the nearly twofold increase in single-family households between 1960 and 1980 was the rapid rise in divorce rates. Moreover, even when young people did marry, they were much more likely than members of the previous generations to postpone childbearing. For downtown workers falling into any of these categories, older inner-city housing became a convenient alternative to suburban subdivisions as long as they had the money, energy, and patience to undertake the necessary rehabilitation work. Not that the demand for rehabbed housing was restricted to downtown workers. Proximity to downtown offered transportation access to the entire metropolitan area, an important consideration for households with multiple wage earners. Thus, once these neighborhoods began to look like solid investments, they attracted a broad range of buyers, including homosexual couples, single women, professional couples, and even retirees. A common denominator remained the absence of children.[25]

The cultural preference of downtown workers notwithstanding, potential home buyers were unlikely to purchase inner-city property if they did not anticipate a decent return on their investment. It is important to bear in mind that many of the actors responsible for rehabilitating inner-city housing did so to resell property and turn a profit. By the 1970s, general trends in the urban real estate market favored a new cycle of investment in the inner city. By this time, the market value of inner-city properties had plummeted to the point where they could be purchased very cheaply. It did not take much in the way of additional incentives to convince developers that spending a few thousand dollars on structural stabilization, tuck pointing, fresh paint and redesigned interiors could yield handsome returns. Low purchase prices similarly reduced the risk for those who bought homes in which to live. Federal preservation policy, then, encouraged a particular mode of residential investment in a section of the metropolis that was already primed for renewed entrepreneurialism.[26]

Finally, preservation fit in neatly with the broader civic goal of making downtown a tourist destination. Having finally lost faith in industrial production as the cornerstone of urban revitalization, older central cities searched for alternative forms of revenue-generating activity. Tourism leaped out as a promising path of redevelopment because cities already had the necessary infrastructure and its aesthetic requirements coincided with those most likely to attract corporate firms and service-sector businesses. Tourist landscapes did not despoil the environment and they generally appealed to out-of-town visitors, urban professionals, and corporate managers alike. Heritage-based tourism, in particular, complemented efforts to transform the inner city into a district for high-income workers and residents. As the oldest part of the city, the downtown and its environs offered something unique to out-of-town visitors. Not only did it provide the starting point for a narrative about the city's growth, but in most cases it also contained multiple sites associated with important national events. Charleston, New Orleans, Williamsburg, Philadelphia, and Boston already had demonstrated the money-making potential of heritage tourism. Even if profit was not the primary motivation of pioneering preservationists in these cities, the resulting economic windfalls certainly excited the ambitions of investors and planners in other cities that had historic landscapes in the postrenewal era. With generous laws in place favoring adaptive use, one city after another began transforming its historic core into a landscape of consumption. Preserving historic structures and converting them not only into museums but also into pubs, bookstores, nightclubs, and restaurants widened the market for both tourists and downtown employees.[27]

In downtown districts, the most heralded offspring of the marriage of preservation and tourism were the festival marketplaces. James Rouse, a shopping-mall developer, launched the festival marketplace bonanza with his rehabilitation of Faneuil Hall and Quincy Market in 1976. With a three-year property-tax abatement and $12 million in financial assistance from city government, Rouse converted a derelict area wedged between Boston's waterfront and its business district into a bustling shopping and tourist destination. Rather than anchoring the complex with a department store, as was the common practice in suburban malls, Rouse built the project around two restored historic landmarks, a colonial meeting house and an early-nineteenth-century meat-and-produce market. With over 150 small shops and dozens of pushcarts selling everything from clothing and furniture to food and souvenirs, the wildly successful consumer emporium offered a distinct alternative to the suburban shopping mall. The formula was quickly replicated by other developers around the country, and Rouse himself transplanted his concept to additional locales. Faneuil Hall Marketplace and its imitators placed urban spectacle at the center of the consumer experience. Historic building façades and spatial layouts based on the preexisting arrangements of streets and landmark buildings imparted an aura of local authenticity to each festival marketplace. And this unique and indigenous sense of place was precisely what visitors wanted. By the end of the 1980s, virtually every major city had some version of a festival marketplace based on the adaptive reuse of historic structures. In Denver and New Orleans, defunct breweries anchored shopping and entertainment complexes. In other cities, train stations, warehouses, and factories were made over for similar purposes.[28]

Preservation's contribution to heritage tourism, however, extended beyond the festival marketplaces of downtown into nearby residential districts, where it often performed double duty as both an enticement to prospective homeowners and a lure for out of town visitors. Beacon Hill and Society Hill were early examples of neighborhoods that prospered as both tourist and residential districts as a result of preservation activity. As residential districts, they attracted young urban professionals who considered the restored homes a badge of their upwardly mobile status as well as a solid investment. Adjacent to some of the most popular heritage-based attractions in the entire nation—Independence Hall in the case of Society Hill and Freedom Trail in the case of Beacon Hill—these two neighborhoods were primed to receive the spillover effects from tourists looking to prolong their sightseeing activities. With a largely intact colonial and early-nineteenth-century landscape and a generous sprinkling of homes occupied by famous people in the past, they had an intrinsic historical appeal. Equally if not more important, their transformation into affluent residential enclaves made them appear both attractive and safe to out-of-towners. By the 1970s, Beacon Hill and Society Hill were well established as thriving inner-city areas where trendy shops, taverns, and restaurants captured the dollars of out-of-towners while contributing to the ambience that supported high residential property values.[29]

A resilient tourist economy and continued demand for unique and attractive inner-city housing sustained the profitability of preservation through the 1980s despite a series of political, economic, and legal setbacks. In 1986, Congress drastically scaled back the tax incentives that had set off the rehabilitation boom ten years earlier. The intent of the legislative revision was not so much to stall preservation as to close loopholes through which investors had slipped to shelter their taxable earnings. Nonetheless, rehabbers could no longer expect to recoup the same percentages of their costs that they did earlier. The subsequent downturn in the real estate market due to a recession and a savings-and-loan crisis further dampened investor interest in historic rehabilitation. Finally, a property-rights movement inspired legislation, primarily at the state level, that diminished the power of municipalities to regulate the architectural character of privately owned buildings. All of these forces exerted an adverse impact on preservation. Annual applications for certification on the National Register of Historic Places dropped by more than two-thirds between 1984 and 1989; by 1993, the federal tax credit program generated only one-fourth the investment that it had a decade earlier.[30]

Preservation was by no means dead, however. Without juicy federal tax breaks, investors shied away from large-scale festival-marketplace-type projects. Yet on a smaller scale, especially at the neighborhood level, preservation continued to be driven by the promise and realization of profits. By the 1980s, preservation had already proved its economic value by turning around dozens of neighborhoods across the country. In the Beacon Hill and Back Bay districts of Boston, residents gloated over a 200 percent rise in property values between 1955 and 1972. During the 1970s in Alexandria, Virginia property values in the "Old Town" district increased more than twice as fast as they did in adjoining neighborhoods.[31] Accounts such as these were legion and continued to feed the appetites of prospective investors into the following decades. Where preservation had already transformed the socioeconomic character of neighborhoods and inflated property values, residents cemented their gains by establishing district-wide zoning. Following the Charleston model of the 1930s, these neighborhoods adopted architectural controls that prevented any deviation from designated historical traditions. Whereas fewer than two dozen localities had imposed architectural standards on homeowners in 1965, more than 2,000 had done so by 1986.[32] Once in place, zoning controls virtually assured the perpetuation of historic rehabilitation, not only because alternative modes of development were outlawed, but because investors had confidence that the character of the neighborhood would remain fairly stable over the long run.

As a further boon to preservation in the 1990s, many states and municipalities implemented their own tax incentive programs to compensate for the reversal of federal policy. As of 2002, sixteen states operated preservation-tax-credit programs that enabled investors to supplement the deductions they received from the federal government with additional discounts on their state tax bills. Many of these programs were less restrictive than the one administered by the federal government in that they did not require investment in income-producing property. Hence, they could be used by property owners who wished to reside in, rather than rent, their homes. Over the next several years, budgetary shortfalls at the state level made these programs a target for possible elimination. Yet in most cases, assessments of their broader economic benefit convinced legislators to retain them. A Rhode Island study, for example, concluded that $23 million in state tax credits stimulated $95 million worth of residential investment over a two-year period. Similarly, rehabilitation tax credits in Maryland reportedly generated $800 million in fresh investment in the seven years following their implementation in 1997. Indeed, by 2004 an additional seven states had enacted historic-tax-credit legislation.[33]

Even as the federal preservation-tax-credit program grew stingier after 1986, other policy initiatives coming out of Washington, DC opened alternative funding spigots. Most notable in this regard was the passage of the Intermodal Surface Transportation Efficiency Act in 1991. The purpose of this law was to create a more efficient, financially stable, and environmentally friendly system of highways, railways, and mass-transit facilities. To ensure sensitivity to the needs of communities, the law also set aside money for activities that furthered local sustainability and livability. Congress designated historic preservation as one of ten categories of activity eligible for these "enhancement" funds. According to one estimate, in the six years following the Act's passage, almost $500 million was funneled to preservation projects. These included nonprofit ventures, such as museums and historic trails, as well as more entrepreneurial undertakings, such as the conversion of old rail stations into shopping plazas.[34]

Yet another development that kept the preservation movement on track was increased reliance on private-sector funds disbursed through nonprofit organizations. Most notable in this regard was the activity of the National Trust for Historic Preservation. Chartered by the federal government in 1949, the National Trust combined education and advocacy with the management of selected properties of national significance, including the Woodlawn plantation in northern Virginia, Drayton Hall in South Carolina, and several Frank Lloyd Wright homes. When Congress terminated funding for the Trust in 1998, the nation's premier preservationist organization turned to the private sector for funding. Five years later, it had raised $125 million from over 1,400 donors. With its robust endowment, the Trust lent hundreds of thousands of dollars annually to community preservation efforts across the nation.[35]

Even if the momentum of the preservation movement slowed somewhat following the flush days of the early 1980s, its champions at the turn of the millennium found reason to be proud of its accomplishments and confident about its viability as an urban revitalization strategy. As of 2001, the federal rehabilitation-tax-credit program alone had produced more than $23 billion in private investment, demonstrating that although the rate of applications had slowed after reaching the $11 million mark in its first eight years, it continued to leverage big money.[36] More important, preservation had delivered on its promise of turning cities around and making them desirable places to live and visit again. In 1989, after logging thousands of miles across the United States journalist Roberta Brandes Gratz announced, "We are in a period of 'urban renaissance,'" a phenomenon she credit to a multitude of grassroots campaigns to save and refashion historic landscapes.[37] The picture looked just as rosy eight years later when authors Richard Moe and Carter Wilkie reported that "neighborhoods left for dead are being revitalized by self-motivated residents. Small-town merchants are reinvigorating their Main Street business districts. Entrepreneurs and enlightened public officials are turning dreary downtowns into places where people want to be."[38] Even the poster child of urban decay, the South Bronx in New York City enjoyed a well-publicized renaissance after creating several historic districts and rescuing many of its famous brownstones from demolition.[39] Although many older central cities in the Northeast and the industrial heartland continued to bleed population, and plenty of inner-city neighborhoods remained mired in a cycle of poverty, disinvestment, and physical decay, cities seemed to have turned a corner; they were no longer dying. For those who wanted concrete evidence that cities were on their way back, they needed to look no further than the downtown tourist districts and historic inner-city neighborhoods where preservation had produced visible results.

What really excited writers like Gratz, Moe, and Wilkie about recent preservation triumphs was not so much the higher levels of investment they represented, but the superior quality of life they produced. Preserved urban districts exemplified the best of urban living; they were attractive, pedestrian-friendly, culturally diverse, and stimulating. Above all else and in stark contrast to the cookie-cutter subdivisions of suburbia, they were "someplace."

History gave them a distinct identity, which let in turn bred a sense of affiliation and local pride.

Even the most optimistic preservationists at the turn of the millennium never assumed that the war had been won. Indeed, the preservation movement continued to be fueled by a sense of impending crisis; every threatened building was defended as if it were the last one left on the planet. If battles still had to be fought tooth and nail against avaricious developers and ignorant planners, preservationists had nonetheless accumulated an impressive arsenal of success stories. Preservation worked, and cities were clearly the better off for it.

Revitalization without Community

Or were they? Even as preservationists were congratulating themselves for turning around neighborhoods once written off, a growing chorus of criticism drew attention to what preservation failed to achieve and, worse still, what it destroyed.

As an urban revitalization strategy, historic-landscape reclamation spoke to a particular definition of urban decline, one that centered on the flight of middle-class populations and the functional obsolescence of older buildings. In combating these aspects of urban degeneration, many traditional preservationist goals were sacrificed on the altar of profit. The entrepreneurial version of historic preservation that flourished after 1966 placed a greater emphasis on the economic potential of aging buildings and landmarks than on their ability to foster a shared sense of belonging. Whereas few critics of preservation advocated the sort of elitist cultural agenda that motivated the Boston Brahmins or John D. Rockefeller Jr. in an earlier era, many shared their conviction that carefully interpreted landscapes could bind people in a common enterprise and even act as a constructive force for social change. The problem with preservation for profit was that landscapes were barely interpreted at all. And when they were, they all too often reinforced social inequities and aggravated long-standing wounds. However successful economically driven historic-preservation campaigns were from a financial standpoint, they did not always promote community cohesion. Indeed, they served as much to divide and disrupt communities as to unify them. It was on these grounds that critics both within and beyond the movement began to question not so much the premise, but the practice of historic preservation in inner cities.

Historic districts revamped for tourism and shopping excelled at creating distinctive urban spaces but offered little to bind people beyond a shared experience of consumption. Draped in the thinnest veneer of history, festival marketplaces and nostalgia-tinged entertainment districts discouraged visitors from reflecting deeply on their relationship to the past. With little meaning attached to buildings, streets, and other structures, shoppers and strollers had no basis for developing personal attachments to the landscape or considering their connections to each other in the context of those attachments. Referring to this shortcoming, critics coined the term "facadism" to denote a single-minded preoccupation with the aesthetics of building styles and surfaces at the expense of interpretation. Where commercial developers aimed to create a stimulating ambience for consumption, what mattered above all else was the "look and feel" of an area and its facility for creating a pleasurable shopping experience. With little incentive to elucidate the actual historical significance of structures, visitors learned little about how buildings were used in the past or what sort of events took place within or beside them. Where attaining the right look and feel led to the fabrication of historic environments—as was often the case in theme parks, shopping complexes, and gilded downtowns—detractors argued that history was debased; phony buildings begat phony history.[40]

This charge assumed an even sharper bite when joined to accusations of interpretive bias. To the extent that tourist landscapes presented specific historical information, they tended to sanitize and romanticize the past. Signage, where it existed, typically celebrated successful businesses and pioneering individuals. Staged reenactments milked historic events for their entertainment value rather than their capacity to provoke thought. References to social conflict were muted; controversial subjects like slavery, strikes, crime, and poverty were glossed over or avoided to keep visitors cheerful. Even in the absence of interpretive displays, mass-consumption landscapes transmitted implicit messages that distorted the past. For instance, by embedding shopping functions in a meticulously arranged historical fabric, festival marketplaces naturalized consumer spending as part of a mythic urban experience in which strangers interact spontaneously and democratically in a lively public space.[41]

In avoiding what James Oliver Horton and Lois E. Horton termed "the tough stuff of American memory," antiseptic historic districts also risked alienating people who saw their history defined in terms of struggle against injustice. Women, workers, racial minorities, gays, and lesbians rarely found their stories represented in the landscapes preserved or reconstructed for mass audiences. To be certain, there was considerable movement toward redressing these shortcomings as the twentieth century drew to a close. The opening of Memphis's National Civil Rights Museum in 1991 and Cincinnati's National Underground Railroad Freedom Center in 2004 reflected recognition of the enormous spending power of African American sightseers who craved opportunities to explore subjects like race relations and slavery. Both of these groundbreaking museums sprang from the preservation of historic structures. The National Civil Rights Museum was housed in the Lorraine Motel, site of Martin Luther King, Jr.'s, assassination, and the central artifact in the National Underground Railroad Freedom Center was a restored antebellum slave pen. On a parallel track, cities like Boston, Denver, and Portland, Maine developed women's history trails to draw visitor attention to previously unheralded landmarks. Communities were slower to highlight the struggles of gays or lesbians in their preservation efforts. Indeed, it was not until 1999 that a property associated with gay or lesbian history was designated as a National Historic Landmark.[42]

Ironically, historic tourist districts sometimes engendered community strife by virtue of their very success. Wherever heritage tourism drew large numbers of people, cultural resources became vulnerable to excessive wear and tear. Despite the potential financial windfall of heritage tourism, some places rejected it out of fear that hordes of visitors would destroy their local treasures along with the tranquility of their communities. Preservationists in Charleston realized as early as the 1930s that by opening historic homes to a constant stream of visitors, they invited further physical deterioration. While Charlestonians ultimately strove to balance a vibrant tourist economy with the careful maintenance of its antebellum mansions, other communities made the conscious decision not to market their historic attractions to outsiders. In the shadows of Charleston, South Carolina's Mount Pleasant attempted to keep its historic antebellum landscape a secret. Likewise, the citizens of Harrisville, New Hampshire refused to publicize their intact brick-granite colonial mills for fear of tourist inundation. Elsewhere, communities already known for their historic properties took measures to reduce unwelcome intrusions. During the 1970s, residents of Philadelphia's Society Hill district campaigned for a moratorium on new commercial establishments so as to limit the disruption from weekend visitors. Oak Park, Illinois faced a similar predicament from its assemblage of Frank Lloyd Wright homes, prompting some property owners to post decals in their windows notifying gawking visitors that they were not welcome.[43]

Historic districts lacking a tourist orientation rarely experienced disruption from outside visitors, but the consequences of shallow and biased interpretation often produced higher levels of internal discord. Neighborhoods that promoted the rehabilitation of older homes as a way to attract fresh investment and affluent inhabitants were just as likely as tourist districts to keep the dissemination of specific historical information to a minimum or present distorted translations of the past. Describing the historic districts in New York State that had recently been added to the national register, one historian averred, "These places certainly have a history, but as they presently exist, they do not express that history to the viewer. Traffic rushes by, neon glows, the facades are a cacophony of styles, power lines are everywhere, and the merchants hawk modern bric-a-brac. Strolling through one of these districts, one could presume, quite erroneously, that the nineteenth century was similar to the twentieth."[44]

What emerged as the primary mechanism for communicating the significance of older buildings, the neighborhood house tour, was indicative of the prevailing mode of presentation. Typically, a group of proud residents who were property owners agreed to open their recently rehabilitated homes to the public in the hopes that others would be inspired to purchase nearby properties and undertake similar projects. Although visitors to a house might learn something about its original construction and its architectural features, homeowners tended to emphasize the recent makeover and the creative possibilities for retrofitting older structures with the conveniences and luxuries of modern living. On the house tour, history represented an obstacle to be surmounted by technology and the idiosyncratic fashion sense of imaginative owners. Even where neighborhoods relinquished overt historical interpretation—one could often walk for blocks in historic districts without finding a marker, plaque, or other informational exhibits—the aesthetic of rehabilitation conveyed an implicit set of messages that were just as erroneous and celebratory as those in their hokey tourist counterparts.

The embrace of the past in historic districts almost always betrayed a bias toward a particular era and a particular function. A neighborhood might present itself as emblematic of a quaint colonial village, an antebellum Southern town, an old seaport, an elite urban enclave, or a frontier outpost. Whatever the selected archetype, deviant aspects of the past were ignored, as were events that occurred either before or after the period of emphasis. As preservation proceeded according to this logic, neighborhoods froze in time. To some extent, the application process for national-register designation, which required districts to identify a "period of significance" and measure the value of standing structures according to how well they conformed to designated historical themes, encouraged these biases. Few neighborhoods, however, found reason to broaden their preservation criteria, even when they were at liberty to do so. For example, neighborhoods that established architectural guidelines for housing rehabilitation and new construction rarely tolerated designs that evoked alternative historical eras. This reluctance was often justified on aesthetic grounds, the argument being that a hodgepodge of architectural styles and building types is jarring to the senses and visually unappealing. The application of a consistent architectural style across the neighborhood, on the other hand, not only looks more attractive but also renders the historic character of a given neighborhood more evident. Thus, it was not uncommon for residents to express indifference or even glee at the demolition of "noncontributing structures" that clashed with the desired historical image, especially when such structures were replaced by "replica" buildings recalling the period of significance.[45]

Neighborhoods frozen in time may have evoked a distinct sense of place but the also defied the logic of history. As David Hamer explained in his critique of historic-preservation practices in United States cities, *History in Urban Places*, restricting commemoration to a particular chronological span or theme contradicts the two most defining features of urban history: change and diversity. According to Hamer, "The concept of the historic district has to a large extent been based on a commitment to a representation of history as static. . . . It is also profoundly antiurban in the sense that it denies the diversity that is the very essence of urban life."[46] Stripped of any allusions to diversity and change, preservation pursued in this manner could not possibly speak to the broad spectrum of social groups represented in any given urban neighborhood, nor could it provide the visual cues that allow people to comprehend how their neighborhood developed incrementally over time.[47] History, in this guise, became mere ornament.

The problems associated with freezing neighborhoods in time became more disturbing as critics contemplated the chronological slices that typically were selected for veneration and exposition. Neighborhoods undergoing revitalization tended to define the period of significance as those years perceived to encompass its peak, when the majority of extant homes were originally constructed, businesses were thriving, and there were more people moving in than moving out. In many cases, rehabbers and urban pioneers pointed with pride to a moment when their neighborhood contained the most prestigious addresses in the entire city. Cincinnati's Dayton Street, which was compared to New York's Fifth Avenue in the late nineteenth century, was added to the national register in 1973 after decades of abandonment and slum clearance in the surrounding blocks. Hillhouse Avenue in New Haven, Connecticut, which received national-register designation in 1985, was described by Charles Dickens as America's most beautiful street. Even where neighborhoods lacked such a refined pedigree, preservationists invariably invoked the glory days of a remote past, long before their area began its downward spiral (see Figure 1-3).[48]

Figure 1-3. *Prairie Avenue, Chicago, Illinois.* Prairie Avenue was Chicago's most prestigious residential address in the 1890s. In 1976, after a long period of neglect, it was designated as a National Historic District. Restoration of vintage mansions and construction of architecturally compatible infill housing reestablished the street's elite status in the early twenty-first century. *(Courtesy of the author.)*

It is not surprising that residents intent on attracting new investment harkened back to the days when their neighborhood enjoyed growth and prosperity. Highlighting a golden age helped legitimize a neighborhood's historic status and provided a model for emulation. It also established a psychic bond between the urban pioneers spearheading revitalization and the early inhabitants who initially developed the area. Privileging the distant past at the expense of the recent past, however, robbed people of the ability to make connections to the present by tracing neighborhood change across the years incrementally. Moreover, it increased the difficulty of embedding residents' personal histories into a larger community narrative since most inner-city residents could not trace their lineage back more than a generation or two in the place where they lived. Those who possessed local roots were usually those whose own history was most closely intertwined with the era of decline, precisely the period that booster-oriented preservationists wanted to forget.

Rapid population turnover in inner-city neighborhoods added to the difficulty of making history resonate with their inhabitants, and the diversion of preservation from public museums, monuments, and landmarks increased the challenge. As long as there was money to be made in preservation and as long as cities clung to the attitude that any preservation worth doing was preservation that paid, it followed that contributing structures were more likely to fall into private hands. Especially in residential neighborhoods where tourism goals were secondary, preservation in the years after 1970 generally entailed the rehabilitation of private homes. While a restored private home and some knowledge about earlier occupants may have allowed owners to feel a greater attachment to their property, it did little to preserve the collective memory of a place. According to Robert Archibald, one of the leading proponents of place-based public history, the preservation of historic structures contributes most to society when those structures are repositories of shared memories. Thus, the most valuable places for capturing the diverse perspectives on the past are those that have served and continue to serve some sort of public function. Author Ray Oldenburg has termed these public sites of congregation "third places," distinct from the first places of home and the second places of work. They might be neighborhood stores, parks, plazas, schools, beauty parlors, or community centers. Yet, in residential districts where historic restoration was employed as a strategy for selling homes, developers often converted third places—stores, meeting halls, and even churches—into private residences, further diminishing the possibility of recovering multiple perspectives on the past and of explaining how communities evolved according to the interaction among people of varying class and ethnic backgrounds. Whether a particular neighborhood developed initially as an elite enclave, a working-class district, or a middle-class suburb, it most likely moved through various stages of development and demographic transition, thereby placing very different populations into contact with one another. The trend in inner-city preservation toward homogeneity and privatization rendered this essential dynamic of urban growth invisible.[49]

The unfortunate consequence of a selective interpretation of the past in inner-city districts was that it served to alienate certain residents as much as it worked to cultivate a feeling of attachment among others. Whereas the affluent occupants of newly restored homes might come to see themselves as inheritors of a local urban pioneering tradition, the people who remained from a preceding era found little that affirmed their rightful place in the community. An exclusive preoccupation with a remote and glorious past provided little basis for connection among residents whose lives bore little resemblance to those who lived and thrived during the designated golden age. A landscape shorn of recent history became a mechanism of disinheritance. The message conveyed by prevailing preservation practices in the late twentieth century was that affluent newcomers belonged and those who remained from the era of decline did not. Typically, this distinction between the welcome and the unwelcome corresponded to a division between homeowners and renters, the well off and the poor, and at times those with light skin and those with darker skin. History thus fragmented community.

In the worst-case scenarios, which regrettably transpired all too often, an elite bias in the application of history justified the displacement of poorer residents, or at the very least inured newcomers to the social costs of the process known as gentrification. At a certain tipping point, the infusion of capital for housing rehabilitation exerted a ripple effect on surrounding properties. A neighborhood once perceived as hopeless or dangerous suddenly made headlines for its position on the threshold of a renaissance. Risk-averse investors, eager to get in on the action before it was too late, rushed to purchase, repair, and modernize remaining properties.. With the renewed demand for housing, property values shot upward. In the initial stages of this process, some existing property owners benefited financially from the opportunity to sell their dilapidated holdings at a reasonable price. Their tenants, typically the poor and the elderly, enjoyed no such windfall and became victimized by forces largely beyond their control. The conversion of rental apartments into condominiums or single family homes left former occupants with little recourse beyond gathering their possessions, sometimes on short notice, and searching elsewhere for cheaper lodging.[50]

Residential displacement was further abetted by the effect of gentrification on property taxes. As homes values rose, tax assessments increased commensurately. Landlords who had not yet sold off their holdings, passed these extra costs onto their tenants. Households unable to meet the higher rents found themselves in the same situation as those who had lost their homes to property conversion. Eventually, rising assessments exerted a similar effect on owner-occupants who may have had no desire to leave their homes but could no longer afford the taxes. In time, entire populations turned over, with affluent newcomers having in essence evicted the poorer residents, both renters and owners. Among the earliest residential enclaves to experience preservation-based revitalization, Georgetown in Washington, DC, Beacon Hill in Boston, and Society Hill in Philadelphia bore witness to this process prior to 1970. Subsequently, instances of economic hardship and the displacement of low-income residents multiplied, especially where saturated housing markets operated in conjunction with renewed interest in historic urban neighborhoods.[51]

Ultimately, the destabilizing consequences of historic preservation under-mined its effectiveness as a revitalization strategy by generating not only criticism but also outright opposition among the residents of targeted neighborhoods. By the 1970s, inner-city preservation had become associated in the public mind with gentrification and displacement. Even though preservationists could point to many places where renewed investment in historic properties did not destabilize neighborhoods, the fear of dislocation was enough to provoke fierce resistance. In the initial phases of the revitalization process, working-class residents usually welcomed the influx of middle-class buyers, although some might have chafed at the austere aesthetics enforced through local architectural guidelines. At the point where they perceived their own homes to be threatened, reactions ranged from a fatalistic acceptance to a militant defense. The latter course of action was most likely to be taken when rehabbers attacked the institutions that had long supported poorer segments of the population—heath clinics, food pantries, homeless shelters, substance abuse treatment centers, and Section 8 housing.[52]

It is important to recognize that from the 1960s onward, historic preservation marched uneasily alongside a more socially oriented alternative to urban renewal that cultivated a vocal constituency among existing inner-city populations. This alternative policy strand, which found its fullest expression in the antipoverty crusades of the Lyndon Johnson administration, diverged from historic preservation in both its diagnosis of urban ills and its prescriptions for recovery. Johnson's War on Poverty flowed from the conviction that urban decay was primarily a social problem, namely America's failure to extend its opportunities and resources to all segments of the population. Although the ambitious undertaking was not restricted to cities, much of its firepower was directed at distressed urban districts that were either bypassed or harmed by large-scale slum clearance. Toward the end of his presidency, Johnson launched the Model Cities program, which promised to coordinate a wide array of antipoverty services in designated low-income neighborhoods. These initiatives broke from the urban renewal mold in two important ways. First, they emphasized social services on the premise that job training, health care, education, legal aid, affordable housing, and other services would provide racial minorities and the poor with the social capital to partake in the nation's economic juggernaut. Second, they mandated the active participation of target populations in the design and implementation of these service programs. If urban renewal invited bureaucrats and developers to transfigure large swaths of inner-city terrain, the War on Poverty would mobilize and empower the poor so that they could control the destiny of their neighborhoods.[53] Even after the Nixon administration dismantled the War on Poverty apparatus, the basic philosophy of building social capital from within continued to resonate with many inner-city residents. More important, the War on Poverty bequeathed an organizational framework that urban minorities and the poor continued to employ when defending their interest at the grass roots. The failure of preservationists to reconcile their goals with the needs of poorer residents guaranteed confrontation.

The Over-the-Rhine district of Cincinnati is probably the most well-documented case of effective resistance to preservation-based revitalization among lower-income populations. Once a largely German working-class neighborhood with a smattering of Italian immigrants, it underwent a dramatic population transition after World War II. Upwardly mobile Germans and Italians moved out, and thousands of poor rural white people from Appalachia and black people displaced by urban renewal took their place. By the 1970s, the district had become "a low-income repository for poor whites, blacks, and elderly German families." Between 1972 and 1978, more than 100 businesses vacated their premises, producing a landscape pockmarked with empty storefronts.[54] Around this same time, the city's leading preservationist organization encouraged the local government to transform Over-the-Rhine into a fashionable residential neighborhood for downtown office workers, with its worn but distinctive nineteenth-century architecture as the primary lure. By this time, however, the evils of gentrification had received plenty of publicity, and well-organized residents of Over-the-Rhine were determined to stand their ground. Dismissing assurances that the poor would not be uprooted from their homes, neighborhood activists fought national-register designation and sought the legal protection of low-income housing. As a result of an intense grassroots campaign, historic preservation stalled and the neighborhood remained a low-income enclave (see Figure 1-4).[55]

The tragic dimensions of gentrification extended beyond the injustice inflicted on the poor and the rancor produced within communities. As the process played out to its logical conclusion, it perpetuated the geographical segregation of social classes and racial groups across the entire urban terrain. The separation of rich and poor and of dark-skinned and light-skinned has plagued American cities for over a century and has led to some of some of the ugliest and most violent episodes in our nation's history. Moreover, it has abetted a politics of mistrust, vengeance, and contention that has hindered cities' ability to address collective problems. An outcome of historical preservation that simply inverts the pattern where the poor concentrate in the core while the wealthy defend the fringe moves urban America no closer to social and political reconciliation.

Figure 1-4. *Over-the-Rhine, Cincinnati, Ohio.* Despite its impressive stock of historic buildings, the Over-the-Rhine district still struggles to attract investment. *(Courtesy of the author.)*

Gentrification's apologists insist that the situation is not so dire and dismiss their opponents and critics as misguided and misinformed. Armed with surveys and statistical data, they maintain that the percentage of inner-city residents forcibly removed from their homes is small, that more people lose their homes as a result of deterioration and decay than rehabilitation, and that most of those dispossessed by gentrification end up with better housing conditions than those they leave behind. Furthermore, they claim that the extent of displacement varies considerably from one city to another and that there are plenty of inner-city districts where middle-class rehabbers coexist with their poorer, more deeply rooted neighbors. In neighborhoods that fall into this category, it is the poor who benefit most from the lower crime rates, better street maintenance, and improved city services that accompany the influx of upwardly mobile homeowners. Some preservation advocates contend that what really matters is the pace of the transformation. Where upgrading occurs slowly, vacant properties get filled and outside speculators who have no vested interest in the long-term stability of the neighborhood are kept away. Even in cases where some people are forced to move against their will, so the argument goes, historic preservation on the whole does more good than harm.[56]

Gentrification's defenders are not entirely wrong in their claims, but to the extent that they encourage a laissez-faire attitude toward displacement, they do the poor, the larger metropolis, and the preservation movement itself a grave disfavor. It is true that the hardship imposed by historic preservation will vary from one neighborhood to another. The volume of displacement depends on a variety of factors, including the stage in the transition process and the tightness of the overall housing market in the larger metropolis. Higher vacancy rates within a transitional neighborhood mean less displacement; greater availability of low-income housing in surrounding areas means less hardship for those displaced. Certainly, the more moderate the pace of change, the easier it is for existing residents to adjust. Yet even in neighborhoods where property rates rise slowly and plenty of low-cost rental units remain available, there are always people on the margins for whom incremental advances in the gentrification process exact higher costs. Left alone, market-driven historic preservation in inner-city districts invariably results in some destructive displacement. But the process does not have to be left alone. While it may be unrealistic in the context of the current political and economic environment to eliminate all negative impacts of neighborhood upgrading through historic preservation, they can certainly be minimized. Indeed, there are several instructive examples of preservation-oriented communities that have minimized displacement by intervening in the market to ensure the continued availability of low-income housing. Some of these will be discussed in later chapters.

The basic premise of this book is that historic preservation can be employed more constructively in America's inner cities. Having established itself as an effective strategy for luring investment back to the urban core, it has yet to fulfill its potential to foster stable, diverse, and enriching communities Given the mixed record of historical preservation over the past forty years, it is not surprising that many inner-city residents remain wary about employing it as a revitalization strategy. The long view, however, reveals preservation as a fluid enterprise capable of promoting a variegated set of societal goals. Without question, century-old frameworks for making sense of the urban landscape are deficient for the purposes of cultivating social harmony and stability in the multicultural inner cities of today. Nonetheless, something may be gained by recovering an earlier emphasis on interpretation and social engineering in the pursuit of a revitalization agenda that does not measure success in dollars alone.

Inner-city preservationists embarking on such a path can anticipate a host of difficult decisions as they wrestle with the inevitable tension between community- building and economic-development goals. For neighborhoods teetering on the edge of extinction, both pursuits are necessary, and reconciling them or striking an acceptable balance between them presents a formidable challenge. Yet this is precisely where public landscape interpretation can help. Creating a process by which ordinary citizens make meaning from a place allows communities to articulate their priorities and increases the likelihood that preservation activities remain consistent with a grassroots vision of neighborhood development. Fortunately, this process does not need to be invented from whole cloth. Over the past several decades, public historians and archaeologists have contrived increasingly sophisticated techniques for engaging diverse urban constituencies in the act of historical interpretation. These innovative practices and perspectives lie at the core of a new agenda for historic preservation.

2

Taking It to the Streets

Public History in the City

The philosophy and practice of public historical commemoration has changed dramatically in the last forty years. The rise of social history as a field of study in the 1970s, along with theoretical advances in the disciplines of cultural geography and urban sociology, gave scholars powerful conceptual tools for making the past meaningful to diverse populations and empowering previously marginalized groups. Academically trained public historians and archaeologists have taken the lead in sharing these insights with popular audiences and developing collaborative projects. Some of the most exciting ventures have boasted a strong preservation component and have relied on the built environment as the primary vehicle for communicating the past to present-day audiences. To grasp the potential of public history as a tool for preservation-based revitalization, it is useful to review the developments that have simultaneously democratized and professionalized the public interpretation of urban landscapes.

Historians in Public

Until very recently, public historians ignored much of the diverse mosaic of American life. Broadly defined, public history encompasses all history delivered to nonacademic audiences. Documentaries appearing on television, museum exhibits, books written for mass markets, and historical markers fastened to building facades all fall under the public-history classification. Public archaeology is a related enterprise that seeks broad public engagement in the excavation and interpretation of material artifacts. Before the rise of the modern university in the late nineteenth century, all history was public history. The men and women who chronicled the past received no special training in historical research; the people for whom they wrote shared a similar social profile as well-educated members of the elite. As late as 1911, amateurs constituted 70 percent of the American Historical Association's membership. Over the course of the twentieth century, however, historical research and writing became increasingly professionalized. University-trained scholars, working in academic settings, disseminated their findings to colleagues and students. Popular history was relegated to journalists, filmmakers, museum employees, and the members of local historical societies. Despite this bifurcation among history practitioners, the themes used to interpret the past remained remarkably consistent. Through the 1950s, both academic and public history recounted a tale of progress. Academic history gave more emphasis to the rise of democratic political institutions and the crystallization of a distinctive American character while the history delivered to public audiences focused more on the heroic acts of individuals, but in both cases the dominant storyline glorified the European march across the American continent, the solidification of national identity after the Civil War, the growth of the industrial economy, and the rise of the United States to world-power status. The history encountered by men, women, and children out in the streets and public places of the city reinforced the dominant narratives. That is, most of the history produced for public display in town squares, along roadsides, and on building facades tended to celebrate the achievements of elite white men.[1]

The flip side of this bias was a blatant disregard for the contributions and sacrifices made by other social groups. Conducting a cross-country survey of monuments, markers, and preserved historic sites during the late 1990s, author James Loewen discovered to his dismay that women and African Americans were severely underrepresented. In the State of Illinois, for example, mention of women was almost completely absent from historical markers despite the fact that both the League of Women Voters and the General Federation of Women's Clubs were founded in Chicago and the Women's Christian Temperance Union was headquartered in Evanston.[2] While Loewen was surprised to find ample reference to Indian wars, Native Americans typically were depicted in unflattering terms. Statues featuring Native Americans, for instance, almost always showed them in a subservient relationship to white Europeans.[3] Even more offensive to Loewen was the public veneration of historical figures who worked actively to suppress the rights of racial minorities. Astoundingly, Nathan Bedford Forrest, founder of the Ku Klux

Klan, appeared on more historical markers in Tennessee than any individual in any other state. At the foot of Canal Street near the Mississippi River, New Orleans maintained an obelisk to commemorate the violent overthrow of the biracial Reconstruction government at the hands of the aptly named White League in 1874. The so-called Liberty Monument, built to honor the White Leaguers who were killed in the attempt to restore white supremacy, was itself a remnant of a bygone era, having been authorized by the New Orleans city council more than a century ago in 1882. Yet, as recently as 1989, Dearborn, Michigan erected a statue of its longtime mayor, Orville Hubbard, a staunch and outspoken defender of racial segregation.[4]

Loewen acknowledged that the situation seemed to be improving in many parts of the country. After 1970, the State of Georgia made a self-conscious effort to place more women and African Americans on its historical markers. In 1990, Pennsylvania received a grant for sixty-six markers devoted to African American history in Philadelphia. In Boston advocates of cultural diversity created a Women's Heritage Trail, a Black History Trail, and a Map of Lesbian and Gay Boston to complement the more traditional Freedom Trail. Had Loewen visited Richmond, Virginia he surely would have noted the presence of native son and African American tennis pro, Arthur Ashe, standing alongside the venerable stone-sculpted Confederate generals on Monument Avenue. Had he toured the Algiers section of New Orleans, he might have observed the large mural painted on the wall of an elementary school by teenagers in 1988 showing recently liberated slaves gazing upward at Harriet Tubman. In almost every major United States city, the past thirty years have witnessed street-renaming campaigns to honor important women and racial minorities. In addition to the ubiquitous Martin Luther King Boulevards, streets have been rededicated to more controversial activists, including Cesar Chavez, Josephine Baker, and Malcolm X.[5]

The expanded capacity of nonelite groups to claim their identity in public landscapes was a product of the tumultuous 1960s and the intensified questioning of traditional hierarchies and authorities. A reevaluation of history was part and parcel of the liberation struggles of the decade: the civil rights movement, the black power movement, the women's movement, and the antiwar movement, among others. The Freedom Schools established in the Deep South as part of the civil rights movement included a revised history curriculum that emphasized the struggles and achievements of African Americans. Likewise, the student and antiwar movements on college campuses sought to recover a history relevant to their crusade. Hence, their publications and pamphlets often featured accounts of previous resistance movements.[6] As activists of all stripes sought inspiration and guidance from the past, they turned to a constellation of actors and events that had garnered little attention in either school textbooks or public venues. Moreover, as women, racial minorities, gays, and lesbians attained greater power in society, they demanded a place of their own in the retelling of the nation's past.

It was around the new field of social history that popular and academic history converged once again, providing a potent force for democratizing the history found in public places. In contrast to the traditional emphasis on statesmen, military heroes, and prominent intellectuals, the new social history aspired to tell history from the bottom up. Ordinary people acting through formal organizations and informal networks took center stage as the critical actors in historical dramas. Fresh scholarship began to explore the role of labor unions, women's groups, mobs, civil rights organizations, neighborhood associations, and ethnic societies in shaping everyday life and changing the course of local and national events. Class, race, gender, and ethnicity emerged as the categories of analysis through which historical conditions and processes were charted and understood. To map out the finer grain of everyday life, historians began to plumb alternative source materials, including census records, probate inventories, tax assessments, birth certificates, marriage records, and property deeds. More than a few academically trained historians saw fit to carry these new perspectives and methodologies into the public realm. For some, the foray into public history was the result of a tight job market. With fewer teaching jobs available at the postsecondary level, many students graduating with Ph.D. degrees took staff positions in museums and local historical societies. In other cases it was a matter of a conviction. In focusing their attention on women, workers, racial minorities, gays, and lesbians, historians found a new basis of connecting with a broad public audience. For the first time, previously marginalized groups saw themselves represented in historical accounts, and therein lay the potential for solidifying group identities and providing direction for social activism. Thus, many social historians came to believe that their work was useful beyond the ivory tower of academia and might even contribute to the transformation of society.[7]

During the 1970s, a group of historians—many of them veterans of the civil rights, antiwar, and women's movements—began to talk of a "people's history" that would not only make history more relevant to the struggles of working people but would involve them directly in the production of knowledge. History could not possibly spark social change, they argued, if scholars continued to pose as expert authorities handing down their wisdom to the masses. Rather, historians could contribute most effectively to the creation of useful public history by serving as facilitators and guiding people toward self-authored accounts of their past. In the Boston area, this mission led three activist historians to found the Massachusetts History Workshop in 1978. Disciples of the new labor history, a subset of social history, had recently begun to explore the nation's radical traditions with the aim of inspiring a more aggressive brand of grassroots activism. The Massachusetts History Workshop sought to bring much of this new research to the general public through a series of public forums in Lynn, Lawrence, and Boston. At the same time, the meetings served as a vehicle for rank-and-file workers to tell their own stories and engage in dialogue with historians. In the eyes of the organizers, the most productive sessions facilitated the transfer of wisdom and a militant spirit from the old-timers to a younger generation.[8]

The Brass Workers History Project in the Naugatuck Valley in western Connecticut also reflected the growing social-history orientation of public-history initiatives. Like many of the most ambitious projects, it developed out of collaboration between academic and nonacademic personnel. In this case, a labor historian teamed up with a video producer, a community organizer, and a union education director to record the history of brass-industry workers in the region and then deliver it back to general audiences in book and video format. Scholarship in the field of labor history provided a set of themes that guided the inquiry. Through contacts with local unions and senior citizen centers, the project team secured the participation of current and former brass-industry workers who contributed by sharing photographs and memories. From the perspective of the workers, the project was considered a success because it gave favorable exposure to a group that had long suffered a poor reputation in the region. By shining a public light on the experience of brass-industry workers, the project legitimized their struggles and instilled in them a sense of dignity.[9]

The excitement generated by these initiatives and others like them prompted activist scholars to formalize and institutionalize their movement through the formation of professional organizations, journals, and degree programs. In 1976, the University of California at Santa Barbara launched the first academic program to train professional historians for work in public settings such as museums, heritage sites, government agencies, and nonprofit organizations. Two years later, it followed up with the inaugural issue of *The Public Historian*, the first journal devoted exclusively to the enterprise. 1979 witnessed another landmark event, the formation of the National Council for Public History, which provided a forum for discussion among public-history practitioners through its newsletters and annual meetings. By 1980, the demand for professional training in public history had spawned roughly fifty university degree programs that churned out dozens of professionally trained scholars who could now boast legitimate credentials as "public historians."[10]

One outcome of the professionalization of public history was a growing consensus around general principals and objectives. Among the early champions of taking social history into the streets, Michael Frisch offered perhaps the most cogent articulation of its fundamental premise when he insisted that useful public history derived from "a shared authority" among scholars, designers, and their audiences. This did not mean that academic scholarship merited no place in the practice of public history. Rather it demanded that popular knowledge, rooted in experience and culture, be accorded equal weight with professional perspectives and that museum exhibits, popular-history books, and public programs develop out of an inclusive dialogue. Frisch's own forays beyond the university gates certainly informed his stance. Early in his professional career, Frisch became active in the ambitious Philadelphia Social History Project (PSHP), based at the University of Pennsylvania. In the spirit of the new social history, the PSHP accumulated massive amounts of historical data about the lives of ordinary Philadelphians. Frisch and several colleagues believed that the raw data could be translated into some type of public programming to coincide with Philadelphia's tercentenary celebration in 1982 and thus be put to some use other than arcane scholarship. They were impressed with how well their source material, especially census records and fire-insurance maps, illuminated the changing conditions of neighborhood life. Anticipating that city officials would sponsor a self-flattering chronicle of the past told from a citywide perspective, they were excited about generating alternative stories from more local and personal vantage points by letting people analyze authentic historical materials on their own terms.

Their program comprised three interrelated activities. The first involved a traveling kit of historical documents and hands-on artifacts, a fold-down stage, workshop materials, and modular exhibits that would enable interested individuals at street fairs, schools, and community gatherings to select the data they wanted and build their own exhibits about the history of their neighborhood. The second consisted of a summer institute in Urban Public History designed to train local teachers and residents in the skills of research and analysis. Third, the group proposed a series of thematic city tours, constructed as "movable discussion groups" that encouraged people to apply historical knowledge to contemporary dilemmas. Although funding difficulties squelched all but a modified version of the first activity, the overall plan illustrated how the concept of shared authority might be implemented in a major metropolitan setting.[11]

As Frisch's proposal for Philadelphia's birthday bash demonstrated, the methodologies employed to recover the histories of previously marginalized social groups were easily transferred to the study of urban neighborhoods. Oral history, the practice of recording the memories of rank-and-file historical participants, became the basis of many such community-history projects. The Baltimore Neighborhood History Project, begun in 1977, relied heavily on oral interviews to reconstruct life in several of the city's working-class ethnic neighborhoods. True to the democratic spirit of public history, the project involved neighborhood residents in every aspect of its development. In the earliest phases of the project, narrators tended to focus on highly personal aspects of their lives: the hard times they endured during the Depression, harsh working conditions, and family relations. In later phases, the interviews were structured more tightly around the question of how neighborhoods maintained their integrity in the face of larger metropolitan pressures. The yield from the interviews included published histories in the *Maryland Historical Magazine*, a picture book, and a play that was performed at over thirty local venues.[12]

The principle of shared authority and the concept of a "usable past" also changed the way many urban historical societies conducted their business. Eager to shed their reputation as stodgy institutions run by little old ladies in tennis shoes primarily for the benefit of blue-blooded genealogists, many historical societies plunged into the more controversial waters of contemporary urban concerns. Closer collaboration with academic historians during the 1980s permitted new ideas about social history and people's history to cross-pollinate among professionals employed at museums and universities. One result was novel exhibit content. Instead of using their museums to showcase collections constructed from donations of the rich and famous, historical societies increasingly displayed photographs and broadcast excerpts of oral interviews that explored the development of neighborhoods and particular ethnic communities. Some went further, sponsoring community forums and promoting social change by addressing hot-button issues like AIDS, racism, and gay rights. Typically, museum staff taking on such projects invited community representatives to collaborate in the curatorial process. Some of the most innovative programs took museum professionals beyond their museums and directly into the communities they served. As one museum professional noted, "Mission statements of museums increasingly refer to their role as public forums and networks of information rather than as authoritative sources."[13]

With all the ferment in the field of public history during the closing decades of the twentieth century, it was perhaps inevitable that traditional historic-preservation practices would come under attack. Appeals for more historic sites that acknowledged the contribution of women, racial minorities, ethnic Americans, and workers reflected more than simply the popularity of the new social history. Advances in the study of urban space were equally critical to the rise of an alternative preservation agenda, one that differed dramatically from both the older national progress-oriented approach and the commercially driven wave of adaptive reuse. Building on the work of geographers and sociologists, historians in the 1980s and 1990s began to view space as more than a container for events; it also acted as a dynamic force in the shaping and articulation of social processes. Landscapes or "places" could best be understood as spaces created for specific forms of production (e.g., cattle ranching, steel manufacturing) that were continuously produced and reproduced by a variety of actors. On the one hand, the creation of space for production required buildings and infrastructural networks essential to the operation of crucial economic functions (e.g., wire fences, blast furnaces). On the other, it spawned community spaces such as schools, churches, and residences that ensured the reproduction of societies. The roles assigned to people within specific political economies corresponded to prescribed limitations on their use of urban space in terms of their freedom to own it, traverse it, and deploy it as an instrument for particular social objectives. In this way, the arrangement of space constrained social possibilities. Yet, as scholars were quick to emphasize, urban terrain was continuously contested as various groups pressed for a restructuring of social relations. Urban space, as the object of contestation, thus became politicized, and urban history became no less than the persistent interplay between spatial and social arrangements.[14]

This understanding of urban space had two important implications for historic preservation in cities. First, it suggested that historic significance encompassed the entire urban terrain and all of its component parts. In other words, the city's bungalows, tenements, parks, sewers, streets, electrical grids, and rail tracks were just as important as structures of architectural distinction. This expansive view of historic landscapes paralleled the trend within preservation circles of moving beyond single buildings and considering entire districts, although it pressed preservationists to go even further in incorporating elements of the physical environment into their definition of "historic." Second, it broadened the cast of characters associated with particular sites. No longer was it appropriate to see landscapes as simply a reflection of the initial designer's intention. Rather, each and every element of the built environment represented a complex web of social relations that evolved over time. As architectural historian Eric Sandweiss explained with reference to the history of a city street, it "means little if it's not tied to the story of the farmer who sold the land, the developer who bought it from him, the families who campaigned to have it paved, the men who laid the asphalt, or the children who rode their bikes on it."[15] Conceptualizing space as a perpetual object of social production and contestation thus provided a powerful antidote to the preservationist flaw of freezing the built environment in time.

For preservationists, one of the most radical implications of this intellectual turn was that interpretations of place required consideration of the natural as well as the built environment. If landscape elements could only be understood in the context of larger systems, and if the essence of places could no longer be reduced to a single moment in time, the raw materials from which people produced cultural forms and the environment that preceded human occupation also belonged in the story.[16] This logic helped propagate the idea of cultural landscapes, places that acquired historical significance by virtue of their combined cultural and natural attributes. Preserving a cultural landscape required the protection of flora, fauna, and geological features along with buildings. Until very recently, this all-encompassing approach to historical preservation made little headway in urban areas.[17] The possibilities for adopting this model in inner cities will be explored in a subsequent chapter. For public historians working in cities in the late twentieth century, the primary windfall from these theoretical advances was an opportunity to connect multiple social constituencies to elements of the built environment.

No urban public-history project was more ambitious and influential in its attempt to integrate new perspectives on space into the field of preservation than the Power of Place. A small nonprofit corporation founded in Los Angeles in 1984, the Power of Place strove to weave women's history and ethnic history into the downtown landscape. In addition to providing a formula for rethinking the meaning of urban places, it joined historians, designers, and artists in the enterprise of engraving those meanings directly into the city's physical infrastructure. Departing from the traditional emphasis on architecture, the Power of Place implored the public to consider the full range of social groups whose collective memories were associated with particular buildings and sites. Dolores Hayden, the corporation's founder, insisted that shapers of the urban landscape included "indigenous residents as well as colonizers, migrant workers as well as mayors, housewives as well as housing inspectors."[18] This socially comprehensive formulation elevated the status of vernacular structures—tenements, markets, factories—that, while lacking architectural appeal, nonetheless assumed historical significance as sites of struggle and achievement for women, workers, immigrants, Latinos, and African Americans.

Two preservation campaigns inaugurated by the Power of Place under Hayden's directorship illustrate the approach. With its crenellated tower and stepped parapets, Fire Station Number 30 exemplified the Craftsman style of architecture that was popular in the early part of the twentieth century. What captured the attention of Hayden and her associates, however, was the station's role in the once-vibrant African American commercial enclave on the southeastern fringe of downtown. The racially segregated firehouse was not only a source of pride in the African American community but also the locus of a campaign to integrate civil service employment in the 1950s. The Power of Place hoped to use the still-standing building to keep the firefighters' legacy alive. To that end it invited fifty retired firefighters and their families to share their memories at an on-site public-history workshop and nominated the station as a Los Angeles Cultural-Historic monument. To the dismay of the people involved in the project, a fire on the property aborted plans to redevelop the abandoned building as an office and an exhibit space commemorating the firefighters.[19]

Another Power of Place preservation campaign targeted the Embassy Auditorium, which hosted hundreds of political rallies and community meetings following its construction in downtown Los Angeles in 1914. Hayden and her colleagues used the auditorium to celebrate the history of women's social activism in the city by publicizing the story of three extraordinary individuals: Rose Pesotta of the International Ladies' Garment Workers' Union; Luisa Moreno of the United Cannery Agricultural, Packing and Allied Workers Association; and Josefina Fierro de Bright of El Congreso, a Latino civil rights organization. Each woman took advantage of the Embassy's liberal rental policies during the 1930s, 1940s, and 1950s to stage mass political events on behalf of their respective causes. To trumpet their accomplishments, the Power of Place designed a commemorative poster, staged a public workshop, and published a bilingual booklet. More ambitious plans included two replica sidewalk showcases that would present information about the auditorium and a reading room inside the building containing literature on the history of local community and labor organizing.[20]

In the two examples just cited, public interpretation of the past was directly connected to the preservation of a standing structure. Wherever any remnant of a historic landscape could be employed to tell stories about the diverse actors that animated a particular place, the Power of Place sought its preservation. Ultimately, however, Hayden and her colleagues were less interested in preserving buildings than in preserving the layers of collective memory that gave spaces the power to define social identities. The actual presence of old buildings and structures was enormously helpful, but not essential. Hence, when the Power of Place could find no appropriate standing structures to relate the saga of Biddy Mason, a nineteenth-century African American midwife, it turned to public art as a substitute.

The remarkable and little-known story of Mason demanded public illumination. Born a slave and transported to California from Mississippi via the Overland Trail, Mason sued for her freedom in 1856 and won her case. Mason went on to become a highly regarded midwife and nurse, delivering babies for many of Los Angeles's leading families. She also became a property owner, the founder of the Los Angeles branch of the First African Methodist Episcopal Church, and the matriarch of a successful family. By 1986, when the Power of Place decided to bring Mason's extraordinary life to public attention, her two-story brick home had long since been leveled for a parking lot. A traditional commemorative plaque was one possibility, but in the end the Power of Place opted for something more ambitious—an 81-foot wall that recounted her story through text, photographs of historical documents, and engravings of the types of equipment Mason used in her work.[21]

The Power of Place broke new ground in aligning preservation goals with emerging trends in historical scholarship and employing innovative formats to deliver history to large and diverse urban audiences. The publication of Dolores Hayden's book about the project, in 1997, along with her many speaking engagements, invigorated the fields of public history and preservation and inspired many like-minded projects. Without question, intellectual currents inside and outside of academia had been pressing steadily toward a more democratic approach to the public interpretation of urban landscapes. Yet, if the Power of Place did not single-handedly revolutionize the practice of public history in cities, it nonetheless provided a widely emulated blueprint as well as the most cogent rationale for extracting the historical significance of vernacular spaces in a way that resonated with the lives and experiences of ordinary urban inhabitants. Moreover, it served as a catalyst for projects that went even further, or at least charted slightly different paths, in integrating landscape preservation and public history to meet the needs of diverse constituencies in multicultural cities.

Among them, the Place Matters initiative in New York City stood out as an exemplar of grassroots public history directed toward sustaining vibrant neighborhoods and communities. Two preexisting cultural organizations, City Lore and the Municipal Arts Society, pooled their resources to found Place Matters in 1998. With an explicit nod to Hayden and the Power of Place, they sought to invigorate collective memories through preservation and interpretation of the built environment and to "create, for the first time, a genuinely public history of New York City that can be inscribed in its streets, buildings, and public places."[22] Although the two projects shared similar goals, Place Matters veered more decisively in the direction of neighborhood regeneration. Whereas the Los Angeles project tended to shine a spotlight on sites with the potential to empower marginalized groups through the solidification of cultural identities, its New York counterpart was more inclined to draw attention to "assets in all kinds of human and community development" so that they could continue to "perform their many productive functions."[23]

Place Matters also surpassed the Power of Place in implementing Michael Frisch's concept of "shared authority," in part through its innovative use of electronic media. Rather than relying on professionals in the fields of architecture, planning, or history to select landscape features of significance, it turned the task over to the general public. Its first project involved building a citywide inventory of important historic sites from the ground up by soliciting nominations from ordinary citizens. Preprinted questionnaires circulated by partner organizations and distributed at workshops asked respondents to identify sites and explain what made them worthy for inclusion on the inventory. In this way, Place Matters served as a facilitator, enabling communities to determine for themselves what places were significant and how those places contributed to community well-being. Within two years, the organization had solicited nearly 200 nominations for its Census of Places That Matter. In 2000, Place Matters improved on its capacity to tap grassroots concern about the historic built environment by launching a Web site. Not only did an Internet presence provide Place Matters with a platform for publicizing its census widely but it enabled the organization to solicit many more nominations—over 500 by 2006. In addition, the Web site became the organization's primary exhibition venue; a series of virtual tours narrated stories about neighborhood decline and renewal, cultural interchange among ethnic groups, and local political activism.[24]

One of those virtual tours, "From Mambo to Hip Hop," recounted a history of popular musical innovation in the South Bronx and East Harlem. With information culled from personal recollections, a section of New York City long associated with urban decay, poverty, and crime was recast as a font of artistic dynamism. When Puerto Ricans migrated from Manhattan across the Harlem River in the 1940s, they transplanted the popular Cuban-based music that had recently burst on the scene in the fertile territory of the South Bronx. There, hundreds of Latino musicians sang, danced, and jammed in the area's parks, rooftops, apartments, dance halls, and clubs. Many, including Tito Puente, Machito, and Tito Rodriguez—the three Mambo

Kings—went on to become national stars. By the 1960s they had created a distinctive salsa sound that departed from its Cuban roots with a high-energy and heavy percussive emphasis. A decade later, cultural interchange with West Indian and African American residents spawned a new hip-hop sound that soon took the country by storm. The Internet tour of neighborhood dance halls, bars, parks, and subway stations (also repackaged in a glossy brochure) highlighted the role of the built environment in supporting the productive interplay of entrepreneurial ambitions and cultural influences. Points of interest on the tour included the Casa Amadeo Record Store, the oldest continuously operated Latino music store in New York City; El Mambo candy store, where youngsters gathered to listen and dance to jukebox tunes in the late afternoons; the site of the elegant Tropicor Club, which booked the top acts in Latin music during the late 1960s and early 1970s; the Grand Concourse subway station, where graffiti artists congregated after school in the 1970s; and the former location of the Black Door club, where renowned hip-hop DJ Grandmaster Flash debuted his manually operated drum machine. In accordance with its preservationist mission, Place Matters prompted the listing of the Casa Amadeo record store on the National Register of Historic Places.[25]

A key theoretical maxim advanced by scholars in the fields of social history and cultural geography is that all landscapes are contested terrain. Public historians have used this insight as the basis for laying claim to virtually all parcels of urban real estate on behalf of groups that were, until recently, poorly represented in historical accounts. In legitimizing diverse perspectives on the history of urban places, this new approach made it difficult if not impossible to arrive at any universally agreed-on version of past events and their meaning. If that made history messier and potentially more contentious, it also imbued the process of historical interpretation with an unusual capacity to build mutual respect among the diverse populations that shared particular fragments of urban space.

It was in this spirit that congregants of an African American church seized upon the restoration and interpretation of what were once segregated seating galleries as an instrument for improving interethnic relations on the Lower East Side of Manhattan. St. Augustine's Episcopal Church began its life in 1828 as a house of worship for New York City's elite patricians. Some of its early members owned black slaves and kept black servants, and it appears that church architects constructed the two concealed galleries in the upper balcony to keep those African American dependents separate from the rest of the congregation. In the decades following the Civil War, the neighborhood became a tumultuous stew of European immigrant groups; by the

1990s, 95 percent of the congregants were African American although the surrounding area remained ethnically diverse. It was around this time that intercultural tensions escalated as the pressures of gentrification along with a heavy influx of Hispanic and Asian immigrants began to displace many poorer African Americans from the area. Preservation and public history became a self-conscious strategy for staking a claim in the neighborhood, reminding people of the long-standing African American presence and ensuring that the legacy would not be forgotten. Yet, rather than enter into a symbolic battle over neighborhood ownership, the church adopted a more inclusive approach. With assistance from the nearby Lower East Side Tenement Museum, it invited representatives from ten community organizations to collaborate in the process of restoring and exhibiting the upper balcony pews. A series of "Kitchen Conversations" encouraged African Americans, Asians, Hispanics, and Jews to react to the former slave galleries in the context of their own perspectives on the neighborhood's past and present. Through this interchange, the diverse participants learned that they had much in common; at some time in the past, all had encountered prejudice, discrimination, and marginalization. Because of these discussions, it was decided that public interpretation of the former slave galleries would lead the way as the first of many place-based exhibits on the theme of Lower East Side social relations, all of which would serve as catalysts for community discussion and enhanced understanding.[26]

The projects in Los Angeles and New York just discussed distinguished themselves by crafting grassroots preservation programs that rejected the more typical economic rejuvenation rationales. The Old Town History Project in Portland, Oregon, on the other hand, demonstrated that preservation programs informed by the insights of social history need not run against the grain of inner-city economic revitalization. Portland's Old Town district, long a home to immigrant families and the poor, was known for many years as the city's Skid Row. In the 1970s, after urban renewal destroyed Portland's original Chinese enclave, a second Chinatown sprouted in Old Town. As visitors flocked to the area, city officials and private investors targeted the district for further redevelopment with the goal of making it an arts, entertainment, and tourist quarter. The completion of a $10.5 million Classical Chinese Garden was viewed as a first step in a revitalization plan that promised sidewalk enhancements, 1,500 new housing units, and a 200-room hotel. Existing residents and property owners did not oppose the scheme; indeed, they collaborated in the planning process and ultimately assented to the recommendations outlined in a 1999 report. Yet, as a condition for their acquiescence, they insisted that the district maintain its economic and ethnic diversity even as new investment and tourists poured in. More-over, they took active steps to ensure that their contributions to the neigh-borhood were not forgotten as it underwent its makeover. To this end they formed the Old Town/Chinatown Neighborhood Association in 2000. Its mission was to preserve an endangered history by recording the memories of past and present inhabitants and delivering that history to public audiences through street performances, walking tours, and interpretive sidewalk plaques placed in front of historic structures. Some of the district's older buildings were also converted into exhibit spaces. Striving to influence the course of neighborhood renewal, the Old Town History Project boldly intertwined emerging techniques and philosophies in the field of public history with the dominant practices of historic preservation. While renovated warehouses and storefronts lured new businesses, customers, and residents to the district, they also tempered the dislocating consequences of neighborhood gentrifica-tion by maintaining a link to the past through public interpretation.[27]

Archaeologists in Public

Concurrent with the infusion of academic personnel and perspectives into the realm of public history, professionally trained archaeologists intensified their engagement with public audiences and institutions. By the 1960s, ar-chaeology already enjoyed substantial visibility, largely through its connec-tion with historic preservation. As was the case within the discipline of his-tory, however, the field of public archaeology enforced a gulf between those who worked in public settings and those employed by academia. With the gradual bridging of this gap in subsequent decades, public archaeology be-came explicitly politicized and developed some intriguing models for apply-ing historical research to the needs of urban communities.[28]

The late nineteenth century is the place to begin the story. It was at this time that an American obsession with protecting the national patrimony extended to ruins and artifacts exposed through archaeological excavation. In a landmark 1892 decision, President Benjamin Harrison issued an execu-tive order to establish the Casa Grande Ruin in Arizona as a national ar-chaeological reservation. This Act was designed to prevent the looting of what remained at this fourteenth-century Hohokam Indian site. A sequence of preservation laws in the early twentieth century, most notably the Antiq-uities Act of 1906 and the Historic Sites Act of 1935, extended the domain of archaeology into the more recent past by authorizing the excavation of colonial farmhouses, frontier trading posts, and military battlegrounds.

These sites, many of which were administered by the National Park Service, became popular with the public and thus forged a connection between archaeology and tourism. Colonial Williamsburg epitomized the application of archaeology to preservation-based tourism in the private sector. Philanthropist John D. Rockefeller, Jr., funded the majority of the project, which combined the skills of archaeologists, architects, and historians to recreate the Virginia capital as it had existed in the eighteenth century. Starting in the 1930s, archaeologists were asked to find razed building foundations so that they could be restored and displayed for public view.[29]

The next milestone occurred in 1966 when Congress passed the National Historic Preservation Act, thereby inaugurating the field of cultural-resource management. This law and several others that followed required the survey and excavation of endangered properties that might harbor relics of historic value. The imperatives of cultural-resource management unleashed a torrent of archaeological activity under public auspices, often in urban settings. Yet public mandate did not necessarily translate into public engagement. Typically, archaeologists working in the employ of federal agencies or private firms recovered, documented, and preserved cultural resources on behalf of some vaguely defined public interest without direct consultation with ordinary citizens or their representatives.[30]

Many archaeologists learned the hard way that serious risks attended the failure to reach out to local communities. The uproar over the African Burial Ground excavation in New York City served as a cautionary tale for archaeologists who operated in isolation from the public. The controversy originated with the discovery of a colonial-era African cemetery on a lower Manhattan construction site in 1991. Following federal guidelines, the property owners (in this case a federal government agency) hired a firm to excavate the skeletons and another forensic team from Lehman College to study the bones. In the absence of any consultation with the descendant community, the archaeologists proceeded with a research design that recalled the most heinous examples of anthropological racism. In the early twentieth century, scholars had relied on the physical characteristics of human beings to establish a racial hierarchy that placed Anglo-Saxon whites at the top and people of African descent at the bottom. Now, almost 100 years later, archaeologists were using the African remains from the New York burial grounds to refine racial typologies. African American community leaders became incensed when they learned of the project and were further enraged at the cavalier handling of the exhumed skeletons. A public campaign to terminate the project eventually reached the halls of Congress, and only an agreement to transfer the entire project to Howard University and integrate community representatives in a new research design prevented it from grinding to a permanent halt.[31]

The African Burial Ground excavation sounded a wake-up call within the profession and dovetailed with a movement under way among academic archaeologists to acknowledge the social implications of their research and imbue their work with political significance. During the 1970s, archaeologists in different parts of the country sought to "document the exclusion of non-Anglo groups from the mainstream of American life" by investigating the material culture of slave plantations and other zones of exploitation.[32] The growing influence of Marxist and postmodern theories alerted academic archaeologists to the role of historical contingency in the construction of analytical frameworks and forced them to rethink their exclusive authority over matters of interpretation. These intellectual currents, however, were slow to infiltrate the field of cultural-resource management, which increasingly operated outside the academic umbrella. Between 1966 and 1980 the number of private-contract archaeology firms mushroomed from three to 500.[33] University scholars often dismissed the work of contract archaeologists as being second-rate, and those employed by private firms became increasingly marginalized within the profession. The founding of The Society for Historical Archaeology in 1967, however, signaled a countervailing impulse designed to lend academic credibility and rigor to public archaeology.[34] Over time it also served as a vessel for the cross-pollination of ideas across academic and nonacademic settings.

By the 1980s, public archaeologists intent on combining the theoretical constructs of academia with socially relevant work found fertile terrain in urban areas. In his 1987 introduction to "Living in Cities," Edward Staski argued that "in the next several years urban archaeologists should have developed a comprehensive and effective set of procedures for meeting public needs and desires."[35] Although no "set procedures" for engaging the public emerged, a variety of ambitious projects moved public archaeology firmly into the arena of contemporary urban concerns.

Among the most notable was Archaeology in Annapolis. Launched in 1981 as collaboration between the University of Maryland and the preservation organization Historic Annapolis, Inc., this program adopted a confrontational model of public interaction. Its application of critical theory to the interpretation of archaeological artifacts aimed to raise historical consciousness and help the public grasp the present-day social and political implications of prior developments.[36] Critical theory developed out of the Frankfurt School of Marxist analysis in the 1920s and has continued to provide a framework for scholarship in a wide variety of disciplines. A fundamental premise of critical theory is that all knowledge serves certain social and political ends; there is no such thing as politically neutral knowledge. Public archaeology conducted within this theoretical framework aimed to expose the contemporary social and political contexts that undergirded historical interpretations and also encouraged public audiences to reflect critically on the uses of history. Ideally, "active questioning" and enlightenment would produce a foundation for "corrective action to rectify social inequality."[37]

In practice, Archaeology in Annapolis consisted of four elements: a twenty-minute, twelve-projector, computer-synchronized audiovisual production; a twenty-four–page guidebook to one part of the Annapolis Historic District; a fifteen-minute tour of an active excavation site delivered by an archaeologist; and three small archaeological exhibits located in museum buildings around the district."[38] Each of these programs sought to demonstrate how understandings of the past changed over time because of shifting scientific, social, and political perspectives. The site tour provided the most appropriate setting for the application of critical theory. Here, archaeologists interacted with the public face-to-face, presenting information on the history of the site and explaining the archeological techniques used to recover this knowledge. Critical theory came into play as the archaeologists highlighted changing interpretations of a site's history over time and confronted visitors with questions about how their present-day lives were affected by these various versions of the past. For example, a tour of the eighteenth-century Victualling Warehouse used archaeological discoveries as the starting point for a discussion on contemporary capitalism and tourism. Ceramics uncovered at the site revealed an intensifying pattern of standardization and segmentation, both hallmarks of contemporary capitalism. By presenting the ceramics in this context, the archaeologists broke from the convention of classifying the food-ware according to date and style. The revised interpretation denaturalized capitalism by exposing it as a system with a specific history. The tour script then forced visitors to reflect on their role as tourists in the modern capitalist economy. Guides explained how Annapolis had long employed stories about George Washington's visits to the town as a device to influence tourist behavior. Because the local economy revolved around tourism, the city needed to maintain a steady flow of visitors. Yet residents wanted to avoid the sort of guests that would make a nuisance of themselves with late-night carousing and impolite manners. To encourage the desired conduct, the austere and dignified Washington was presented as a model tourist worthy of emulation.[39]

While Archaeology in Annapolis adopted confrontation as a mode of public engagement, other projects chose a more conversational approach. As defined by Larry McKee and Brian Thomas, the conversational approach is rooted in "the need to carry on a conversation, rather than present lectures, and the need to broaden the use of archaeological evidence in museums and other public interpretations of the past."[40] In contrast with the confrontational mode of engagement employed in Annapolis, the conversational approach requires that archaeologists listen as much as they talk to the community around them.

Archaeological projects that utilized the conversational approach often collaborated with communities in developing and interpreting a research design based on community concerns and interests. Linda Derry's work in Selma, Alabama provided a framework for this type of community engagement. Her recommendations included a plea to involve target audiences from the inception of projects. "If the community does not help define the questions," she contended, "the answers will not interest them." Thus Derry advocated projects built around "questions that count" in the context of particular community circumstances. Moreover, she urged archaeologists to take the time to "work through difficult issues *with* the community" over the course of a project. As an important corollary to her insistence on community consultation, Derry exhorted her colleagues to take a "holistic" approach by recognizing the full range of social diversity among interested parties.[41]

With respect to public participation, few projects were more ambitious than Alexandria Archaeology. Launched in 1977 as a city-funded enterprise, this program brought professional archaeologists and local citizens together to develop a historic-preservation plan, conduct research, curate collections, and interpret community history.[42] Under the banner of community-based archaeology, this joint venture investigated over 100 sites in the city of Alexandria, Virginia and recovered over 2 million artifacts. Decisions about where to excavate were driven by public curiosity. Through the organization Friends of Alexandria Archaeology and discussion at public meetings, interested citizens expressed their curiosity about a wide range of subjects: the evolution of the town's main street, the history of its waterfront district, Alexandria's Quaker heritage, and the city's long-standing free black population.[43] Citizens were particular eager to recover information from sites that were slated for urban redevelopment. Critical to Alexandria Archaeology's success was its large volunteer corps. City archaeologist Pamela Cressey estimated that between 1977 and 1987, "more than 2,000 individuals . . . worked to excavate sites, catalog and illustrate artifacts, draw maps, research documents, write papers, give site tours and enter data into computers."[44] This unprecedented level of civic involvement infused the project with a public dimension at all levels of archaeological work from the research design to interpretation and education.

Over its first thirty years of operation, the public benefits of Alexandria Archaeology proved considerable. Data collected from the excavations fed the creation of museums, a historic walking and bike trail, and educational programs.[45] The 1.2 million visitors who patronized the city's eight museums each year during the 1990s provided Alexandria with an annual economic windfall estimated at over 8 million dollars when lodging and restaurant revenue were included in calculations.[46] Perhaps even more impressive, the project gave citizens a platform for influencing land-use planning. Alexandrians had long bemoaned their access to their waterfront. The excavation and reconstruction of a historic canal lock on the Potomac River provided the rationale for a much-sought-after waterfront park. Building on this achievement, citizens were able to convince the city to designate several additional waterfront parcels as parks that served a combined educational and recreational function.[47]

The excavation and reconstruction of the canal lock testifies to the persistent link between public archaeology and historic preservation. Much of the recent activity associated with community-based archaeology has occurred in conjunction with the preservation or reconstruction of historic buildings. Even excavations that follow the demolition of buildings, or yield little that can be re-fashioned for contemporary use, often advance the cause of preservation by enriching the historical record and contributing to the public interpretation of surrounding structures that have been converted into residential quarters, shops, museums, restaurants, and taverns. Certainly, this has been the case in both Annapolis and Alexandria. The Annapolis example is especially because, because by asking audiences to examine critically the uses to which history is put, archaeological interpretation invites a critique of contemporary preservation practices.

If Annapolis and Alexandria suggest a role for public archaeology in the realm of heritage tourism, a more recent project on the near-Westside of Indianapolis demonstrates its application to preservation initiatives directed at inner-city revitalization. By the early twentieth century, this area just west of downtown was the heart of Indianapolis's African American settlement. By midcentury, however, it was regarded by city planners as a slum, and most of it had succumbed to the destructive forces of urban renewal. An exception was a six-block area in the shadow of Indiana University–Purdue University Indianapolis (UIPUI). Severed from the surrounding urban fabric with which it evolved, this enclave struggled to maintain an identity. Beginning in the

1980s, residents embraced historic preservation to protect what was left of the neighborhood and to cultivate a distinct sense of place. In 1992, the Ransom Place district secured a designation on the National Register of Historic Places. Deeply devoted to a recovery of local history, residents were receptive to a proposal by archaeologists at UIPUI to excavate several sites in and around the neighborhood. In 1997 a partnership was formed among UIPUI, the Ransom Place Neighborhood Association, and the Indianapolis Urban League to illuminate the enclave's historic ties to the obliterated near-Westside and thereby "reclaim a heritage concealed by urban transformation."[48] Once the excavations were under way, the very visible "stream of artifacts" associated with previous African American populations that emerged from the ground had the effect of strengthening residents' claim to a portion of urban space that was otherwise marginalized and vulnerable to continued appropriation.[49]

By the dawn of the twenty-first century, public archaeology had moved well beyond the mission of simply educating the masses. In directing research toward the creation of a more just and democratic social order, some archaeologists began to think of themselves as advocates and activists, rather than as neutral translators of humanity's material relics.[50] This paradigm shift did not relieve archaeologists of the obligation to study the past, but it demanded a thorough immersion in contemporary political contexts. In urban settings, it was not unusual to find archaeologists taking explicit positions on behalf of historic preservation, affordable housing, and the provision of care for senior citizens.[51]

Over the last forty years, then, the movement to involve communities in historical research and interpretation has redefined the practices of both public history and public archaeology. These parallel trajectories testify to the influence of broad societal trends on academic life. Despite a congruent determination to make scholarly research relevant to contemporary society, however, the democratization of history and archaeology did not proceed in tandem. The structure of academic departments and the establishment of separate professional organizations and journals enforced disciplinary insularity, giving rise to two distinct movements: public history and public archaeology. As a result, projects have typically been lodged in either one discipline or the other. The lack of communication across the fields of archaeology and history has surely impoverished each enterprise. Nonetheless, a convergence of philosophies and several decades of experience working in urban communities hold forth the promise of active collaboration in the public interpretation of preserved inner-city landscapes.

One Step Beyond: Reclaiming Urban Space
as the Basis for Community Development

The democratic impulses of public history and archaeology offer tremendous opportunities for ordinary citizens to direct the benefits of historic preservation toward the creation and maintenance of stable and vibrant communities. As we have seen, enormous strides have already been taken. From Los Angeles to New York and many places in between, historic landscapes have been reinterpreted at the grass roots to reflect the full array of social groups and forces responsible for the city-building process. The pioneering projects described here by no means exhaust the range of public projects that have deepened the meaning of urban landscapes. For example, one can wander the restored alleys of San Francisco's Chinatown and learn from bilingual bronze markers how they were superimposed onto the existing city street grid to mimic land-use patterns in China's Guangdong province.[52] Beginning in 1985, the Archaeological Research Centre in Toronto sponsored an annual downtown excavation to expose the architectural remains of demolished buildings and display the material objects once used at the site by ordinary men and women.[53] To preserve a visible reminder of past labor struggles in Pittsburgh, the Battle of Homestead Foundation waged a successful campaign to prevent destruction of the last remaining structure of the Homestead Steel Works.[54] In the mid-1990s a woman in Portland, Maine launched a campaign to restore an early-nineteenth-century church on the industrial waterfront that was once a stop on the Underground Railroad. The restoration project has since turned into a vehicle for exploring the local African American community's hidden past.[55] As back alleys, dilapidated waterfronts, and factory buildings have assumed historical significance, and as the historic contribution of the full cast of urban inhabitants has been disclosed, it has become possible for ordinary citizens to appreciate their roles as custodians of their surroundings and as responsible parties for ensuring that those surroundings are consistent with the sorts of communities they want.

Through history, then, urban inhabitants lay claim to space. Conceptualizing the urban landscape as an inheritance confers on its heirs an entitlement to control its destiny. Indeed, involving communities at the grass roots in the historical interpretation of their neighborhoods is empowering because the very act involves them in the production of that space. For marginalized groups in society, the stakes are especially high. As Dolores Hayden has observed with respect to women and ethnic minorities, "the constant threat of being dispossessed makes each community's attachment to the urban landscape particularly poignant."[56] Going one step further, it is not a stretch to presume that a stronger attachment to place can solidify a community's determination to resist future threats of dispossession. The historic-preservation movement, for all its shortcomings, remains an ideal vehicle for engaging communities in historical interpretation and directing redevelopment toward locally defined ends.

It is in this capacity to reshape urban communities that public history and public archaeology have more to contribute than they typically have achieved. In too many cities, the promise of public archaeology and public history remains unfulfilled. In most grassroots projects, the connection between the past and the future remains somewhat nebulous. Historical research and archaeology may provide communities with generalized insight about where they want go, but rarely are they employed to address specific policy dilemmas or redevelopment decisions. Initiatives such as the Portland Chinatown/Old Town project, however, demonstrate that it is possible to tailor public-history programs to concrete revitalization outcomes. For most public historians and archaeologists this is uncharted terrain. In the following chapters we will attempt to map out a generalized strategy for crafting public-history and archaeology projects that assist communities directly in the revitalization process.

3

≒+

An Experiment in North St. Louis

More than any other section of St. Louis, the north side manifests inner-city decay. In the districts hugging the curve of the Mississipp River beyond the central business district, one can travel for miles amid a depressing spectacle of abandoned factories, crumbling houses, and weed-strewn lots. But within that landscape of dereliction, one also finds pockets of rejuvenation where refurbished building facades, flowering gardens, and busy construction crews disrupt the prevailing bleakness. Despite the bedraggled appearance of St. Louis's north side, few sections of the city hold greater potential for preservation-based revitalization. Not only does the area contain many salvageable structures of architectural merit dating back to the nineteenth century, but it also boasts a population eager to embrace its past as a way of navigating its way toward a brighter future. This chapter will document recent preservation and public-history initiatives undertaken by residents of one particular neighborhood on the city's north side, Old North St. Louis. Working in conjunction with faculty and staff at the University of Missouri–St. Louis, residents drew on some of the most exciting developments in the fields of public history and archaeology to stabilize the built environment and simultaneously strengthen community bonds.

The Preservation Movement in St. Louis

Community activists in Old North St. Louis had no trouble grasping historic preservation's potential for neighborhood regeneration. Few cities in the United States did better than St. Louis at attracting investment to moribund inner-city districts through the adaptive reuse of older buildings in the last quarter of the twentieth century. Undoubtedly, the passion for preservation in St. Louis was attributable to the devastating loss of much of its historic landscape in the decades following World War II. The disappearance of brick row houses, high-spired churches, and corner stores dating back to the nineteenth century was as much the product of policy decisions as neglect. Strategies to save the city relied heavily on the demolition of older, dilapidated structures and their replacement with new construction. Like many other cities in the industrial Midwest and Northeast, St. Louis saw itself on the verge of crisis in the immediate aftermath of World War II. With the general shift of population and manufacturing activity to Sunbelt states and the drain of investment to suburban locations within the metropolitan region, the city of St. Louis faced the prospect of economic and social collapse. In the opinion of city planners, the only viable alternative entailed comprehensive redevelopment of already occupied land, a policy that politicians of the period pursued with gusto.[1] Low-income residential neighborhoods flanking the central business district were systematically obliterated to make room for corporate offices, factories, a baseball stadium, and a limited number of high-rise apartment complexes. According to one estimate, urban renewal accounted for the demolition of 60,000 dwelling units in St. Louis between 1955 and 1980, most of them in the central core. Meanwhile, north and south of downtown, federally funded interstate highways tore through residential districts otherwise untouched by renewal, thereby adding to the tally of demolished buildings.[2]

By the late 1960s, signs of backlash against the destroy-and-rebuild approach to urban revitalization had become apparent. For decades isolated preservationists had fought a rearguard battle against developers and city officials bent on large-scale clearance. In 1959, as some of the most ambitious urban-renewal projects were set in motion, a group of outraged citizens formed the Landmarks Association of St. Louis. Defending much beloved mansions, skyscrapers, and civic buildings against highway construction and redevelopers, the organization gained members and considerable publicity over the next several years. An important milestone was reached in 1965, when St. Louisans cast their mayoral ballots for A. J. Cervantes, who opposed the incumbent Raymond Tucker in the Democratic primary, campaigning on a platform that explicitly rejected the practice of destroying residential neighborhoods.[3]

In part, the turn of public opinion reflected disillusion with prevailing policy. For all the hype surrounding urban renewal, it produced little obvious improvement in urban conditions beyond the central business districts. Redevelopment proceeded slowly in the recently cleared Mill Creek Valley, just west of downtown, and the public housing erected on the northern and southern edges of downtown were a disaster. The Pruitt-Igoe apartments, once considered an exemplar of modern low-income housing, deteriorated so rapidly in terms of both social and physical conditions that the city dynamited all thirty-three buildings in the complex in the early 1970s. Yet the reversal of attitude was also a product of urban renewal's success and the upsurge in demand for historic housing in several inner-city neighborhoods. With the central business district on a firmer footing and some of the worst slum areas either pushed further west or confined to public housing reservations, nineteenth-century row houses and four-family flats close to downtown suddenly became attractive to an assortment of artists, young professionals, and office workers. Most of these households lacked children, leaving adult members with time and money to rehabilitate and modernize their new homes.

Two neighborhoods on the city's south side spearheaded the preservation renaissance. Lafayette Square had once been one of the city's most exclusive residential enclaves. Developed around a thirty-acre landscaped park in the 1850s and 1860s, it drew railroad executives, politicians, and other members of the social elite to its terra-cotta mansions and stone-fronted row houses. Following an 1897 tornado, however, it fell into disrepair as some of the property owners chose to move rather than rebuild. By World War II, many of the properties had been converted into rooming houses, and when city planners assessed the area in 1947, they declared it "obsolete." According to official wisdom, the Square's salvation lay in tearing down all remaining structures and replacing them with garden-apartment complexes. But before the city got around to the task, a group of energetic young families launched a grassroots preservation campaign. In 1969, they formed the Lafayette Square Restoration Committee and sought national historic-district status from the National Park Service. With money obtained from the National Trust for Historic Preservation and some supportive local banks, they acquired twelve dilapidated properties, made emergency repairs, and then recouped their costs by selling the homes to new owners who pledged to continue the restoration work. With the money acquired from the resale, they established a revolving fund to carry the work forward.[4] A similar process unfolded in the nearby Soulard district, where enterprising rehabbers and affluent young professionals gravitated to nineteenth-century Federal-style row houses clustered around a public market. Like Lafayette Square, Soulard bore the hallmarks of a slum, with high unemployment rates and plenty of abandoned buildings. Building on the precedent set by their neighbors, a group of residents new to the district formed the Soulard Restoration Group in 1974 and began actively recruiting prospective home buyers. With the inception of historic-property tax credits for income-producing properties in the 1970s, developers began to take an interest in the area as well, rehabilitating properties for middle- and upper-income renters.[5]

The most direct connection between central-business-district revival and neighborhood historic preservation occurred in LaSalle Park, also on the city's near south side. During the 1950s, Ralston-Purina, one of the city's largest and oldest companies, decided to retain and expand its corporate headquarters on the southern fringe of downtown rather than join other firms in a suburban exodus. The area surrounding the site, however, was in the throes of urban decline, and as Ralston-Purina's new office buildings went up in the late 1950s, the neighborhood deteriorated even further. The corporation wanted to take some kind of action, not only because the surrounding slum was an eyesore and a threat to its real estate investment, but also because it wanted to provide housing for its white-collar workforce. Initially, it hoped to clear the area and build new mixed-income housing units under the auspices of the federal urban renewal program. Yet, as the rehabbing phenomenon began to demonstrate its impact in the nearby Soulard and Lafayette Park districts, the corporation abruptly shifted course and decided to revitalize the area through preservation and rehabilitation. In 1975, the corporation broke ground for LaSalle Park Village. Working with the local development agency, Ralston-Purina secured $2 million in federal funds for a renewal scheme that relied heavily on restoration of nineteenth-century row houses and detached two- and three-story houses. Through a subsidiary, the LaSalle Park Redevelopment Corporation, Ralston-Purina contributed its own funds to buy and reconstruct twelve crumbling homes, which were then sold to attorneys, nurses, management consultants, and company employees. This initial foray spurred further private investment, and by 1984 nearly 200 homes, town houses, and apartments had been rehabbed.[6]

Within the central business district, a similar shift in strategy was under way, although the critical impetus here was the federal tax code revision, which offered irresistible incentives to developers willing to adapt historic properties for commercial purposes. The most notable project was the conversion of the city's grand railroad terminal into a major retail and restaurant center in 1985. St. Louis Union Station originally opened in 1894 amid tremendous fanfare and adulation. Conceived as a monumental gateway to the city, it dazzled the eye with a lofty stone clock tower and Romanesque-style façade and arched entrance. Inside, a barrel-vaulted great hall allowed passengers to wait for their trains in the splendor of marble columns, ornamental friezes, stained-glass windows, and a gold-ribbed ceiling. Its massive balloon train shed spanned thirty-two tracks. By 1960, however, passenger railroad traffic had diminished considerably and the station was underutilized. City leaders scratched their heads pondering its future. A variety of ambitious plans for converting parts of the terminal complex into a motel, supermarket, parking lot, and convention center foundered on the lack of investment funds. With the availability of historic-property tax credits after 1976, prospects for revitalization brightened considerably. James Rouse, fresh from his triumphs in Baltimore and Boston, eyed St. Louis as his next profitable festival marketplace venture. Forming a partnership with Omni Hotels, Rouse embarked on what would become the nation's most expensive rehabilitation project using federal tax credits. No longer a terminal for railroad trains, the landmark building was reincarnated as a tourist and shopping spectacle complete with restaurants, bars, boutiques, souvenir marts, an artificial lake, and a luxury hotel.[7]

After a lull in local preservation activity following the passage of the Federal Tax Reform Act in 1986, momentum resumed when the State of Missouri stepped in with a generous tax credit program of its own. Launched in January 1998, the Missouri Historic Preservation Tax Credit program provided a 25 percent tax credit on the cost of renovating commercial and residential properties. Under its provisions, developers were permitted to offset their state tax obligations over a thirteen-year span, beginning two years before renovation and extending twelve years beyond the year of construction. The program invited applications from individuals, corporations, and partnerships; the credits themselves were fungible in that they could be sold or exchanged. Eligible structures were those listed individually on the National Register of Historic Places along with those identified as contributing to either a nationally designated district or a local district certified by the United States Department of the Interior. One further stipulation was that the total cost of renovation be equal to or greater than 50 percent of the value of the building.[8]

At the state level, the impact of the Missouri Historic Preservation Tax Credit program was dramatic. Within three years of its inception in 1998, 74 million dollars worth of tax credits leveraged nearly 295 million dollars worth of historic rehabilitation activity.[9] One notable consequence of the successful state program was a more aggressive pursuit of federal tax credits. Missouri law allowed developers to piggyback federal incentives atop any award granted by the state. With both federal and state credits in hand, developers were able to recapture up to 45 percent of their investment costs. Thus, the state law inspired a higher rate of applications for the limited—yet still significant—federal program. According to an annual report issued by the National Park Service, Missouri surpassed all other states in 2004, with $357 million in federal tax assistance for rehabilitation projects.[10] Within the State of Missouri, St. Louis garnered the lion's share of government assistance. Approximately 62 percent of the state's program activity occurred within the city, accounting for $183 million in project costs and $46 million in credits. The combination of federal and state tax subsidies was instrumental in jump-starting preservation projects downtown, where numerous old warehouses were converted into loft-style condominiums.[11] Beyond the city's central core, the state program reignited a boom in the rehabilitation of residential properties, particularly in the south-side neighborhoods just beyond the Lafayette Square, Soulard, and LaSalle Park districts.

Despite St. Louis's impressive record of preservation-based redevelopment, the phenomenon remained geographically selective. While hundreds of homes were restored on the city's south side, and a wide variety of historic structures were adapted for new uses downtown, preservation lagged on the north end of town. It was not for any lack of opportunity or effort. North-side neighborhoods shared the same architectural traditions that drew throngs of rehabbers to the south side. Much like their peers in Lafayette Square and Soulard, north-side residents established historic districts and aggressively solicited middle-income home buyers. Several factors stymied their efforts. Historically, the city's north side had always enjoyed better connections with the central business district. As a result, it developed earlier and saw more intensive industrial activity. What was once an advantage, however, became a burden, as a poorer and denser working-class population placed tremendous stress on the physical environment. Housing, in particular, deteriorated faster on the north side. Inferior housing conditions, however, proved less of a handicap than demographic trends. Even as the south side became poorer with the in-migration of families from the Missouri countryside after World War II, it remained predominantly white. North St. Louis, on the other hand, absorbed African Americans displaced from public housing and urban-renewal projects. As North St. Louis became synonymous with African American residency, it also became stereotyped as a haven for criminals, drug addicts, and welfare mothers. In fact, inner-city neighborhoods on both the north and south sides harbored their share of social maladies. But the presence of African Americans north of downtown kept away many would-be homeowners willing to take a risk in otherwise similar neighborhoods several miles away.

The Limits of Historic Preservation:
Old North St. Louis

The Old North St. Louis neighborhood was one of several on the north side where preservation, despite valiant efforts, achieved only limited gains (see Figure 3-1). As early as the 1960s, aficionados of nineteenth-century vernacular urban architecture began to display an interest in the area's red brick row houses, mansard-roofed Victorian homes, and numerous churches. Picturesque streetscapes enhanced by colliding street grids inspired painters to erect their easels at quiet intersections. The Landmarks Association of St. Louis organized bus tours through the near north side to publicize its largely unknown architectural gems. The city's premier preservationist organization also maintained a vocal opposition to urban redevelopment schemes that sought to plow under the neighborhood's historic infrastructure in the name of slum clearance and progress.

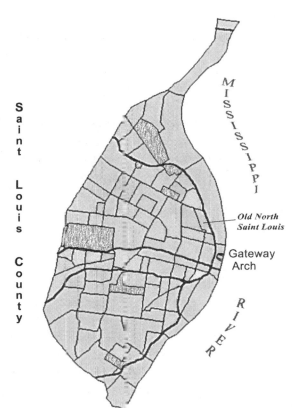

Figure 3-1. *Map of St. Louis Neighborhoods. (Illustrated by Kathryn Hurley.)*

Old North St. Louis, then known as Murphy-Blair, was one of the inner-ring neighborhoods designated for total physical reconstruction by city planners in 1947. Its supposedly obsolete stock of housing made it unsuitable for modern living; only the construction of entirely new housing units could guarantee its viability as a residential quarter. It also found itself in the path of one of the proposed interstate highways deemed so critical to the city's future.[12] For three decades, demolition and blank-slate redevelopment remained the predominant city planning objective for Old North St. Louis.

The interstate scheme came to fruition first, with the passage of the Federal Highway Act in 1956 as the catalyst for action. With only minimal citizen opposition, the Mark Twain Expressway opened to traffic four years later. Along three parallel streets for a distance of about twelve blocks, hundreds of homes, dozens of shops, and two active churches were sacrificed to accommodate the six-lane, high-speed thoroughfare. The destruction wrought by the Mark Twain Expressway extended beyond the buildings that stood in its path. Erecting a physical barrier between the neighborhood's predominantly industrial section near the Mississippi River and the more residential area to the west, the highway split the community in two. In the wake of the highway construction, the residential enclaves in the eastern part of the neighborhood could no longer sustain themselves as they were severed from the community's shops, schools, and remaining churches. Meanwhile, the attrition of the eastern residential district eroded the customer base of surviving businesses on the western side of the highway.[13]

The opportunity for planners to reconstruct the remainder of the neighborhood came with the Model Cities program of the late 1960s. Designed to reduce unemployment, provide better housing, and improve education in distressed inner cities, Model Cities distributed federal funds according to the priorities of local residents. In the Murphy-Blair district, a well-established social-service agency, the Grace Hill Settlement House, took the lead in organizing the necessary citizen committees and administering funded programs. Grace Hill was favorably disposed to the city plans that had lain dormant for two decades, convinced that their implementation would result in better housing for its low-income constituents. Based on a comprehensive study of housing conditions, the local Model Cities apparatus decided to tear down dilapidated buildings in a nine-block area and build new residential units for low-income families in their place. Working with the city's Land Clearance for Redevelopment Authority, the newly created Murphy-Blair Residential Housing Corporation demolished homes and buildings, both occupied and unoccupied, in the early 1970s. To replace them, federal funds subsidized a low-rise apartment complex known as Murphy-Blair Townhomes. Through the early 1980s, the Murphy-Blair Residential Housing Corporation continued to pursue federal funding for low-cost housing in the neighborhood. Near the town houses it built smaller one- and two-bedroom apartments, known as the Murphy-Blair Gardens, to accommodate the growing number of retired people in need of housing. Elderly and disabled residents moved into the new Murphy-Blair Senior Commons starting in 1983.[14]

The last major project utilizing Model Cities funds was a pedestrian mall on Fourteenth Street, traditionally the neighborhood's major shopping corridor. Reeling from the diminished patronage resulting from area population loss, members of the North Fourteenth Street Businessmen's Association partnered with a Model Cities subcommittee in 1970 to resurrect local commerce. Together, they devised a plan to make the shopping strip friendlier to pedestrian shoppers by closing the street to traffic and improving the sidewalks. Sketches from the proposal show a street completely transformed, bustling with strolling shoppers and adorned with cheerful shop-window displays. With a price tag of $500,000, it became the first pedestrian mall of its kind in St. Louis. While the mall itself did not require the demolition of any buildings, the parking lots built to compensate for the removal of street parking did, and hence several blocks of housing behind Fourteenth Street met their demise.[15]

It was not policy alone that emptied the neighborhood of its buildings; many succumbed to fire while others crumbled from lack of upkeep. Climbing vacancy rates and bleak prospects deterred absentee landlords from sinking large sums of money into the repair and upgrading of aging buildings. Rather than install indoor plumbing or retrofit interiors with closets, some owners preferred to milk their properties for whatever they could get from renters and allow them to disintegrate pipe by pipe, brick by brick, and lintel by lintel. Broken windows, collapsed stairways, and caved-in roofs marked a sequence of dereliction that ultimately led to demolition. When owners defaulted on their taxes, which they often did when buildings outlived their economic usefulness, properties were deeded to the City of St. Louis. Although city officials might order their demolition when they reached a point of no return, they were just as likely to let them stand and rot. Many of these decaying buildings became fire hazards, and during the late 1970s and early 1980s a rash of conflagrations swept the neighborhood. When vacant homes mysteriously ignited in the middle of the night, they bore the imprint of arson. No clear evidence exposed the precise motivation of the arsonists, although residents often cited the brisk market for recycled brick as a likely incentive. Some owners may have collected insurance money, although a fair number of the burned buildings were not covered by any policy.[16]

1981 marked something of a turning point for the neighborhood. In that year, a group of homeowners founded the Old North St. Louis Restoration Group (the Restoration Group) with the aim of stabilizing the neighborhood's physical environment. Its initial activities included the formation of an arson patrol and the creation of a pocket park where a group of buildings had recently been torn down. Its stance was decidedly preservationist. One of the catalysts for establishing the homeowners' group was frustration with the Model Cities program and its emphasis on social services for the poor and urban-renewal-style reconstruction. Inspired by the success of south-side neighborhoods in using preservation to attract private investment in an aging housing stock, the Restoration Group sought similar goals on the north side. It moved aggressively in that direction by embarking on a program to purchase, rehabilitate, and sell endangered but salvageable homes.

The preservationists of Old North St. Louis hardly fit the profile of chardonnay-sipping, BMW-driving gentrifiers. The core of the Restoration Group consisted of several families with deep roots in the neighborhood and a cohort of urban pioneers who had recently migrated from another part of town to open an inner-city mission for their Presbyterian Church. In later years, the Restoration Group's social composition more closely approximated the stereotype as artists and young professionals added to the mix. Yet the organization continued to retain and attract many members who earned their living in blue-collar and pink-collar occupations—contractors, clerks, carpenters, and postal workers. Racially, however, white members far outnumbered African Americans.

A passion for investigating and publicizing local history developed as a logical extension of the Restoration Group's preservationist aims. The organization recognized that its goal of physical stabilization would not be realized until the community-at-large gained respect for the built landscape and saw it as something worth saving. An appreciation for the area's rich history was deemed essential to the cultivation of that respect. In their quest to stimulate interest in local history, preservationists had several factors working in their favor. First, the neighborhood boasted an independent tradition that was distinct, albeit intertwined with that of St. Louis. Its beginnings dated back to 1816, when three wealthy landowners—William Chambers, William Christy, and Thomas Wright—purchased a rural parcel of riverfront property from a French settler by the name of Louis Labeaume. In that same year they incorporated the Village of North St. Louis. Their aim was to plat and develop a town that would compete with their neighbor to the south for the growing volume of river commerce to and from Alton, Illinois. Their civic venture was rooted in the hope that a favorable location on the

Mississippi River would attract enough commerce and investment to enable it to overtake St. Louis as the region's major trading center. Such was not the case, but even after the Village was annexed by the City of St. Louis in 1844, its inhabitants retained their parochial loyalties. Second, the neighborhood's major draw for outsiders was Crown Candy Kitchen, a vintage soda fountain business established in 1913 by Harry Karandzieff, a Macedonian immigrant. With its barely altered interior, the ice-cream parlor invited customers to step back in time while they slurped on malts and gobbled chili dogs. The proprietor, at that time the son of the original owner, promoted a nostalgic ambience by decorating the walls with American memorabilia (see Figure 3-2). By the 1980s, the soda fountain was attracting curiosity seekers from the entire metropolitan area. With history already serving as a lure, the Restoration Group found reason to believe that its continued promotion could become the basis for a distinctive identity, one that would deliver the neighborhood from unfavorable associations with crime-ridden and impoverished "north St. Louis."

Figure 3-2. *Crown Candy Interior.* The popularity of Crown Candy Kitchen, with its nostalgic interior, alerted Old North St. Louis residents to the possibilities of using history to generate interest in their neighborhood. *(Courtesy of the author.)*

Recasting the neighborhood as "historic" gave rise to two initiatives during the early 1980s. The first was a campaign to secure designation as a national historic district. The recently formed Restoration Group, along with the Landmarks Association of St Louis, identified the northernmost section of the neighborhood as a promising candidate for inclusion on the National Register of Historic Places. It was in this part of the neighborhood where housing was most intact and thus most ripe for rehabilitation. Moreover, the Landmarks Association had recently written successful nominations for two small districts in the southern portion of the neighborhood. Listing the northern part in the national register, which was accomplished in 1983, brought the entire neighborhood west of the interstate highway under the purview of the national program. Typical of applications seeking to place inner-city neighborhoods on the national register, those written for Old North St. Louis emphasized the historic significance of the vernacular architecture, the succession of immigrant groups that passed through the area, and the notable people who inhabited extant homes.[17]

The second initiative involved changing the neighborhood's name. For most people, the area was simply part of St. Louis's north side, or "near north side" for those who sought greater precision. For city planning purposes, the district was carved into multiple units that bore the name of certain streets or parks, such as Webster, Murphy, Blair, and Mullanphy. For members of the Restoration Group, these designations were just as harmful as the generic "north side," as they bore the imprint of the urban-renewal and antipoverty programs that had done so much to ruin the neighborhood in their minds. As an alternative, they proposed "Old North St. Louis," an explicit reference to the neighborhood's roots as an independent village and, simultaneously, its current status as a historic district. Under the mayoral administration of Vincent Schoemehl, the new appellation received official sanction from the City of St. Louis.

Over the next fifteen years, the Restoration Group continued to market the neighborhood's heritage by sponsoring tours of its historic homes and publishing a cookbook of recipes handed down through the generations by the various ethnic groups that populated the area. Yet the impact of the strategy proved underwhelming. The Restoration Group's wide reach in the neighborhood and a persistent trickle of incoming rehabbers sustained optimism among the preservation-minded. But it was hard to make the case that the neighborhood had turned a corner. Between 1980 and 2000 the population exodus was unrelenting, accounting for a 40 percent decrease in the number of inhabitants. On the cusp of the twenty-first century, Old North St. Louis remained overwhelmingly poor and in danger of extinction by neglect. The mean household income of $6,863 was well below the city average of $19,458. According to the US. Bureau of the Census, roughly one-third of the population was considered "very poor." Although low real estate values and high vacancy rates created an opportunity for purchasing and rehabilitating aging structures, few local residents had the financial capabilities to undertake the task. Thus, it was in the hopes of jump-starting the revitalization effort and taking the strategy to the next level that the Restoration Group formed a partnership with the University of Missouri–St. Louis and submitted an application to the Department of Housing and Urban Development (HUD) to establish a Community Outreach Partnership Center (COPC).[18]

HUD established its COPC program in 1994 to help colleges and universities conduct applied research about contemporary urban problems and simultaneously improve outreach to surrounding communities. It aimed not only to improve urban conditions but also to increase the capacity of higher-education institutions to address pressing urban issues on an ongoing basis through the involvement of students and faculty. The COPCs created through the program provided a mechanism for universities to collaborate with community organizations in developing research agendas and applying research findings to a set of programmatic goals. COPCs in their various incarnations were created to spur economic growth, fight crime, combat housing discrimination and homelessness, provide job training and counseling, and establish mentoring programs for youth.

The University of Missouri–St. Louis's interest in the COPC program grew out of its own commitment to applied urban research, primarily through the activities of its Public Policy Research Center (PPRC). The decision to partner with the Restoration Group was based on an already existing relationship between the homeowner's association and the PPRC. In 1997 and 1998, the Restoration Group had sought assistance from the university in structuring a planning process that involved neighborhood meetings, focus groups, and a design charette. Through these initial contacts, PPRC staff became convinced that Old North St. Louis was an ideal setting for a COPC because of a set of clearly defined needs and a cadre of dedicated activists. The COPC grant proposal took shape around the neighborhood's existing preservation goals and the relevant resources the university had to offer. In September 2001, the federal government awarded the Restoration Group $400,000 to establish the Old North Neighborhood Partnership Center and to develop a series of community-stabilization programs in conjunction with the university over a three-year period.[19]

Crafting the Old North Neighborhood Partnership

The Old North Neighborhood Partnership Center, established in 2001 with a $400,000 budget and a three-year window of opportunity, pursued community stabilization primarily through the protection and rehabilitation of historic homes. Its activities fell into four functional categories: Community Organizing and Leadership; Home Maintenance and Financial Literacy; Environmental Health and Safety; and Neighborhood Stabilization and Historic Preservation. Within each category, a series of research and outreach initiatives targeted specific community problems and challenges. Although this multipronged approach enabled the Center to address a wide range of community needs—including Web site development, leadership training, air quality evaluation, vacant lot cleanup, and mosquito control—its real strength lay in providing interdisciplinary resources to the central mission of converting an aging housing stock into a community asset. For example, the environmental assessment component of the program, which involved faculty and students from the University of Missouri–St. Louis's School of Nursing, emphasized the remediation of environmental hazards in older homes.[20] The Home Maintenance and Financial Literacy segment offered instruction on weatherproofing, improving indoor air quality, and low-maintenance landscaping.[21]

It also aimed to place preservation on a socially responsible footing. As noted in Chapter 1, there is a tendency among preservationists to dismiss or minimize the social costs associated with the successful recycling of old houses. Not so in Old North St. Louis. One of the primary objectives of the Old North Neighborhood Partnership was to avoid gentrification and the displacement of low-income families. This is not to suggest that neighborhood preservationists were acting out of pure altruism. Quite the contrary. Many of Restoration Group members scraped by on very modest incomes and stood to be among the first to feel the pinch of rising property values in their tax bills. For these homeowners, some of whom had lived in the area for decades, rising property values promised tidy profits from future sales, but most were not anxious to sell their homes and relocate. With respect to the area's low-income renters, members of the Restoration Group viewed them less as disinterested transients than as potential homeowners and rehabbers. Given the difficulty of attracting new home purchasers from outside the neighborhood, the Restoration Group hoped to cultivate capital formation and investment from within. Converting renters into homeowners meant less social dislocation and a larger contingent of residents with a long-term economic stake in the neighborhood.[22]

Tenant organizing and financial literacy training emerged as corner-stones of the antidisplacement strategy. To provide area tenants with a vehicle for voicing their concerns about the direction of neighborhood development and acquiring home maintenance and money-management skills, the Restoration Group and the university pledged to organize a tenants committee consisting of families that leased apartments in some of the neighborhood's older homes. In addition, the Old North Neighborhood Partnership Center offered a series of financial-management workshops for low-income tenants interested in buying property as well as homeowners encountering difficulty keeping up with mortgage payments and repair bills.[23]

Although historic preservation was not articulated as a focus of Community Organizing and Leadership activities, the strategic planning exercises that emerged from this segment of the Old North Neighborhood Partnership forced the Restoration Group to think more rigorously about how to expand and fulfill its preservationist agenda. At the time of the project's inception, the Restoration Group had already embarked on the purchase and rehabilitation of a several randomly scattered homes in the neighborhood. Yet it remained wary of direct involvement with large-scale housing development. Some members believed that an overly cautious approach spelled disaster. If the Restoration Group did not advance and implement a plan of its own, they argued, the neighborhood lay vulnerable to the whims and calculations of external profiteers. With abundant parcels of vacant and cheap land, Old North St. Louis was tempting terrain for large-scale developers who anticipated an imminent upsurge in the demand for inner-city housing. The easiest way to amass and prepare property for such large-scale development was to purchase contiguous parcels and demolish existing structures so as to create a blank slate for mass reconstruction. This was the Restoration Group's nightmare scenario. It was only through the strategic planning process that the Restoration Group committed to drafting its own plans and seeking out sympathetic developers, thereby retaining control over the neighborhood's future. More specifically, the Restoration Group's strategic plan, completed in 2003, was instrumental in carrying through to completion the North Market Place project, which combined new infill home construction with the renovation of historic residential properties.[24]

What set this COPC program apart from its predecessors was its heavy reliance on historical and archaeological research and dissemination. Several Partnership Centers in other cities had employed oral history to document recent urban transitions. Yet, in virtually all of these cases, historical knowledge contributed only loosely to other project goals, such as improved health care, better education, economic revitalization, and crime prevention. Moreover, it invariably represented a relatively small and peripheral component of the overall research agenda.[25] In the Old North Neighborhood Partnership, on the other hand, history was central to the entire endeavor and there was plenty to investigate. Although Old North St. Louis could trace its history back further than most places in the metropolitan region, there was not a tremendous amount of written material on which residents could draw to craft a distinctive heritage. As a fairly generic working-class neighborhood with few civic luminaries, it did not elicit much attention in the standard historical surveys of St. Louis, nor did it inspire any published books or scholarly articles devoted solely to its development. The snippets of information that appeared in the local media from time to time created a fragmentary record, and much of what people knew about the neighborhood's past had been handed down from one generation to another through word of mouth. The task of the Old North Neighborhood Partnership Center was not simply to recover a lost history but also to develop a set of historical narratives that would correspond to specific neighborhood objectives and then deliver those narratives to residents in accessible formats. In preparing these usable narratives and conducting the underlying research, the Partnership Center drew on some of the models discussed in the previous chapter. Fitting history to the specific needs of one neighborhood also required a heavy dose of improvisation. At all points in the process, decisions about what to research and how to present the findings flowed from extensive and sometimes contentious dialogue among faculty, students, and local residents.

In the year or so leading up to the project's inauguration, the Restoration Group lacked a clear idea about what history needed to be recovered. Some residents simply wanted to fill the gaps of historical knowledge. The assumed outcome of this approach was a comprehensive chronicle of the neighborhood's development that would encompass a wide variety of topics and cover a broad span of time. There was also a fear that with the passing of another generation much of the history that was stored as memory would be forever lost. Hence, one of the Restoration Group's priorities was to record the recollections of longtime residents. This rather vague scheme of priorities, while not atypical for homeowners' associations, promised little in the way of direct support for the neighborhood's preservationist agenda. To the Restoration Group's credit, it did not want to limit historical research to architectural themes, which had been the emphasis of the national register application. It had not yet, however, developed a strategy for tailoring research to a contemporary agenda, a task that was further complicated by the Restoration Group's expectations about how the research would be deployed.

Initially, the Restoration Group saw history as a mechanism for marketing the area's special character to outsiders. Its members, particularly its leadership, hoped that through the development and dissemination of promotional materials, more people in the region would visit Old North St. Louis and, after seeing it for themselves, consider living there. The city's plan to pave a bicycle trail along the riverfront running north from downtown excited expectations of cyclists detouring from the prescribed route and venturing deep into the neighborhood. It was thought that more publicity about Old North's historic attractions would provide the necessary incentive.

There is nothing inherently wrong about using history as a marketing tool. In an age of globalization and increasingly homogenized experience, heritage tourism satisfies a real hunger for the distinctive and the autochthonous, that which springs from local sources. For overlooked inner-city neighborhoods like Old North St. Louis, it is a perfectly logical and reasonable way to command greater attention and generate more revenue for local businesses. But as we have seen, heritage tourism has a poor track record of anchoring residents to their communities and harmonizing social relations within them. Social stability was certainly a goal of the Restoration Group, and its members well understood the importance of inculcating an appreciation of history among existing residents, primarily for the purposes of preserving the built environment. Over time, discussions between faculty and residents moved the project's orientation closer to a community-building approach. Regionwide marketing, however, remained an important goal, and throughout the course of the project a tension endured between the imperatives of delivering history to internal versus external audiences.

One of the more notable consequences of moving toward a community-building approach was the prospect of using history to repair long-standing social rifts. The Restoration Group had expressed a desire to improve its relationship with previously neglected constituencies, particularly low-income renters. There was a realization that lingering antagonism between preservation-minded homeowners, on the one hand, and social-service-oriented renters and low-income households, on the other, was counterproductive, especially when attempting to advance the interests of the neighborhood within the broader political terrain. The Financial Literacy portion of the Old North Neighborhood Partnership Center was designed, in part, as a bridge-building endeavor, but it was only as the historical research component began to move forward in the early phases of the project that community cohesion across class and racial divides emerged as an explicit goal.

How project goals were refined and how those goals were translated into practice had everything to do with the social composition of project participants. It was understood that as far as local residents were concerned, members of the Restoration Group, the primary community partner in the project, would take the most active role. Because working with the entire organization would have been unwieldy, the Partnership Center established a smaller local-history committee to perform most of the deliberative work. In addition to faculty from the history and anthropology departments and to staff from the PPRC, the committee included four local residents. The Restoration Group's initial impulse was to fill its four slots with residents who had deep roots in the community and a firm knowledge of local history. After some discussion, however, the Restoration Group was persuaded that this approach was not necessarily the most conducive to the project's community-building goals. Rather quickly, the Restoration Group and university personnel agreed that it was far more valuable to recruit people who could connect the research to contemporary community agendas and do so in a way that would ensure the representation of diverse perspectives. It was seen as especially important that the committee reflect the neighborhood's racial composition, so even though the Restoration Group remained a predominantly white organization, two of the four appointed members were African American. Both had purchased older homes in the late 1970s as part of the first wave of African American families to diversify the neighborhood's racial complexion, and both had become increasingly active in the Restoration Group. Joining them were a member of the Presbyterian congregation that had come to the neighborhood to start a mission in 1978 and another white woman whose husband indeed boasted deep roots; his grandfather was among several immigrants who had founded a branch of the Polish National Catholic Church in 1907. Given the prevalence of homeowners in the Restoration Group, reaching lower-income renters required going outside the organization. To this end, the Grace Hill Settlement House was brought in as informal partner, with staff from the social-service organization sitting in on conversations from time to time. One or two students conducting research also attended meetings on a fairly regular basis, as did Restoration Group staff. Other occasionally invited guests included representatives from state and local government and local residents involved with a particularportion of the project.

The committee functioned in the following manner. Operating within the parameters set by the broader project goals, faculty and students drafted a series of proposals for the committee's consideration. After discussion—some of it contentious—the committee determined a course of action and an allocation of responsibilities. As individual projects got under way, the committee reviewed their progress on a monthly basis, making modifications as necessary. From time to time, the committee solicited wider community feedback at general Restoration Group meetings. Following a formal presentation, local residents were invited to ask questions and offer their comments and suggestions. Final products were released to the general public only after careful vetting by the local-history committee.

The first order of business for the committee was defining the scope of work. This phase of the project predated the formal application for funding and determined the content of the COPC proposal. Given the Restoration Group's initial bias toward external marketing, the proposal emphasized tangible products that either could be distributed by the Restoration Group or given high visibility within the neighborhood. Proposals oriented toward internal consumption received a less favorable response. One that was rejected would have renamed selected streets and parks to more accurately reflect individuals and deeds admired by present-day inhabitants. The idea was to invite residents to nominate streets and parks for redesignation and make a case for why their candidates better represented the values and goals of the community than the original historical figure. Committee members saw little to be gained in such an endeavor and feared that it might reopen old wounds if different factions vied for naming rights. Perhaps they were right. Undeniably, open dialogue about the past does not automatically promote mutual understanding and social harmony. Even the most ardent champions of airing controversial historical topics in public concede that there are situations where the harm may exceed any benefit.[26] In this case, however, there was little reason to believe that a sensitively managed community dialogue would not have contributed to the reconciliation of internal differences and divisions through a frank exchange about neighborhood identity. Fortunately, other opportunities for building consensus over community values arose during the life of the project. In any event, the committee ultimately settled on three deliverable outcomes of the COPC grant: a history trail consisting of local landmarks; a video documentary chronicling the neighborhood's development; and a community museum featuring various exhibits on Old North St. Louis's past. A fourth product identified by the committee, which was a publication about the neighborhood's history, was not formally introduced in the COPC proposal but eventually became part of the project's work plan.

The Old North Neighborhood Partnership proposal outlined a research methodology that relied heavily on oral history and archaeology. By the time the project began, much of the easily accessible written information in local libraries and archives had already been exhausted by researchers. If the historical content of the proposed Old North Neighborhood Partnership Center products were to move beyond the little that had already been documented, new sources would have to be mined. Oral history and archaeology promised to unearth fresh data that would not merely corroborate existing research but break new terrain in patterning daily life, social organization, and cultural change. Oral history was attractive to the Restoration Group because it satisfied an eagerness to capture the memories of an older generation of residents before they were lost forever. Several members of the Restoration Group had also developed an interest in amateur archaeology. In the process of digging in backyards and rummaging through old privies, several residents had come across various household objects—bottles, ceramics, and so forth. These discoveries piqued a curiosity about the vast trove of archaeological treasures that presumably remained underground, as well as a desire to interpret their meaning.

From the perspective of university faculty, an important benefit of oral history and archaeology was their contribution to a comprehensive chronological coverage. As noted in Chapter 1, inner-city preservation initiatives have elicited considerable criticism for focusing too tightly on the remote past, thereby isolating present-day inhabitants from history's flow. Indeed, much of the research that the Restoration Group had drawn on to establish the neighborhood's historic credentials emphasized the founding of the independent village and the subsequent arrival of foreign immigrants in the nineteenth and very early twentieth centuries. The application form for the National Register of Historic Places, which supplied the most exhaustive coverage of local history, out of necessity displayed a bias toward the remote past.. According to federal guidelines, fifty years must pass before historical significance can be properly assessed. This meant that when Old North St. Louis applied for historic-district status in the early 1980s, there was no incentive to contemplate developments that postdated the early 1930s. Given the application's emphasis on architecture, it is unlikely that the recent past would have elicited much attention anyway, as the district contained few buildings of mid- or late-twentieth-century vintage. Thus, a gaping information hole separated the era of dense, centered urbanism from contemporary experience. In this respect, Old North St. Louis was no different from most inner-city districts pursuing a preservation agenda. Typically viewed as a period of decline, the decades spanning the Great Depression, World War II, and urban renewal were seen as best forgotten. If members of the local-history committee initially displayed little enthusiasm for revisiting these intervening years, archaeology and oral history forced a consideration. Oral history inevitably privileges the recent past because personal recollections go back no further than an individual's birth. Even the life experience of elderly narrators fell primarily into the period after 1930. Archaeology, of course, can retrieve information about ancient times and remains the best methodology for researching prehistoric civilizations. Yet, no matter the object of inquiry, archaeologists must go through the recent past to arrive at the final chronological destination. Thus, recent artifacts inevitably become exposed and invite attention.

Although the local committee spent considerable time debating nuts-and-bolts matters—what type of materials should be used to construct historical markers, where to carve out space for a community museum, where to store collected materials—the more substantive discussions revolved around the development of a research strategy and the construction of historical narratives. Before beginning work on each of the stipulated products, the committee wrestled with what it wanted to discover and what it hoped to convey to wider audiences. Although each product developed around its own set of research questions and goals, two basic themes underlay most of the work: the value of the built environment and the neighborhood's long-standing tradition of social diversity. Both themes had loomed large in the Restoration Group's previous efforts to publicize the neighborhood's history, but under the auspices of the Old North Neighborhood Partnership Center they underwent rigorous scrutiny, reevaluation, and reinterpretation in the service of specific community objectives.

Preservationists typically establish the value of built landscapes by highlighting aesthetic accomplishment and referencing the various schools of architecture and design reflected in their component parts. The typological approach was very much evident in the national register nominations for Old North St. Louis, and there was plenty of incentive to embrace it in the Old North Neighborhood Partnership project. The neighborhood was a veritable museum of urban vernacular architecture, covering the years from the Civil War to the Great Depression. Almost all the major architectural styles of the period were represented: Greek Revival, Italianate, Romanesque, Craftsmen, and so forth. These styles were manifest not only in the district's private homes, but also in its churches, factories, and schools. By classifying structures according to architectural genre, ordinary buildings became emblems of national design trends, and thus significant. Moreover, the fine craftwork evident in the iron and brick ornamentation adorning area buildings warranted recognition.[27]

While the project showcased some of the area's most attractive homes in the video documentary and educated readers about dominant architectural movements in the booklet, the major interpretive thrust of the theme of "built environment" flowed from questions of social use. Rather than focusing on the set of actors who designed and built the buildings, we who were involved in the project emphasized the multitude of people who inhabited and passed through them over the many years of their existence. By allowing the built environment to open a window onto lives once lived, we encouraged the current inhabitants of Old North St. Louis to locate themselves along a continuum of social struggles and development. In this respect, we adopted the perspective of cultural geographers and public historians (discussed in Chapter 2) who view landscape as the accretion of social experience and a repository of collective memories.

Among the four final products, the history trail most explicitly accentuated the built environment. In explaining the significance of the selected landmarks, which included stores, churches, streets, parks, factories, schools, homes and gardens, short textual narrations emphasized patterns of social life rather than appearance and design. For example, the brochure text about a featured home in the northern part of the neighborhood made little mention of its Victorian architecture but instead recalled the owners of the local hardware store who lived there for many decades and the family that moved in during the late 1970s intent on retaining its original features and beautifying the entire block with a tree and flower garden. Likewise, while noting the art deco façade on a bathhouse built in 1937, the brochure description stressed the lack of indoor plumbing in the neighborhood that sustained a need for public showering facilities well into the 1960s.

One of the most powerful arguments advanced regarding the built landscape was that its nineteenth-century remnants still conferred social benefits on residents. The question of how to best redevelop inner cities from an architectural and planning standpoint continues to generate intense debate and divergent design schemes. One popular school of thought, especially among large-scale developers, is to recreate the suburbs in the city. This approach usually entails clearing any remnants of a prewar landscape and retrofitting the terrain for ranch style homes with expansive lawns, wide driveways, and two-car garages fronting the street. Short blocks may be combined into longer ones and reconfigured streets may even terminate in circular cul-de-sacs. This suburban redevelopment model was precisely what the Restoration Group sought to avoid. While its most active members had come to accept the necessity of new construction to fill the ever-proliferating vacant lots, they wanted to make sure that new housing was architecturally consistent with the remaining nineteenth-century stock that they revered. The desire for architectural congruity was not based solely, or even primarily, on the aesthetic appeal of visual uniformity. Rather it was justified by its contribution to a more desirable mode of social interaction and neighborliness. Indeed, new infill housing was deemed essential to the neighborhood's goals because it promised to recreate the central feature of nineteenth-century urban life, density, along with all the accompanying advantages.

The Old North Neighborhood Partnership strove to support the neighborhood's redevelopment vision by researching and publicizing the social and economic advantages associated with dense housing arrangements. Few aspects of neighborhood life loomed larger in the memories of interviewed old-timers than a vibrant street life. Although horse-drawn omnibuses made their appearance in most cities just prior to the Civil War, only to be supplanted by more extensive electric streetcar networks several decades later, nineteenth-century urban neighborhoods were designed to accommodate pedestrian movement. One of the major consequences of high-density urbanization, in Old North St. Louis and other neighborhoods like it, was the capacity to support local businesses that were accessible by foot. Ubiquitous corner groceries, drug stores, saloons, and candy shops in conjunction with the five-and-dimes and more specialized clothing, furniture, hardware, and shoe stores that flanked major commercial corridors placed daily necessities within walking distance of neighborhood households. Doctors operating out of their homes and itinerant vendors roaming the alleyways further contributed to a largely self-sufficient retail economy. One member of the local-history committee, Gloria Bratkowski, had lived in the neighborhood at the tail end of this era and shared some of her personal memories with the group. She recalled that when she and her husband moved into the apartment above her in-laws in 1972, a chain grocery store did business less than two blocks away; two shoe stores, two pharmacies, a dry goods store, and Woolworth's were within easy walking distance.[28]

Uninterrupted rows of two- and three-story homes with minimal setbacks from the street and a paucity of open green space created distinct forms of social behavior. Neighbors interacted with one another across back porches or on the front steps of their homes. Children routinely played on the sidewalk with others who lived on their block under the watchful eye of adults. The constant comings and goings of people from work and shopping expeditions, along with the informal congregations of neighbors and children on the sidewalk, produced a sense of safety, freedom, and community. Some interview subjects spoke of leaving their front doors unlocked at night, knowing that constant street traffic and the close proximity of neighbors served as a sufficient deterrent to crime. Likewise, parents remembered feeling comfortable allowing their children to wander in the neighborhood to buy ice cream or candy at a corner store. Highlighting these features of urban life thus became a way of building community consensus over a housing-development plan that featured the rehabilitation of existing homes and the construction of infill facsimile town houses. Indeed, trumpeting the virtues of dense, nineteenth-century-based housing arrangements served not only to discourage suburban-style redevelopment in the inner city but to advocate a more ecologically sustainable and socially desirable alternative to suburban-style living more generally.

A second interpretive thrust regarding the built environment that fed directly into the Restoration Group's preservationist mission was to portray adaptive reuse as a long-standing and salutary local tradition. Again, this required redirecting attention away from the original architecture and builders and toward subsequent modifications and occupants. The big lesson to be learned here was that successful neighborhood development did not require the demolition of obsolete buildings and the construction of new ones in their place. To the contrary, historical research furnished numerous examples of structures that were successfully recycled for alternative uses: the institution built for impoverished immigrants in 1867 that was reconfigured slightly for its new life as a chemical factory in 1900; the nineteenth-century kindergarten that was rehabilitated for private housing and art studios in the late twentieth century; the venerable corner drug store that the Restoration Group ended up converting into its office in the 1980s. Each of these standing buildings earned a spot on the history trail. Through their inclusion, we were able to argue that as a result of their preservation and adaptation, current residents, and presumably future generations, could encounter tangible evidence of the layers of social experience and come to understand how with each new life given to an old building, a link was established between successive generations.

Making the case for preservation also demanded some discussion of the costs attending the alternative to adaptive reuse—demolition. Alongside the neighborhood's tradition of retrofitting old buildings for new uses was an equally if not more powerful trend of tearing down and building anew. The historical record in Old North St. Louis could easily be read as a testament to the built environment's fragility, or at least as a cautionary tale about the cultural costs of landscape annihilation. These two themes were developed most explicitly in one of the exhibits prepared for the community museum, titled, "Coming Out of the Dust." Through the presentation of photographs, artifacts, and direct quotes excerpted from oral histories, this exhibit enumerated some of the most unfortunate losses to the community. The first notable casualty was the prehistoric Indian burial mound that once stood in the southern part of the neighborhood close to the river. Measuring 34 feet in height, this massive earthen pile, dubbed "the Big Mound" by French settlers, had functioned as a ceremonial platform and tomb for an advanced native civilization that flourished on both sides of the Mississippi river around A.D. 1200. Although the early settlers of North St. Louis saw it at as an interesting curiosity, they decided that the dirt would be put to better use filling holes and laying roads, and so the mound was gradually dismantled in the 1850s and 1860s. Another victim of progress documented in the exhibit was the swath of homes, shops, and churches swallowed by the interstate highway in the 1950s. The exhibit design juxtaposed photographs of the highway construction with quotes from residents recalling its devastating effect on the neighborhood.

The most important message we hoped to convey by tracking the chronological threads associated with adaptive reuse and demolition was that the fate of the built environment rests in the hands of ordinary citizens. Each of the aforementioned lines of inquiry enabled us to follow a trend from the remote past to the present, thereby anchoring contemporary residents firmly in the flow of history. By highlighting the role of human agency in resolving the enduring conflict between preservation and redevelopment in the past, scholars and residents on the history committee strove to empower local citizens to control the direction of land-use policy in the present. Despite the larger economic and political forces that have always operated on the local environment, individual and collective action at the grass roots, or lack thereof, often played a decisive role. In this regard, one of the most inspiring stories was the successful community battle against a proposed distributor highway in the late 1970s. Of all the major routes proposed in the city's postwar traffic plan, the last to remain on the drawing board was an inner belt that skirted the downtown and linked the major spoke highways that led to the suburban fringe. If constructed, the highway would have sliced through Old North St. Louis, obliterating hundreds of occupied homes. Having stood by silently when the first interstate highway carved a chunk out of the neighborhood's heart, and having witnessed the ensuing damage to the community fabric, residents mobilized in opposition. Joining with neighbors in other threatened parts of the city, they formed the Coalition to Stop the North-South Distributor and packed public hearings. With the issue at a standstill in 1980, the Coalition secured the support of mayoral candidate Vincent Schoemehl, who on election kept his campaign promise and officially terminated the project.[29]

It should come as no surprise that a neighborhood once filled with foreign immigrants and still troubled by racial and class frictions would choose to investigate social diversity as a historical theme. What was not self-evident, however, was the manner is which the neighborhood's racial, ethnic, and socioeconomic history would be analyzed and interpreted. The Old North Neighborhood Partnership was by no means operating on a fresh cadaver; ethnicity, as much as architecture, had long served as an organizing device for making sense of the area's past. The history committee, however, found the previous narrative seriously wanting. Thus, much of its work revolved around rewriting the neighborhood's racial and ethnic history in the service of strengthening community.

A key challenge in interpreting the second major theme in Old North St. Louis history, ethnic and racial diversity, was moving away from a succession model of in-migrating populations. A succession model periodizes history according to the sequential ascendance of different ethnic groups. The ethnic succession model is the one that has been used most frequently to make sense of Old North St. Louis's social history. Accordingly, Old North St. Louis has long served as a "gateway" or "port-of-entry" neighborhood, a place where people of diverse backgrounds come from afar to gain a foothold in the city before moving on to other parts of the metropolis. The procession began with the pioneer founders of North St. Louis, primarily of English descent, who hailed from Kentucky and Virginia. The town grew slowly in its early years, as most settlers to the general area gravitated to the adjacent City of St. Louis. Rapid development awaited the town's annexation to the City of St. Louis in 1841 and the ensuing influx of European immigrants. For the remainder of the nineteenth century, Germans stood out as the dominant group in the neighborhood, accompanied by a smattering of Irish immigrants. By the beginning of the twentieth century, the tide shifted again as immigrants from Poland, Italy, and Russia took the place of previous residents who were climbing the social ladder by purchasing homes in more prestigious neighborhoods to the north and west. This pattern of geographical mobility and social transformation was repeated during and after World War II when white people and then African Americans from the rural South and surrounding countryside migrated to the area.[30]

In terms of specifying the prevailing ethnic and racial migration trends, the sequence was undeniably accurate. Moreover, it was quite reasonable to see the neighborhood as a springboard for social mobility, as reflected in eventual out-migration. The fallacy occurred when it was implied, or in some cases stated explicitly, that incoming groups displaced their predecessors, resulting in a complete demographic turnover. The neighborhood, in this flawed scenario, passed through its Anglo period, its German period, its Polish period, its African American period, and so forth; each ethnic experience appeared discrete and isolated from all others. One shortcoming of this approach was that it grossly oversimplified the demographic profile of the neighborhood at any given time. Ethnic and racial populations continually overlapped, and the contributions and actions of any group had enduring influences well beyond the period of their numerical supremacy. The biggest danger, however, was the approach's potential for alienating the contemporary populations from much of the neighborhood's past. One of the biggest challenges in using history to strengthen community in inner-city neighborhoods is the overwhelming presence, in most cases, of people who do not have deep roots in the locality. When those people are told that *their* history goes back only as far as twenty years, or conversely that it corresponds to a period that has long ago come and gone, the risk of psychological estrangement increases.

In their account of Cincinnati's Over-the-Rhine district, Zane Miller and Bruce Tucker observed a decided preference for an accumulation model among preservationists who hoped to upgrade the neighborhood and attract more middle-class homeowners. An implication of an accumulation model is that the neighborhood's future is not aligned with one particular group and that decisions about who stays and who leaves are matters of individual choice rather than coercion. The specter of forced displacement recedes into the background as the neighborhood's history points to a future where individuals of varied social backgrounds can share a common environment without tremendous conflict.[31]

As it turned out, members of the Restoration Group were already predisposed toward an accumulation model and had begun moving in this direction by publishing their cookbook, with its panoply of ethnic recipes. The members of the history committee were especially eager to document and publicize the enduring contributions made by each major ethnic and racial group that had populated the neighborhood. In part, this desire reflected the particular passions of the committee members, each of whom displayed a fierce advocacy for the history of the racial or ethnic group to which she felt an affiliation. The two African American women were eager to crack the "whites-only" version of history that had prevailed to that point. The other two women wanted to make sure that Polish and German accomplishments received recognition. Although we would not have predicted how strongly newcomers to the neighborhood would identify with those of similar ethnic and racial background in the remote past, this sense of connection was a promising development. It suggested that a multicultural approach to the past would resonate with virtually all members of the present community and make them feel as though they had deep stakes in the community's past. Indeed, a beauty of the accumulation model was that it enabled those stakes to penetrate multiple chronological layers of the past.

Our inquiry into Old North St. Louis's African American heritage surely produced the most dramatic revision of the standard historical narrative. The succession model, while not entirely to blame for the exclusion of African Americans from previous accounts of the neighborhood's past, certainly contributed to the omission. Among previous chroniclers, a preoccupation with the first century of growth, up to the point of saturated development in the 1920s, translated into an exclusive focus on the white and predominantly immigrant populations. Because the "African American period" postdated World War II, it was not of great interest to those who wished to highlight the neighborhood's supposed golden age, nor was it particularly relevant to the authors of the historic-district nomination who were required to find significance in a prewar landscape. Thus, it came as a surprise for some involved in the project to discover that African Americans had a long-standing presence in Old North St. Louis, going back to the earliest days of nonindigenous settlement. Several town founders kept slaves of African descent, and free black people had also inhabited the area and owned property. African Americans played an even more prominent role in the neighborhood after the Civil War, when many freed men and women left southern plantations for cities such as St. Louis. Whereas free black households in the city's northern wards numbered fewer than fifty on the eve of the Civil War, this figure had more than quadrupled by 1870. African Americans came to North St. Louis from virtually every state in the old Confederacy, although most had been born in Missouri. Black men found employment as freight haulers on the waterfront and as laborers in nearby sawmills and brickyards. Women commonly supplemented household income by working as laundresses or servants. It was not uncommon for young black women to work as live-in servants in white homes in the neighborhood. By the 1920s, a relatively small but solid enclave of African Americans lived in the vicinity of a segregated school in the southern part of the neighborhood.[32] This formerly obscured history of African American presence in Old North St. Louis received ample coverage in all of the project's final products.

Yet another virtue of the accumulation model was its facility for accommodating an investigation of cross-ethnic and cross-racial social relationships. If different groups occupied the neighborhood simultaneously in the past, history promised to offer some guidance about how similarly divided populations might interact constructively in the present. Indeed, the question of how groups got along with one another in the past emerged as the central theme guiding the project's research agenda on race and ethnicity.

Adopting an accumulation model and researching patterns of group interaction still left the project vulnerable to one of the major shortcomings of local public history: the tendency to glorify the past. As Carol Kammen noted, "Most local historians write supportive things about their communities. Their histories," she continued, "tend to be upbeat and boorish."[33] This celebratory impulse arises from several factors, all of which were present in Old North St. Louis. Communities are generally reluctant to generate negative publicity for themselves but they tend to be hypersensitive when they suffer poor reputations to begin with. In such cases, reference to unpleasant events in the past may be viewed as detrimental to contemporary marketing goals. In Old North St. Louis, crime was a pariah topic. Although the neighborhood's history was replete with instances of violence and criminal activity, some members of the history committee feared that too much attention to this aspect of Old North St. Louis's past would reinforce popular prejudices and negative impressions of the area. When elements of present-day populations identify with their counterparts in the past, a similar dynamic operates. Certain groups may avoid staining the reputation of historical protagonists for fear of the shadow it might cast on them. For the sake of internal social harmony and the maintenance of ethnic or racial pride, it often seems safer to cover up misdeeds committed in the past. In Old North St. Louis, this proclivity was compounded by the desire to paint the neighborhood as a bastion of ethnic and racial tolerance.

For all the pressures conspiring toward a rosy interpretation of the past, there were countervailing arguments in favor of a more balanced approach. First and foremost, portraying previous eras of high diversity as times when friendliness, camaraderie, and toleration pervaded social relations clearly belied the historical record. Moreover, inventing a golden age of racial and ethnic harmony would have established an unrealistic and unattainable standard of social behavior. However, by depicting social relations in terms of a constant tension between intolerance and prejudice, on the one hand, and cooperation and openness, on the other, current residents could better understand the pivotal role of individual choices in their own lives and the impact of those decisions on wider community harmony. It was in this spirit that the history committee ultimately strove to serve up a version of history that was plausible and honest, especially when it came to the topic of social relations.

The project's archaeology component served as the driving research methodology behind our investigation of social relations and the role of ethnicity in organizing daily life. Members of the history committee were eager to see what the archaeological record had to say about the depth of people's ethnic attachments. Did German families live differently from Irish, Italian, or African American families? Did foreigners retain Old World customs in the

New World? Did ethnic affiliations wane with the passing of generations? In addition, residents wanted to explore the social relationships that developed among these ethnic groups. Was there any evidence that material culture served as the basis of shared experience and direct interaction? Historical accounts confirmed that the German community in St. Louis opposed slavery and supported the Union cause in the Civil War. [34] But did the political alliance of German immigrants and African Americans have implications for the way ordinary Germans in Old North St. Louis and those of African descent engaged with one another on a more personal level?

In 2002, the project began to address these questions through University of Missouri–St. Louis archaeological field schools attended by students and community residents. Three sites were chosen: German American households at 1204–1208 Hebert Street, a mixed ethnic block at 1102–1112 Chambers Street, and a postbellum African American school and community along the 1200 block of Hadley Street (formerly North Twelfth Street.)

The Hebert Street site consisted of three two-story, brick row houses with a razed alley house and outbuildings. An 1895 Sanborn fire-insurance map showed that a stable and various sheds once lined the rear edge of the property. In the nineteenth century, the homes were occupied primarily by first- and second-generation German families, but by 1910 other ethnic groups—Hungarians, Austrians, and French—had begun to arrive. Almost all of these residents rented their homes. With the exception of a salesman and a clerk, the men who lived in these flats toiled in blue-collar occupations. Female occupations typically were listed in census manuscripts as "keeping house" or "servant," but there were exceptions. In 1900 Emily Mund was listed as a saleswoman of ceramics, in 1910 Sophia Ponath was employed by a hatter, and in 1920 Lillian Lemke worked at a dress and dye company.

Archaeological work focused on the rear yard area of this site to document general yard refuse and the outbuildings. Excavations in 2002 uncovered portions of the razed alley house, a stable, a shed, and a fence. A review of the artifacts collected revealed abundant ceramics, food remains, toys, bottles, and architectural material. The only artifact pattern that indicated a distinctive German tradition was a higher percentage of redware (19 percent of the assemblage) than in other ethnic households in the neighborhood and other sites in the greater St. Louis region.[35] Previous archaeological studies conducted in other parts of the United States have suggested an association of redware with German heritage. In particular, the Pennsylvania Dutch had a long tradition of producing redware for household tables between the 1600s and the 1800s.[36] In a rural context, redware has been found in higher percentages on German farms that produced butter and other milk by-products.[37] The evidence suggested that this German tradition also extended to Old North St. Louis.

The excavation on Chambers Street provided an opportunity to study the material remains of a different ethnic group, the Irish. Archival research on the former row of brick homes, originally constructed in 1859, documented a residential cluster that included German, Irish, and Polish households. The most notable occupants, at 1110 Chambers Street, were brothers George and Karl Bernays. George and Karl were German refugees from the 1848 revolution who became prominent locally in the fields of medicine and journalism, respectively. During the Civil War, Karl also collaborated with compatriots to organize a pro-Union, German militia.[38] The fame of the Bernays family notwithstanding, other considerations compelled the committee to select an adjacent Irish homesite at 1112 Chambers for excavation. First, it was the least disturbed of the lots between 1102 and 1112 Chambers. Second, while German households had been studied at the Hebert Street site, the project had no archaeological evidence pertaining to Irish Americans, who constituted the second most populous ethnic group in nineteenth-century North St. Louis. Third, in sharp contrast to German immigrants, Irish exiles competed with African Americans for menial jobs and were less likely to support civil rights causes.

Excavations at the 1112 Chambers address uncovered an ash pit, a waterline trench, and a shallow pit feature. The trove of recovered artifacts included ceramics, bottle fragments, doll parts, buttons, and both faunal and floral remains. Ceramic comparisons with the Hebert Street site revealed smaller percentages of whiteware, redware, and porcelain. Conversely, ironstone and stoneware were more common. Aside from the differences in redware, it was not clear how these discrepancies might be explained by ethnic attachments. The greater frequency of porcelain at the Hebert Street site would appear to reflect a higher standard of living among German families, but an analysis of other ceramic fragments did not reveal any marked difference in economic resources.[39]

The third site was intended to shed light on an African American residential enclave that thrived from about 1870 until 1930. The small settlement grew around one of several schools in St. Louis built exclusively for African Americans immediately after the Civil War. For the first few years of its existence, the school, known as Colored School Number Two and later renamed Dessalines School, operated out of a church basement on the city's north side. In 1871, the city purchased the former home of a local lumber merchant and converted it into a permanent schoolhouse. During its first year of operation, over 300 students attended classes; in subsequent decades, over two dozen African American families made their homes in the blocks surrounding the school. In the 1900 census, all of the African Americans listed in this district rented their homes and most held blue-collar jobs such as domestic servant, fireman, day laborer, laundress, porter, and teamster. Foreshadowing the urban-renewal upheavals of the post-World War II era, this African American residential pocket was demolished for the construction of an interurban rail line connecting St. Louis with towns across the Mississippi River in Illinois in 1930. The school, however, remained active until 1974. Shortly after its closing, the building was razed as well.

Largely unknown to current inhabitants, Dessalines School and the surrounding enclave sparked tremendous curiosity. People wanted to know why the school was located in their neighborhood, how the attitudes and political views of German and Irish immigrants might have influenced the decision, and to what extent the African American residents were integrated into the wider community. The recent construction of a cinder block industrial building precluded any archaeological work on the former school site. A property across the street at 1750 Hadley Street seemed more promising because it appeared to be among the least disturbed plots in the district. Investigators used surface collection and a systematic posthole testing survey across the site. The posthole tests documented a layer of cinder and coal just below the ground surface. This was clearly related to the coal yard and loading dock that were located at this address after the rail line was routed through the area in 1930. Unfortunately, few artifacts were found below this layer and no cultural features were encountered that could be associated with the African American occupation. Ultimately, we concluded that the entire area had been so severely disrupted by the rail line that no further testing was warranted.

Despite the setback at Hadley Street, archaeology provided important material evidence relevant to themes of social organization and daily life when analyzed in conjunction with other types of source material. Indeed, one of the most exciting aspects of the project was the way that faculty, students, and residents combined various forms of historical inquiry in the attempt to resolve thorny issues. To interpret nineteenth-century artifacts, faculty and students read the secondary literature on material culture and pored over census records, fire-insurance maps, and city directories. In this way, we were able to move beyond the identification of objects to informed speculation about their function and use.

Our investigation also benefited considerably from the marriage of archaeology and oral history. Over a three-month period in the fall 2002 semester, students conducted interviews with about thirty people who had some firsthand knowledge of the neighborhood. Some of these informants grew up in Old St. Louis and then moved away, while others spent their entire lives there. Although many resided in the neighborhood at some point in the past, others lived elsewhere but worked, worshipped, or shopped there. Interview subjects varied in age, gender, and ethnic background. One technique used in the interviews was to interrogate people about the uses and meanings of artifacts recovered in archaeological digs. For example, numerous marbles were unearthed in the excavations at Hebert Street. Thus, interview subjects were asked to share memories about playing with marbles. In this way, the project was able to compile a rich assemblage of marble stories. Informants described the specific games they played, the types of marbles they used, and perhaps most importantly, whom they played with. The recollections revealed that marbles were a means of transcending the ethnic divisions that otherwise organized social life; children played marbles with other youngsters who lived nearby, regardless of their ethnic background. Moreover, the conversations about marbles yielded some unanticipated information about the ways in which gender organized childhood recreation. Several informants noted that only boys played with marbles.

One of the most productive techniques for eliciting stories involved presenting the artifacts directly to interview subjects. In addition to the marbles, items offered for inspection included bottles, fuses, and ceramic fragments. Interview subjects were asked whether the artifacts were recognizable and how they were used. When handed a coffeepot fragment that had been uncovered in the backyard of a German American household, one startled woman of Italian descent pointed to her glass showcase to indicate that she still owned an intact version. She explained that the pot was part of a coffee and tea set acquired by redeeming coupons from the Jewel Tea Company in the 1950s. Although this woman maintained many Italian customs in her home, especially with regard to foodways, the coffee and tea set was yet another example of engagement with a consumer culture that crossed ethnic lines.

In this particular case, the interview proved instrumental in identifying the ceramic fragment. The utility of the direct inspection technique went beyond the precise identification of artifacts, however. In most cases, the informants were familiar with the objects and were able to describe their use or origin in a way that enhanced our understanding of daily life. Through the technique of direction inspection, then, the interview subjects assumed interpretive authority over the artifacts. Moreover, by repeating the process with several interview subjects, the project accommodated multiple perspectives on past events.

Although ethnic and race relations dictated the selection of archaeological sites and governed the analysis of the recovered objects, the excavations also revealed ways in which the neighborhood was connected to the wider world through trade, transportation, and employment networks. Despite the neighborhood's reputation as a place where people could walk to their jobs, a work tag from the East St. Louis Stone Company unearthed at the Chambers Street site indicated that by the twentieth century, some people traveled beyond the neighborhood to find employment. The East St. Louis Stone Company was located across the Mississippi River in the state of Illinois and operated there as early as the 1920s. By this time, an extensive metropolitan streetcar network facilitated the movement of people throughout the region and across the river, thereby widening employment opportunities. Another indication of external connections was provided by the discovery of a 1970s key ring advertising a post office box in Warren, Michigan. Because we were unable to identify the owner of the key ring, this particular artifact raised more questions than it answered, but along with the work tag, it reminded the community that the history of the neighborhood was and continued to be tied to the history of other places. Rather than developing in isolation, it was shaped by broader economic, social, and demographic forces.

Archaeological evidence proved particularly illuminating with respect to the changing relationship between the local and national consumer economy. A number of nineteenth-century soda bottle fragments recovered during our excavations testified to the prevalence of localized consumption patterns, as most of the bottles were manufactured in St. Louis. To further investigate the local soda pop economy, a student working on the project interviewed Ollie Garger, whose Austrian-born parents founded the Garger Bottling Company in 1919. The Gargers originally manufactured and bottled soda in their home and sold their product door to door by wheelbarrow. Although the family maintained the business into the 1980s, consumer allegiance to national brands such as Pepsi Cola and Coca Cola eroded the vitality of local producers like Garger's in the post-World War II era. Reflecting the growing participation in a mass consumer culture, many of the collected artifacts of more recent vintage were manufactured far from Old North St. Louis. Yet the archaeological evidence also revealed a long-standing engagement with global consumption networks, dating back to the nineteenth century. For example, one ceramic fragment recovered at the Hebert Street site was identified as part of an ironstone bowl manufactured by Charles Meakin in Hanley, England between 1883 and 1889. For Christian and Maria Rolf, who inhabited the house at that time, the imported bowl, likely part of a matching set, represented a link to a flowering culture of mass consumption. Although we never learned precisely where the Rolfs purchased their bowl, we discovered that wares produced by the Meakin family were routinely sold through the Sears, Roebuck and Company catalogues around this time.[40]

With regard to the themes of ethnicity and wider connections, archaeological evidence complicated the historical assumptions held by many people in the community. The notion of a completely self-sufficient community governed by stark ethnic segmentation was challenged by what we found underground. Supplemental research in archival sources and oral history confirmed the need for a more nuanced and fluid picture of social relations. Ethnic and racial affiliations, while important, were not the sole basis for social interaction. Local taverns, schools, city streets, athletic clubs, and organizations such as the Boy Scouts and the Grace Hill Settlement House facilitated the crossing of ethnic and, to a lesser extent, racial boundaries in the pursuit of leisure, education, and health care. The intermingling of people from varied ethnic and racial backgrounds by no means made for a blissful melting pot. Indeed, the oral interviews starkly exposed an ugly side of social diversity. It was clear from the oral accounts that ethnic relations were quite strained at times. Narrators recounted numerous examples of racial prejudice, intimidation, and even violence. An elderly Italian American told the story of how her husband, on entering a predominantly Irish American church, was greeted with an ethnic slur and told to worship elsewhere. Another informant recalled the fights that regularly broke out between parochial school and public school students. Bringing these nasty incidents to light served a dual purpose. By condemning them, it gave the community an opportunity to articulate its values. In these cases, history served as a negative example. Moreover, by acknowledging the injustices that once occurred, it opened the door toward the ever-important goal of reconciliation.

Reflections

It is difficult to evaluate the success of the public-history initiatives associated with the Old North Neighborhood Partnership. More than four years after the project's termination, the Restoration Group continues to express its satisfaction with the outcome. The organization has a package of products it can use for marketing the neighborhood. Visitors to the Restoration Group office encounter the miniature museum as they walk through the front door, a public television station broadcast the video documentary, and both the history booklet and the history trail brochure have enjoyed wide distribution. Publicity about these various products has, in fact, drawn people into the neighborhood. According to Restoration Group staff, dozens of visitors have stopped by the office to view the exhibit or pick up a booklet or brochure.

Perhaps more important, the products have become a tremendous source of pride in the neighborhood. The involvement of community representatives in all phases of the project gave residents a sense of ownership in the products and a feeling of accomplishment. Perhaps the strongest praise for the public-history programs came from a resident who called into a local radio show and observed, "Until we began focusing on our historical roots, our historical context, ideas for redevelopment of our particular neighborhood went absolutely nowhere. . . . .But since then, things have begun to snowball."[41] The evidence of progress in Old North St. Louis is tangible. The pace of housing rehabilitation has picked up. As of March 2008, twenty historically designed town homes had been constructed and purchased by resident-owners. Three separate housing developments and commercial developments, all building off the model of the North Market Housing project, were either in the planning stage or under way (see Figure 3-3).[42] Whether public history

Figure 3-3. *Fourteenth Street Redevelopment, 2009.* The Crown Square development project in Old North St. Louis involves the rehabilitation of twenty-seven buildings, many of which had been abandoned storefronts along the Fourteenth Street pedestrian mall. When completed, 34,000 square feet of commercial space and more than eighty renovated apartments will be available for lease. *(Courtesy of the author.)*

was single-handedly or even primarily responsible for enabling the neighborhood to turn a corner may be a legitimate matter for debate. Indeed, to the extent that history has assisted in revitalization, it is unquestionably due to its synergistic relationship with other components of the Old North Neighborhood Partnership: the financial literacy and home repair workshops, the environmental health and safety initiatives, and the leadership training program. Yet what is also undeniable is that through an examination of their history, residents have developed a keener sense of who they are, what they value, and where they are going. In many respects, the Old North Neighborhood Partnership Project stands as a worthy model of community-driven public history and archaeology with much to offer other inner-city neighborhoods looking to enhance preservation efforts with more meaningful interpretation.

Still, there are aspects of the project that failed to meet expectations or that, when viewed in retrospect, might have been handled differently. For instance, initial project design did little to develop the community's capacity to conduct and disseminate historical research in the service of contemporary agendas on a sustained basis. One of the drawbacks of organizing the project around the delivery of products was that tight timetables precluded a thoroughgoing transfer of research skills from university faculty to neighborhood residents. As the project unfolded and this shortcoming became more obvious, steps were taken to address it. One summer, for instance, time was set aside to compile a bibliography of published books and articles pertaining to the neighborhood's development. All members of the history committee contributed to the bibliography, and with its completion residents became less dependent on faculty to conduct local research. Another capacity-building activity, not originally anticipated in the overall project design, was the preparation of a guide to conducting oral history interviews. The original project design limited oral history instruction to the university students assigned to conduct the interviews. This left the community with a dead-end activity once the university curtailed its involvement. The short handbook, which included sections on preparing questions, ethical considerations, recording techniques, and transcription, enabled residents to carry the oral history project beyond the three-year grant period. At least one member of the history committee used the guide to conduct additional interviews outside the auspices of the Partnership Center.

No challenge proved more difficult than expanding the orbit of local participation beyond the Restoration Group. There is a tremendous utility in executing public-history projects through an established community organization. It is difficult if not impossible for a project to assume a life of its own if there is no permanent organizational vehicle to sustain it. Moreover, active community organizations are in the best position to tailor public-history programs to fit pressing community needs. In this regard, the Restoration Group proved a perfect partner. Not only did the organization have a clear agenda for neighborhood development to which history could be applied, but it had an appreciation for the value of ongoing historical research to that agenda's fulfillment. As a result, it was easy to obtain the cooperation and active involvement of local residents affiliated with the Restoration Group, even those who were not members of the local-history committee.

Oral history and archaeology proved to be excellent mechanisms for widening and deepening citizen engagement in the project. Oral history provided approximately forty individuals with the opportunity not only to share their personal recollections but to offer their interpretation of the neighborhood's history. Among the standard questions posed to narrators were, "What changes have you observed in the neighborhood over time? How do you account for those changes? How do you evaluate them?" In other words, the function of the oral history initiative was not limited to the collection of information about the past, but also allowed historical narratives to spring from the grass roots. Many of the views and insights drawn from the oral interviews shaped the central interpretations put forward in the history booklet, video documentary, and history trail brochure. But they also stood alone as excerpted quotes included as sidebars in the history booklet and as labels in the museum exhibit.

Archaeology facilitated broad citizen participation in a somewhat less formalized but equally constructive way. All the neighborhood excavations occurred in full public view. Not only were wandering pedestrians encouraged to observe the work, but local residents were invited to pick up tools and muck about in the dirt with university students. Over the course of the two summer digs, several residents took up the offer and assisted in the surveying, digging, sifting, and cleaning. The intention in inviting residents to participate in the excavations was to nurture a respect for the production of knowledge. By making the research process transparent, it was hoped that the community would have confidence in the final interpretations.

Once the recovered artifacts were cleaned, inventoried, and analyzed, they were prepared for display in a community museum, where they sat alongside household objects donated by current residents. Contributed items included old menus from a local soda fountain, piano sheet music, a sewing machine, a dresser, and an assortment of kitchenware. Soliciting donations of material artifacts from local residents not only provided yet another mechanism for community involvement but also served to integrate current residents into the flow of history. The juxtaposition of objects disposed of years earlier with possessions recently removed from twenty-first-century households highlighted the active presence of the past in people's lives and served to remind visitors that just as the actions of previous generations shaped the present, today's actions will determine the future. Framed in this manner, the archaeological displays linked past, present, and future in a very personal way. The incorporation of donated items was particularly valuable because many people in Old North St. Louis could not trace their own history back very far in the neighborhood and therefore had no direct connection to many of the excavated artifacts. Our approach to collecting thus reinforced the idea that the history of a place is the history of many places. By attaching stories about the owners to the artifacts, both donated and excavated, present-day inhabitants were able to compare their lives to those of people who preceded them and develop a sense of connection to place through a sequence of past lives and material culture.

Although these multiple paths for involvement greatly facilitated residents' sense of investment and ownership in the project, the Restoration Group constituted the project's primary recruitment pool throughout its duration. Perhaps this was to be expected, but it was not entirely desirable. After all, the Restoration Group's aims for cultivating widespread community respect for the physical environment and stabilizing social relations across racial and class divides required outreach beyond its immediate constituency. It was precisely to extend the project's reach that the Grace Hill Settlement House was brought in as a secondary partner from the very beginning. This well-established social-service agency with deep roots in Old North St. Louis remained the most effective vehicle for publicizing our activities to the most impoverished members of the community and the local rental population. Through several of Grace Hill's ongoing programs, we were able to make short presentations and to solicit feedback as well as formal participation in the oral history project. Contacts with staff at a senior citizen home and a low-income housing development also provided limited interaction with otherwise disconnected segments of the local population. Some of the museum exhibits were deliberately designed two-dimensionally on poster board so they could be duplicated and displayed in the senior citizen housing facility or in one of Grace Hill's service centers. Finally, the HomeWorks classes offered as part of the Old North Neighborhood Partnership gave us access to a slightly lower-income audience than was represented by the Restoration Group. On the other hand, efforts to secure the cooperation of several local churches were unsuccessful. Yet even where we gained access to residents unaffiliated with the Restoration Group, recruitment remained an uphill battle. Low-income renters and senior citizens, for instance, were not generally wedded to the preservationist goals that inspired the Restoration Group to embrace public history. Appeals to more abstract community-building and social reconciliation objectives, while not entirely falling on deaf ears, lacked an immediate and tangible payoff and thus failed to animate the involvement of those on the margins, struggling to make ends meet on a daily basis.

Had we anticipated these obstacles and potential pitfalls at the outset, the project surely would have been designed differently. Indeed, subsequent university-community partnerships aimed at leveraging local history for revitalization purposes in inner-city St. Louis developed programming to build greater capacity among local residents and expand participation across a more complete spectrum of the local population. In 2004, the PPRC at the University of Missouri–St. Louis established the Community History Research and Design Services (CHRDS) unit to build and improve on the public-history experiment attempted in Old North St. Louis. Over the next few years, CHRDS launched several new community-based projects with civic and neighborhood organizations in the city's inner core. Of course, each neighborhood had its own peculiar set of characteristics, challenges, and goals. Nonetheless, many of the same thorny issues arose repeatedly: addressing the scars of racial discord, utilizing university resources effectively, balancing skill transfer and product delivery, and wrestling with conflicting perspectives on the past. The chapters that follow this one take up these issues and others in the spirit of crafting inner-city history projects that move beyond preservation.

4

≈+

History that Matters

Integrating Research and Neighborhood Planning

Inner-city neighborhoods eager to reinvent themselves as historic districts readily grasp the advantages of public landscape interpretation. The promise of public archaeology and history can be especially compelling in communities (like Old North St. Louis) that require strong preservation initiatives to stave off physical annihilation. Old North St. Louis preservationists instinctively identified history as an indispensable ally in their campaign to cultivate widespread respect and interest in the neighborhood's residual housing stock. Public history and archaeology emerged as ideal mechanisms for engaging local residents in that process. Even neighborhoods far from the brink of material extinction comprehend the benefits of raising consciousness about the built landscape's significance. The prospect of favorable media publicity, a stronger sense of belonging among residents, and higher levels of investment in underutilized properties make local-history initiatives an easy sell in neighborhoods that possess a plentiful stock of salvageable old buildings.

All too often, the full potential of history to reinvigorate older neighborhoods remains unrealized because of interpretive schemes that do not speak directly to the challenges contemporary residents face and to the kind of places they want to create. By incorporating grassroots public history into preservation initiatives, communities gain an opportunity to refine their collective vision and exert greater control over redevelopment activities. This chapter will explore some of the ways that the interpretation of historic landscapes can help communities chart constructive paths by serving as an adjunct to the planning process. Through a series of case studies in St. Louis, it presents several models for aligning historical and archaeological research with locally defined community goals. Of course, research and analysis alone will not stabilize or revitalize inner-city neighborhoods; historical knowledge can contribute directly to community development only when possessed by those who make or influence decisions. Fortunately, the past twenty years have energized democratic engagement at the local level, expanding the range of organizations and people with the capacity to create strong and vibrant communities. If public history itself is to matter, its practitioners must learn to collaborate with these agents of community change.

Historical Research and Community Planning

The formal integration of public history with official urban planning mechanisms is one way to ensure that historical research informs policy. Historians have occasionally chided professional planners for failing to take long-term trends into account when assigning future land uses to particular neighborhoods and urban districts.[1] Over twenty years ago, Shelley Bookspan expressed the hope that local governments would rectify such errors by employing public historians to assist in the writing of master plans. "These historians," she wrote, "will read U.S. Geological Survey maps, fire insurance maps, archaeological reports, and the sites themselves in order to determine who has used the land, how, and for what purposes."[2] Presumably, this exercise would allow planners to identify trends and formulate their prescriptions for future development accordingly. Although few city governments appear to have adopted Bookspan's suggestion, it remains an intriguing idea. Nonetheless, the best opportunities for fusing public history and planning reside within the scope of neighborhood action.

At the neighborhood level, planning is more likely to germinate from the grass roots. Indeed, it is from the elemental cells of the urban anatomy that the most successful innovations in democratic planning and redevelopment have materialized in recent years. Cities that have taken the greatest strides in restoring vitality to their residential cores are those that have empowered citizens by decentralizing decision making. With citywide planning agencies losing much of their political muscle in the waning decades of the twentieth century, power has devolved to thousands of neighborhood-based nonprofit organizations that have translated the aspirations and needs of ordinary citizens into action, not so much through the mechanisms of government but through volunteerism and the strategic recruitment of private investment.

In the last twenty years, the community-development corporation (CDC) has emerged as the archetypal organizational vehicle for executing neighborhood planning agendas. While some CDCs can trace their roots to the 1960s, most came into being after 1980. Their efflorescence at this juncture grew out of a general frustration with top-down renewal schemes and the federal government's concomitant retrenchment from direct intervention in urban affairs. In many respects, CDCs mimicked the functions of more traditional neighborhood organizations by addressing issues of crime prevention, beautification, and image marketing. They departed from their more traditional counterparts, however, by engaging in private-investment decisions. CDCs have taken an active role in economic redevelopment through formal partnerships with private investors and direct entrepreneurial initiative. While most have directed their energies toward providing housing through the restoration of existing homes and new construction, some have also ventured into commercial retail, small manufacturing, and community services. Their tremendous success—by the mid-1990s they were responsible for adding roughly 60,000 housing units to the nation's supply, annually—and favorable publicity has inspired many traditional homeowner associations to assume greater oversight of local economic development, so that in recent years the distinction between the types of organizations have blurred somewhat. In some places, CDCs collaborate with other neighborhood organizations, while in others where no CDCs operate, more traditional neighborhood organizations have incorporated local planning into their mission.[3]

At least one scholar, June Manning Thomas, has advocated the incorporation of oral history techniques into local community planning, on the basis of her work with CDCs in the Detroit area. Oral histories with longtime community activists, conducted by Thomas and her associates, mined the wisdom of those who had come to know the neighborhood through many years of direct experience. The recovered memories provided a narrative context that was useful for devising and legitimizing contemporary neighborhood-improvement plans. Descriptions of community life in the past were used to establish benchmarks for what was achievable in the future. For example, one community leader remembered growing up when the neighborhood was full of people and shops. These recollections became the basis for including a commercial center in a new neighborhood-development project.[4] A yearning for a return to the days when residents met all their daily needs at small street-corner shops animates the aspirations of citizens in many inner-city neighborhoods and could conceivably shape planning priorities elsewhere. Similarly, recollections of abundant recreational outlets, social services, or job opportunities might bias planning agendas toward alternative redevelopment goals, such as more park space, health clinics, or vocational schools.

The interviews conducted by Thomas in Detroit also solicited information about previous community-improvement campaigns so that present-day leaders could learn what type of programs were attempted, how they fared, and what variables conditioned their effectiveness. One informant, drawing on her memories of the 1970s, spoke glowingly about the success of African American block clubs in encouraging homeowners to maintain their property. Based on her recollections, she advocated their reinstatement. Another activist urged the resumption of an annual door-to-door survey of needs assessment that often revealed unanticipated matters of concern. With a rich arsenal of documented memories, the accumulated experiences of former community leaders was put to productive use in the formulation of planning goals and the generation of ideas for stimulating citizen engagement.[5]

Oral history offers substantial benefits to communities that are eager to apply historical lessons to contemporary dilemmas. As Thomas observed, it is a particularly useful means of retrieving the perspective of people on the margins of society and of securing the participation of people that might not otherwise take part in a planning process.[6] An oral history project need not be confined to community activists, however. Even those who formerly took a passive stance toward community affairs can provide valuable information about how a particular community functioned in the past as well as its desirable attributes. Of course, conventional historical research into newspaper accounts, old photographs, archival maps, and census data should not be overlooked in the attempt to reconstruct past modes of community life. What oral informants supply, however, above and beyond documentation, is the experience and wisdom to interpret and explain historical change. The real key to effective use of that experience and wisdom lies in plugging those historical perspectives back into the machinery of contemporary planning. Considering the rapid turnover of inner-city populations as well as leadership in community organizations, such accumulated historical intelligence is otherwise lost.

The approach outlined by Thomas is one in which historical research informs the community planning process. It is also worthwhile to invert the equation so that history serves, rather than directs, planning goals. In instances when communities have already established redevelopment priorities, history may be used to clarify and publicize them through the construction and dissemination of relevant chronological narratives. Historic preservation, especially when it takes the form of architectural restrictions on new construction and rehabilitation, represents de facto planning. Thus, communities engaged in preservation efforts have already initiated a planning process, one to which historical interpretation can profitably cleave. Ideally, communities will employ history in a dual capacity—that is, to both support existing planning goals and to further refine them. Indeed, Community History Research and Design Services (CHRDS) has endeavored to combine the two applications of history in its work with inner-city neighborhoods in the St. Louis area.

To return again to the example of Old North St. Louis, recall that from the project's beginnings, residents had arrived at a general revitalization strategy. The rehabilitation of older homes was central to their vision of neighborhood renaissance, but they were also committed to maintaining the population's social diversity. While local preservationists immediately saw the potential of public history and archaeology to advance the first goal by fostering a greater appreciation of the built environment, they did not anticipate that it would also contribute to the second. Yet an interpretive scheme that highlighted the neighborhood's tradition of social diversity allowed residents to craft a local identity around the principle of ethnic and racial tolerance. Thus, public commentary on the past gave residents the opportunity to communicate contemporary values. Using history to establish what a neighborhood considers important and what it stands for takes preservation beyond the repair and reuse of old buildings and into the realm of sustaining and improving broader patterns of urban life. And while the promotion of social diversity may constitute an appropriate focus for public-history projects in many places, it is but one among many themes that can help neighborhoods move forward.

The following case studies illustrate a variety of applications for historical research in richly interpreted urban preservation initiatives. All three local-history projects described took place in St. Louis. Despite sharing some similar characteristics—for example, a predominantly African American population and a built landscape that inspired preservationist impulses—the three host neighborhoods were sufficiently different in terms of socioeconomic makeup, organizational capabilities, and historical trajectory to warrant divergent thematic approaches and delivery formats. Moreover, each project operated under unique budgetary constraints. None of the initiatives discussed here are presented as perfect models for emulation, but when viewed together they reinforce the importance of tailoring implementation as well as interpretive strategies to particular neighborhood resources and contexts.

Lewis Place

For several decades, residents of Lewis Place, a three-block corridor in North St. Louis (see Figure 4-1), had managed to insulate themselves from the steady creep of urban decay on surrounding streets. By the spring of 2004, however, this oasis of stability seemed in jeopardy. As a new generation of occupants rotated into the homes on Lewis Place, some of the more established homeowners worried about an erosion of community solidarity and a diminished commitment to property maintenance. After attending a public presentation at the University of Missouri-St. Louis on the application of public history in Old North St. Louis, three members of the Lewis Place Improvement Association began to wonder whether a similar project effort might make a difference in their neighborhood. Within weeks, representatives from CHRDS and the homeowners organization met to hammer out the contours of a modest public-history initiative.

Across a conference table, the three Lewis Place residents explained their frustration with the lack of historical knowledge among families moving

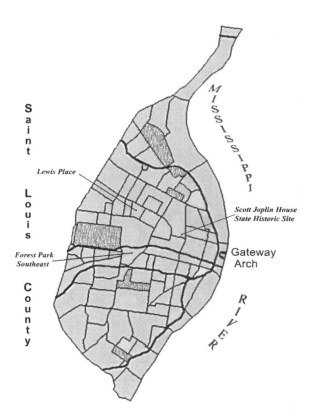

Figure 4-1. *Map of St. Louis Neighborhoods. (Illustrated by Kathryn Hurley.)*

into the neighborhood, along with their desire to insure that everyone living on the street understood what made it so special. They knew that during the 1940s Lewis Place played a pivotal role in the residential desegregation of St. Louis. As they understood their story, at some point white homeowners on Lewis Place had signed restrictive covenants to forbid the sale of their homes to non-Caucasians. The color line held firm on the eastern boundary of Lewis Place until the mid-1940s, when a group of intrepid civil rights activists challenged the covenants in court and launched a clandestine assault on the street's racial exclusivity by buying property supposedly through Jewish straw parties. Their success paved the way for further legal challenges, most notably the Shelley v. Kraemer case that went to the U. S. Supreme Court and outlawed the use of restrictive covenants across the nation in 1948.[7] More than fifty years later, the number of Lewis Place residents who personally remembered those civil rights pioneers was dwindling rapidly, and there was concern that a powerful unifying influence would disappear. To this end, they insisted on a full accounting of a story that was known only through the fragmentary recollections of participants, many of whom were very elderly or deceased. The representatives from the Improvement Association believed that educating Lewis Place residents about their predecessors' struggle for racial advancement would bolster community pride and inspire a stronger sense of stewardship. Above all, they wanted confirmation that their community occupied a prominent place in the history of St. Louis and the nation.

As our discussion turned to some of the specific challenges facing current residents, we quickly recognized the utility of opening a second line of inquiry about another distinctive aspect of Lewis Place: its status as a private street. When it was initially subdivided in the 1890s, Lewis Place became one of several streets in St. Louis that relieved the city of responsibility for general maintenance. Residents agreed to pool their resources to take care of basic services like lighting, paving, and landscaping. Approximately fifty such private streets were established in St. Louis between 1869 and 1920. By 2004, only about half of these still functioned in this capacity and Lewis Place itself was in jeopardy.[8] Because of difficulties in collecting assessments, much of the street was in disrepair. Moreover, some homeowners had begun to question the wisdom of keeping the street private and advocated turning control back to the City.

What was at stake on Lewis Place was not simply the fate of beautiful old homes but the entire infrastructure of the street. Certainly, residents were curious about the architectural significance of their homes. Developed as an exclusive residential enclave, the street boasted several exemplary Queen

Figure 4-2. *Lewis Place Gate.* The arched entranceway to Lewis Place, designed by the firm of Barnett and Hayes, remains the community's most distinguished architectural landmark. *(Courtesy of the author.)*

Anne and Georgian-style homes. It also contained a generous sample of pre-World War I bungalows that developers added to the mix after they experienced difficulty selling some of the larger homes. A final burst of single-family construction in the 1920s further expanded the range of housing styles.[9] The street's most notable architectural structure, however, was not a house at all but rather a yellow brick arched entrance gate designed by the nationally renowned firm of Barnett and Hayes (see Figure 4-2). Other distinctive landscape features included ornate sidewalk gas lamps and an expansive median "parkway" planted with trees and grass. Once the Lewis Place Improvement Association realized that a historical investigation would clarify the current debate over street privatization by exposing what previous residents saw as the major benefits and drawbacks, these common properties assumed more importance than the individual homes.

Before the meeting concluded, the group's most vocal spokesperson raised a third issue. What, he wondered, did residents on surrounding streets think about Lewis Place? His assumption was that from the time that attorneys, educators, and business leaders waged their fight for racial equality in the 1940s, Lewis Place represented a beacon of courage and hope among African Americans who lived nearby. The question was of no small importance, as residents of Lewis Place had come to the realization that the preservation of their street required a wider community vision. Perhaps the street's current residents would recognize their responsibility to engage in broader social activism once they the understood that African Americans in North St. Louis had long looked to Lewis Place for leadership.

Limited funding restricted our investigative efforts to one semester. In consultation with members of the Lewis Place Improvement Association, two graduate research assistants scoured local archives and libraries for relevant documentation and conducted oral interviews. Their findings were delivered to the community through a small history booklet and several presentations at meetings and picnics sponsored by the Improvement Association. Archival research corroborated much of the folklore that been handed down through the generations regarding the desegregation struggle and also corrected some misunderstandings. Although many contemporary residents were under the impression that most of the straw parties that purchased homes for African American families were courageous Jews and light-skinned blacks, this did not appear to be the case. Most homes that ended up under black ownership were purchased and then quickly resold by individuals associated with "wildcat" real estate companies that broke the tacit agreements about which blocks were open to blacks. This was a less heroic version of the story than the one that had gained widespread acceptance. Wildcat realtors were not motivated by social justice or altruism but rather by the financial gains to be made by turning over property. Ultimately, however, the research validated the community's claims of historical significance. The campaign to desegregate Lewis Place was not the first challenge to restrictive covenants in St. Louis, nor was it the decisive one. Yet, in breaking a color line that had held fast for decades, it emboldened activists to expand their struggle several blocks to the northwest, where a court challenge did make it all the way to the U.S. Supreme Court and where civil rights attorneys were able to rearticulate the key arguments they had brandished in the Lewis Place cases.[10]

Historical research also provided fresh perspectives on the issue of street privatization. Residents learned that privatization initially was pursued to avoid dependence on a city government that was notoriously slow to provide its citizens with basic services. In the 1890s, residents were more likely to get their streets paved, their street lamps lit, and their trees trimmed if they did it themselves than if they relied on public authorities.[11] Although that particular rationale for privatization no longer seemed relevant, further inquiries into the struggle to maintain the street through the twentieth century introduced other considerations. An interview with James Buchanan, a former president of the Lewis Place Improvement Association, revealed that during the early 1990s many property owners refused to pay the fees that supported street maintenance. At one point, the budgetary situation became so dire that the Improvement Association could no longer afford to light the street at night. Yet members of the community refused to release their common property to the city. As residents of the only African American private street in St. Louis, they saw their demonstration of self-sufficiency as a positive reflection on their race. According to Buchanan, residents took pride in showing the entire population of St. Louis that "African Americans could invest like other people and maintain property without the help of the city." Moreover, Buchanan insisted that the imperative of setting a constructive example on behalf of African Americans remained as important in 2005 as it did fifteen years earlier, when the street engaged in a similar debate over privatization.[12]

Unfortunately, the research team had insufficient time to fully explore the subject of wider community relations. Preliminary findings, however, took Lewis Place residents slightly aback. As they suspected, the desegregation of Lewis Place led directly to the opening of housing opportunities for African Americans on adjoining streets. Yet neighbors did not necessarily view Lewis Place homeowners as role models or as advocates for the larger community. Quite the contrary. Over time, Lewis Place families had developed a reputation for being aloof and for displaying an air of superiority toward their less exclusive neighbors. The prevailing sentiment toward the inhabitants of Lewis Place, according to a woman who had moved onto an adjacent street in 1966, was "those people think they're important, they're a little bit different from us, we don't have what they have."[13] This revelation explained some of the resistance Lewis Place residents had recently encountered as they pursued collaborative relationships with outside groups and individuals to address areawide problems.

Despite its modest scale, Lewis Place's foray into public history appeared to stabilize the community. In subsequent years, officers of the Lewis Place Improvement Association reported greater success in collecting assessments, better turnouts at community events, an end to divisive arguments over deprivatization, and improved maintenance of private and common properties.[14] They agreed that the dissemination of historical knowledge was at least partly responsible for progress on all these fronts. More impressively, public history became the springboard for a wider community effort to combat blight. Perhaps because of a greater sensitivity to external perceptions, several members of the Improvement Association succeeded in bringing together representatives from twelve surrounding blocks in an organization called Lewis Place

Historical Preservation, Inc. In addition to promoting the rehabilitation of older homes, it incorporated community planning, economic development, and neighborhood beautification into its orbit of responsibilities.[15] Over a period of about three years, the organization inventoried abandoned lots in the neighborhood, launched a major cleanup campaign, and pressured the city to pave area alleys. In 2009, the organization's president announced the inauguration of inexpensive lawn-care service to help homeowners keep their properties in tidy condition.[16] Some members also dove headlong into city and statewide campaigns to fight the usurpation of land through eminent domain. They recognized that as long as they lived in the midst of abandoned lots and dilapidated buildings they remained vulnerable to the loss of their property—and hence their community—through this method of public acquisition and private redevelopment.

As residents of Lewis Place intensified their political and civic engagement, they continued to rely on public history to galvanize citizens. In 2007, Lewis Place Historical Preservation, renewed its ties with the University of Missouri–St. Louis in mounting a photography exhibit at a local elementary school. Alongside contemporary images of Lewis Place, the neighborhood's amateur shutterbugs hung older pictures gathered from family photo albums. To replicate the strategy that had worked so effectively within the gated community, the preservation organization began researching and sequentially highlighting the history of each of its twelve constituent blocks.

The rhetoric of the Lewis Place Improvement Association explicitly linked neighborhood revitalization to a local identity grounded in history. Indeed, its explorations in history proceeded in tandem with the maturation of a local development agenda. Revitalization had come to mean something very specific, and although it certainly included the preservation of older buildings, it had nothing to do with cultivating a market for pricey housing or attracting throngs of tourists. At its core was a vision of affordable, well-kept homes, intense local pride, and indigenous control over community affairs. Somewhat humbly but accurately, the president of the preservation organization summed up its mission in 2007 with this statement: "We're trying to save the neighborhood and honor the struggle that was waged for people to live here."[17]

Forest Park Southeast

Shortly after the Lewis Place project began, the CHRDS office received a communication from the executive director of another neighborhood organization, the Forest Park Southeast Development Corporation (FPSEDC). He had seen the brochure produced for the Old North St. Louis History Trail and wanted something similar for his constituents. His organization certainly had the credentials we sought in a community partner. For over twenty-five years, it had functioned as the umbrella organization guiding the revitalization of several racially diverse, lower-income inner-city neighborhoods flanking the once-thriving Manchester Avenue commercial corridor. As the route of one of the city's radial streetcar lines, Manchester Avenue ignited a real estate boom in the 1890s and attracted a multitude of businesses that served both local residents and commuters. During the 1960s and 1970s, however, many of them vacated their premises as the surrounding residential areas suffered from depopulation and steady impoverishment.[18] Determined to reverse this pattern of decline, a coalition of neighborhood organizations and local businesses founded the FPSEDC in 1977. In addition to promoting private investment, the organization renovated dilapidated properties, planted community gardens, sponsored a variety of youth, public safety and beautification programs, operated as a clearinghouse for information, and served as a conduit between residents and government agencies to ensure the efficient and timely provision of city services.[19] In these capacities it operated as a fairly typical CDC.

Unlike the Lewis Place Improvement Association and the Old North St. Louis Restoration Group, however, the FPSEDC had never given much thought to utilizing history as a tool for urban regeneration. The organization wanted to capitalize on the recent addition of several sections of the community to the National Register of Historic Places, but it had no preconceived notions of what themes or questions were appropriate for a public-history project. Like many other inner-city precincts in St. Louis and beyond, it simply hoped to boost interest and investment by publicizing its status as a historic district. In an initial meeting with the organization's president, representatives from CHRDS spent considerable time explaining how public history could be employed more strategically by tailoring research and interpretation to specific community goals. We also found it necessary to sell the idea of broad community involvement in the creation of a history trail. The FPSEDC's executive director had initially anticipated that CHRDS would operate in the role of an independent contractor—that is, choosing the sites, researching the history, preparing photos and text, and then submitting a complete package to the FPSEDC for eventual publication. On grasping the philosophy behind the CHRDS approach, he assented to a more ambitious community enterprise and managed to convince his Board of Directors to allot $6,000 for the project.

To balance the goal of broad-based citizen participation with the need for efficient governance, we devised a two-tiered operating structure. Ultimate decision-making authority was vested in a five-member steering committee that met every few weeks and included me, the executive director of FPSEDC, and several longstanding members of the community. We also sought more extensive public input by scheduling three community workshops at a local elementary school.

Of the three workshops, the first was the most important, as it was here that residents had the opportunity to articulate a path of community development that would govern the historical research and the content of the history trail. The turnout was lower than we had hoped: only ten people attended. Nonetheless, the event was productive. Following an introductory presentation about CHRDS and the ways in which other communities had employed history to advance urban revitalization, the attendees split into two discussion groups. The first explored the subject of neighborhood identity. With flip pad and felt-tipped markers, this team took notes about what it believed made the neighborhood special and what values it wanted to promote in its redevelopment. The second group focused on places, compiling a list of buildings, parks, and streets that were in dire need of attention and another list consisting of neighborhood gems that might be showcased in promotional literature. Over lunch, each group summarized its main conclusions in a brief presentation.

Later, the entire assemblage reconvened to identify sources of community stability and pride that could be reinvigorated through preservation and interpretation. Participants agreed that education, religion, recreation, and architectural beauty constituted key indicators of community health, deserving priority in any plans for neighborhood improvement. No subject, however, excited greater passion than the decline of local business activity and the departure of beloved consumer establishments. In turn, residents wistfully recalled the grocery stores, laundromats, bakeries, pharmacies, and drygoods establishments that had once been so integral to their lives and the neighborhood's vitality. Finally, a woman who had lived in the neighborhood since 1963 attempted to distill the prevailing sentiment, declaring that the defining characteristic of Forest Park Southeast for much of the twentieth century was local commerce—the small shops, markets, and taverns that met people's daily needs and supplied the area with jobs and entrepreneurial opportunities. Other workshop participants nodded and murmured in assent. Seizing the moment, we quickly reached a consensus on the primary goal of our public-history endeavor: reviving local businesses, especially along the once-thriving commercial corridor of Manchester Avenue. Promoting education, spiritual development, access to recreational venues, and an appreciation for artistic accomplishment ranked as secondary objectives.

As the end of the session approached, participants nominated specific sites for inclusion on the Forest Park Southeast History Trail. Here, we borrowed a technique that had been developed and tested by public historians in New York City several years earlier. To compile a census of historic landmarks, the Place Matters organization invited ordinary citizens to nominate places that were meaningful to them in the past and to record relevant memories on either paper or online survey forms. Although the Forest Park Southeast project had a narrower thematic focus than the Place Matters census, the basic concepts and mechanisms were transferable, with slight modifications. Given the modest turnout for our workshop, we decided to dispense with paper questionnaires and rely solely on oral testimony. Residents were encouraged to make multiple suggestions as long they explained how each might be interpreted to advance one of the five prescribed goals. By this means, the group compiled a list of nearly forty historic sites. Reflecting the neighborhood's priorities, the largest set of nominations consisted of former and current businesses along Manchester Avenue. A number of buildings—including a fire station, a Masonic lodge, and a corporate office—made the list by virtue of their visual appeal. To highlight the role of religion and education in the community, several schools and churches received endorsements. A race track, a movie theater, an amusement park, and a gymnasium represented the theme of recreation.

The next step in the process involved winnowing down the list to a smaller number that could be described briefly in a foldout brochure. This task fell to the smaller steering committee, which convened the following week. Because the FPSEDC wanted to promote the adaptive reuse of older buildings, only standing structures made the final cut. Among them were successful examples of rehabilitation: a dry-goods store recently converted, with historic tax credits, into a soul food restaurant; a former athletic hall resurrected as a warehouse; and loft apartments that in a previous incarnation had constituted Lambskin Lodge Number 46 of the Order of Ancient, Free, and Accepted Masons. Roughly half of the landmarks were dilapidated structures awaiting an infusion of investment. The FPSEDC hoped that by publicizing the historical significance of these neglected properties it could facilitate their conservation and stimulate interest in bringing them back to life in some alternative form.

Another strategic decision emerging from the steering committee was the addition of two sites that lay just beyond the neighborhood's boundaries: the Missouri Botanical Garden and the Barnes-Jewish Medical Center.

Both the garden and the hospital complex boasted fascinating histories that were intertwined with the development of St. Louis. Moreover, both remained among the busiest and most iconic institutions in the entire city. Indeed, their specific location in relationship to the neighborhood fed hopes of increased commercial development along the north-south axis connecting the two sites. Given that many neighborhood residents had direct contact with these places as visitors or patients, their inclusion in the brochure seemed consistent with the initiative's spirit.

The key event in the research phase of the project was an oral history workshop held in the elementary school gymnasium. Here again we borrowed from our Place Matters counterparts in New York by using "memory forms" to gather information about the nineteen landmarks designated for the history trail. In previous projects, we had collected firsthand information through lengthy tape or video-recorded oral histories. We anticipated that in a workshop setting, conventional oral history techniques would be unwieldy and would result in hours of recorded material for which we lacked the resources to transcribe. Thus, we opted for a simpler written format. Taking advantage of the gymnasium's spaciousness, the attending residents were divided into pairs so they could interview one another using prepared questionnaires. While interview subjects answered a series of questions, interrogators recorded the testimony on paper. After a while, they switched roles. By capturing stories about the aggrieved neighbors who met at Adams Elementary School to orchestrate a campaign against an offensive soap factory and the opening of a pay station for utility bills at Mazar's Drug Store, the memory forms demonstrated the role of place in forging community. Along with more traditional archival research, the oral history workshop yielded the raw material from which a paid graduate student authored brochure copy. After the steering committee reviewed an initial draft, a final version was released to the community in a third workshop. To extend the community's capacity to conduct further research, CHRDS also prepared and distributed a manual for investigating local history.

The Forest Park Southeast project provides a good example of how historical interpretation can be aligned with specific preservation-based revitalization goals. It also illustrates some challenges and difficulties associated with this brand of public history. Given the model of shared authority employed in CHRDS projects, the ultimate success of any initiative hinges on the capabilities and energies of our community partners. The FPSEDC was an ideal collaborator because in its role as a CDC, it had the capacity to enact change and make a difference. With little experience in the field of public history, however, it required considerable coaxing to buy into the concept of a democratic and goal-oriented research and interpretation strategy. Even after the project was well under way, FPSEDC staff struggled to grasp the necessity of recruiting civic activists, regardless of how long they had lived in the neighborhood. We found ourselves frequently reminding our partner organization that while older residents with rich memories constituted a valuable resource, it was just as important to enlist people involved in contemporary discussions about community planning and development.

In the end, we were somewhat disappointed by the lack of broad community involvement in the project. Meager levels of participation might have been expected had our community partner lacked deep reach into the grass roots. This was not the case with the FPSEDC. In this instance, the problem stemmed from the project's relatively low ranking on the organization's scale of priorities. With so many activities and ventures on its plate, the organization was unwilling to invest a tremendous amount of time and energy mobilizing mass citizen participation. Although CHRDS attempted to compensate by distributing flyers around the neighborhood, it did not have sufficient cachet to inspire an overwhelming response. Fortunately, the few residents who consistently attended meetings maintained their enthusiasm throughout the project and made significant contributions. Another casualty of limited commitment on the part of FPSEDC was timely publication of the history trail brochure. As of 2009, it had not yet made its way into print.

This research and interpretation was not entirely wasted. FPSEDC staff recounted historical details about specific properties when courting investors and also made use of the written narratives when scripting neighborhood tours for developers, local dignitaries, and casual visitors. Much of the information we generated, then, was disseminated by word of mouth in a calculated manner. Although the project's precise influence is hard to ascertain, it is worth noting that in its aftermath, the FPSEDC focused its redevelopment efforts on the Manchester Avenue commercial corridor. In 2007 the organization was heavily involved in the development of a Manchester Streetscape plan, and shortly thereafter it helped procure a $1.45 million grant for improved pedestrian lighting along a six-block segment.[20] Moreover, the rehabilitation of dilapidated storefronts proceeded steadily; within three years all the abandoned properties highlighted on the history trail had been resuscitated as active businesses (see Figures 4-3 and 4-4). In its 2007 newsletter, the organization identified Manchester Avenue as "the focal point" of the neighborhood's resurgence, adding that "with historical structures lining its streets, Manchester is quickly becoming the centerpiece of the neighborhood."[21] In Forest Park Southeast, as in other neighborhoods in which CHRDS has worked, it would be preposterous to claim that public

Figures 4-3 and 4-4. *4198 Manchester Avenue.* Built in 1905, this building on the corner of Boyle and Manchester Avenues in the Forest Park Southeast neighborhood operated for many years as a pharmacy. By 2005 it had been abandoned. Three years later, the same property was one of many along Manchester Avenue that had been restored to active use. It currently operates as a Mexican restaurant. *(Courtesy of the author.)*

history single-handedly turned a neighborhood around. Yet it seems reasonable to claim that in a modest way the project clarified and contributed to the progress of the community's revitalization plans.

The Scott Joplin House State Historic Site

Despite its location on the fringe of one of St. Louis's poorest and most physically ravaged neighborhoods, the Scott Joplin House State Historical Site seemed an unlikely catalyst for urban revitalization in the spring of 2005.[22] On the streets surrounding the four-family flat once occupied by the famous ragtime composer and subsequently converted into a museum, crumbling old Victorian homes strained to retain their dignity amid grassy lots and more modern but architecturally bland low-rise apartment complexes. Widely recognized as one of the neighborhood's few cultural assets, it was nonetheless only weakly integrated into the life of the surrounding community. Its estrangement was somewhat ironic given the fact that the house had been the object of a spirited grassroots preservation campaign thirty years earlier. On learning that the City of St. Louis had slated the dilapidated building for demolition in 1977, Jeff-Vander-Lou, Inc., a CDC, stepped in to purchase it. Although the building had always served a residential function, local activists within the organization were confident that with sufficient structural intervention, it could be refurbished as a cultural attraction, one that would focus local pride and stimulate more preservation activity in the area. The CDC, however, failed to raise the necessary funds, and so, to facilitate its rebirth as an interpretive center the organization donated the property to the State of Missouri in 1984.[23]

State ownership turned out to be a mixed blessing. The restoration project went forward, but the community had relinquished control over the redevelopment scheme. Although the building's new guardian, the Missouri Department of Natural Resources (DNR), pledged to turn the property back to either the City of St. Louis or Jeff-Vander-Lou after making repairs, it did neither.[24] Instead it assumed responsibility for operating the property as a house museum. Seven years after the acquisition, with the exterior shored up and the interior restored to its appearance circa 1901, the time of Joplin's residence, the State opened the building to public visitation. Interpretive displays focused primarily on Joplin's life and music. The installation of an antique player piano enabled visitors to hear some of Joplin's original compositions while interpretive panels provided biographical information and described the composer's contribution to ragtime music. Ideas that had percolated in the local grassroots phase of the process—for instance, reserving the attic for an exhibit on local black artists and performers and transforming the entire block into an "inner-city cultural center"—were either abandoned or shelved. Not surprisingly, the focus on Joplin and ragtime music fostered a clientele that was predominantly white and suburban. Few of the African American residents who lived and worked on the surrounding streets visited the museum or attended its musical festivals.[25]

As the twenty-first century approached, several circumstances and developments conspired to rekindle the original vision of the site as a community resource. In addition to owning the Joplin town house, the DNR had acquired nearly 4 acres of adjoining property as a buffer against incompatible development. This acreage included both vacant lots and dilapidated brick buildings that were similar in appearance to the Joplin residence. By the late 1990s, with the museum fully functioning, the DNR began to turn its attention to these contiguous properties, thereby taking on the de facto role of an urban redeveloper. In 2000 it completed renovation of an adjacent building and opened it as a replica of the Rosebud Café, a saloon widely considered the premier venue for ragtime in Joplin's day (see Figure 4-5). To defray operating costs, the DNR leased the space for parties and receptions on weekends. It was originally intended as a venue for the performance of ragtime music, but the DNR hoped that its rental policies would also generate

Figure 4-5. *2600 Block, Delmar Boulevard.* The renovated Scott Joplin House and Rosebud Café occupy the two buildings in the foreground. Additional properties owned by the Missouri Department of Natural Resources are located farther down the block. *(Courtesy of the author.)*

some local patronage. Indeed, they did; about 90 percent of Rosebud's business came from African Americans who lived nearby. Suddenly and unexpectedly, then, the Joplin house was presented with an opportunity to reengage with the surrounding African American community. Moreover, the obvious void filled by the Rosebud alerted DNR staff to the real possibility of serving other community needs as they proceeded with site redevelopment. Now managers of the Scott Joplin House had a compelling incentive, if not an obligation, to reorient the site's mission.[26]

An interest in archaeological research gave the DNR another reason to strengthen its community presence. Under pressure to demonstrate some movement toward the construction of a backyard patio for performances and receptions, the site administrator proposed an archaeological investigation as a logical first step. Given that Joplin lived in the house only for a few short years, it was unlikely that archaeological research would turn up the composer's toothbrush, tuning fork, or any other personal effects. Far more likely was the recovery of material evidence pertaining to patterns of daily life across more than a century of urban development. Incorporating this information into the museum's displays would necessarily expand the scope of interpretation beyond Joplin to include his social context. The prospect of a more sophisticated exhibit storyline certainly appealed to the site administrator and other staff members who were eager to bolster their scholarly credentials. Even more valuable, however, was the opening it created to resonate more viscerally with the surrounding African American population. When Joplin moved into the neighborhood it was in the process of transitioning from an ethnically and racially mixed working-class area to one that would become almost exclusively African American by 1920. Archaeology, then, would narrate the evolution of an African American neighborhood and tell a story that featured the area's current inhabitants along with their predecessors.

Preliminary conversations between DNR staff at the Joplin House and CHRDS culminated in the idea of using local history as bridge between Scott Joplin and contemporary urban revitalization, with a community-driven plan for site redevelopment as an ultimate goal. With little previous experience interpreting local history or working with local community organizations, the Scott Joplin House State Historic Site eagerly embraced a formal partnership with CHRDS and secured state funding for a three-year project that included a series of archaeological excavations. Shortly thereafter, the U.S. Department of Education provided additional resources to develop a local-history curriculum for area high schools.

Lingering community resentment toward Joplin House for its perceived aloofness presented the project with a serious challenge from the start, although the involvement of the University of Missouri–St. Louis, a neutral party, may have softened community opinion somewhat. In addition to recasting itself as the friendly neighbor, the museum also needed to create formal mechanisms for community engagement. In line with previous practice, we proposed the formation of a small steering committee composed of influential community activists along with the scheduling of several large public forums. We had hoped that Jeff-Vander-Lou, Inc., the local CDC responsible for saving the Joplin house nearly twenty years earlier, would serve as our primary conduit to the community-at-large. Its response to our project, however, was tepid. Although the organization expressed support for the project, it rarely sent representatives to meetings. Thus, we set about recruiting committee members by informing museum visitors about the initiative and contacting local social-service, civic, and religious groups. Gradually we cobbled together a group of seven or eight dedicated volunteers that included educators, artists, retirees, members of one of the area's largest church congregations, and the founder of a small community organization.

After several months of discussion and a reconnaissance survey of research materials, the group concluded that it made the most sense to orient neighborhood identity and a redevelopment agenda around the area's rich tradition of entertainment and performing arts. Oral histories, newspaper accounts, and other archival sources confirmed that Scott Joplin merely represented the first wave of artistic innovation that preceded a series of contributions to jazz, vaudeville, gospel music, poetry, and avant-garde performance. Indeed, it was during the period after Joplin's residence that the neighborhood emerged as a premier African American entertainment district and, by extension, a crucible of political activism. Eager to burnish the neighborhood's historic credentials, the committee produced and distributed a three-fold brochure that informed local residents about the Booker T. Washington Theater, which had opened in 1913 as one of the first auditoriums in the country to be built by and operated for African Americans; the 1939 protest to compel the manager of a local movie theater to hire African American cashiers and projectionists; and the politically charged multimedia art created by the Black Artists' Group (BAG) in the late 1960s.

The attention given to BAG in our research and interpretation produced an immediate and unexpected payoff in terms of advancing the neighborhood's cultural efflorescence. Inspired by the Black Power movement, BAG had sought to raise black consciousness and mobilize African Americans politically through creative expression. From its headquarters in an old warehouse near the Joplin residence, the collective fused Afrocentric forms of theater, visual arts, dancing, poetry, and music in provocative avant-garde performances. The group gradually dissipated after its leading musicians left St. Louis in 1972 and went on to achieve international renown in the world of experimental jazz. Other BAG artists also relocated to cities with more progressive reputations in Europe and the United States.[27] By 2005, however, some of the cooperative's founding members had returned to St. Louis, among them a poet who moved back into his mother's house a few blocks from the Joplin site. On learning of our project, two original BAG members agreed to join our steering committee. The timing was fortuitous. As it happened, the group had been contemplating a reconstitution but was having trouble finding a performance space. Recognizing an opportunity to provide a valuable community service, the site administrator at the Joplin House offered the use of the Rosebud Café for rehearsals and shows. Renaming itself the Black Artists Guild, the group accepted the proposition and began scheduling poetry readings and concerts. Subsequently, the Scott Joplin House State Historic Site became the de facto headquarters for BAG.

Employing the site as a crucible for indigenous cultural innovation and a venue for community events was precisely what the steering committee hoped to achieve, and in the project's third year it worked assiduously to flesh out these objectives more fully in a series of recommendations for the disposition of state properties. Each monthly meeting began by exploring some aspect of local history as a springboard for discussion about contemporary possibilities. Resident historians pored over census data, read oral histories, searched through old newspapers, and handled artifacts recovered from archaeological excavations to discern how the neighborhood once functioned and how the Joplin site could best leverage the past (see Figure 4-6).

While there was wide agreement on reviving the area as a popular destination for art and entertainment, committee members did not necessarily share the same priorities when it came down to working out the details or finding ways to strengthen the site as a community resource. Schoolteachers envisioned a place where young people could learn about and celebrate the African American experience. The prospect of configuring interior spaces to meet the varying the needs of local cultural organizations excited a representative from BAG. For a retired postal worker on the committee, the site was ideally suited for family reunions in which multiple generations could gather and link their personal genealogies to the neighborhood's history. In line with a tradition of mutual support, a church minister suggested operating a food pantry and women's shelter on some portion of the property. A series of open forums held throughout the neighborhood indicated which among the many ideas resonated most powerfully with the wider community and encouraged the committee to focus its vision. In December 2008, the committee

Figure 4-6. *History Committee, 2008.* Members of the Local History Committee inspect artifacts from recent archaeological excavations at a meeting in 2008. *(Courtesy of the author.)*

submitted its final report and presented its recommendations at a meeting with state officials in the Rosebud Café. In calling for an auditorium, artist studios, exhibit galleries, inexpensive accommodations for visiting performers, and music practice and instruction rooms, the report offered a blueprint for the site's role as a cultural incubator. Proposals for a neighborhood garden, a dog park, and an information center met other community needs at a minimal expense. DNR representatives at the meeting responded favorably and endorsed it as the starting point for an official site development plan.

Although the committee's primary focus was the immediate neighborhood surrounding the Joplin house, it also seized an opportunity to espouse a general model for administering urban heritage sites. Many of the proposals contained in the final report differed rather dramatically from the amenities and attractions typically found at historic sites, either in Missouri elsewhere. It was incumbent on the committee to demonstrate that features such as a community garden, lodging facilities for artists, and a community information center were consistent with the state agency's mission to "protect, preserve, and enhance Missouri's natural and cultural resources." At the same time, the committee recognized that it was asking the state to think more broadly about what it meant to "protect, preserve, and enhance" local resources in inner-city settings. The potential payoff was enormous. By integrating its interpretive mission with the needs of its immediate neighbors, the Scott Joplin House offered a new paradigm for cultural heritage sites in urban America.

Conclusion

In three inner-city districts of St. Louis, citizens engaged serious historical inquiry to identify, protect, and reinvigorate precious local assets. Each neighborhood saw preservation as a catalyst for revitalization, and yet the knowledge of local conditions acquired through historical investigation yielded distinctive, homegrown strategies for moving forward. All three communities agreed on the necessity of renewed investment in the built environment. Residents understood that additional resources from either public or private sources were needed to shore up aging buildings, maintain basic services, and stimulate the types of economic and cultural activities that exemplify the best of urban living. Yet preservation was less about making money than about stabilizing physical infrastructure and gaining some measure of control over the fate of fragile communities. Indeed, in each place the desire for economic growth was tempered by fears of overdevelopment and social disruption. Lewis Place activists worried about the reconstruction of their neighborhood through eminent domain and an ensuing scarcity of affordable housing. As much as the revival of merchant commerce appealed to the inhabitants of Forest Park Southeast, members of the local-history committee hoped to avoid the sort of hyperdevelopment likely to produce noise, congestion, and rowdy behavior. To this end, the district's alderman introduced local legislation in 2008 to outlaw certain types of commercial uses along Manchester Avenue, including bars without food permits, check cashing establishments, and fast-food restaurants.[28] Residents living in the vicinity of the Scott Joplin House expressed overwhelming opposition to the idea of selling state property to private developers. And while many wanted to see the return of small shops and residential quarters in other sections of the neighborhood, they implored the DNR to use its political influence to prevent the gentrification of properties surrounding the state historic site.

By narrating the built environment in accordance with grassroots planning, these three projects moved historic preservation well beyond the rehabilitation and reuse of old buildings for the sole purpose of economic redevelopment. What they sought to protect, or in some cases resuscitate, were the social, cultural, and economic webs that sustained viable communities and connected people to place. This was most apparent on Lewis Place, where residents were concerned primarily with maintaining a particular relationship to their common property, but it also applied to Forest Park Southeast in the residents' quest for economic self-sufficiency and to the Scott Joplin neighborhood, where the renovation of historic properties promised to revive the district's status as an entertainment destination and a wellspring of cultural achievement. Aligning narratives with revitalization goals in a comprehensive manner necessarily pushes preservation into new terrain, not only with respect to how information about the past is deployed but also with regard to what landscape elements fall within preservationists' orbit, a topic addressed in the next chapter.

5

≈≑⊢

Making a Place for Nature

Preserving Urban Environments

Historic preservation in cities has focused almost exclusively on the restoration and interpretation of built structures. Even as preservation has emerged as a community-revitalization strategy and, in the best scenarios, incorporated vernacular elements of the urban landscape and diverse interpretive perspectives, this bias has remained. On the face of it, the scant attention devoted to natural landscape elements by historic preservationists is unsurprising. Nature is rarely considered a major force in the development of cities. Instead, it represents that which was eviscerated as the historical process unfolded. Yet many of the challenges facing inner-city communities pertain directly to the way people interact with their natural surroundings—the air they breathe, the water they drink, the soil on which they play, the plants and animals they encounter. Effectively integrating the natural and built environment in a coherent vision of healthy and satisfying communities may well constitute the next frontier in urban historic preservation. Wedded to good public history, it may also hold the key to assuring a sustainable relationship between the urban core and the surrounding metropolis.

The Trajectory of Two Preservation Movements

For many years the preservation of natural areas and the preservation of built environments proceeded along parallel tracks, each guided by distinct laws, constituencies, and agendas. Certainly, since World War II, historic preservationists have concentrated their activities in cities and looked to cultural attributes to measure the worthiness of standing structures. Nature conservationists, on the other hand, increasingly adopted scientifically based criteria to protect endangered species and their habitats in less populated areas. Within cities, environmentalists focused their attention on threats to human health, particularly air and water pollution.[1] On occasion, environmentalists and historic preservationists joined forces to stop offensive development projects that interfered with their goals—for instance, the construction of new highways—but the basis of these alliances tended to be strategic rather than philosophical.[2] As long as environmentalists saw the object of preservation as the exclusion of people from nature and the maintenance of nature in a state of pure wilderness, there was little likelihood of a unified perspective on landscape conservation.

As the twentieth century drew to a close, however, new ways of thinking about place began to erode the boundary between the two preservation approaches and point to an overarching rationale for protecting both natural and cultural assets. Indeed, the same intellectual currents that brought the accomplishments and struggles of more social groups within the orbit of historic preservation made it possible to acknowledge and appreciate the role of natural forces in shaping the character of places. Reading landscapes as layered systems of economic and social production logically took any analysis of place back to the soils, waterways, minerals, flora, and fauna initially manipulated by humans for their sustenance and growth.[3] Further intellectual incentive for a more comprehensive approach to landscape preservation came from a group of environmental historians who shattered the false dichotomy between nature and artifice by exposing the human imprint on settings usually perceived as "natural." Scholars such as William Cronon, Stephen Pyne, Anne Spirn, and Mark Spence demonstrated that some of the most cherished national examples of natural beauty—including the Grand Canyon, Niagara Falls, and Yellowstone Park—were all products, at least in part, of human design.[4] At the same time, nonhuman forces such as wind patterns, geological formations, and hydrology were shown to have played critical roles in the shaping of spaces widely perceived as the epitome of artifice—for instance, factory complexes and urban neighborhoods.[5] Finally, a greater appreciation of nature's inherent dynamism and the corresponding demise of an equilibrium model of ecological succession forced yet another point of congruence between the two preservation movements. Once one concedes that nature never exists in a steady state, restoration requires the selection of a date or historical period to serve as a benchmark. Ecological preservation thus becomes de facto historic preservation.[6]

As important as these theoretical breakthroughs were, it was a set of practical considerations that made environmentalists and historic preservationists receptive to the idea of moving beyond strategic alliances to a more holistic and coordinated set of conservation principles and practices. A heightened appreciation of contexts—in the case of environmentalism, habitats and ecosystems instead of individual species, and in the case of historic preservation, entire districts rather than isolated buildings—shifted both movements toward a total-landscape approach and the conservation of larger territories. As the parcels targeted for protection grew in size, it became inevitable that they would encompass both natural and cultural resources. Moreover, the burgeoning phenomena of heritage and ecotourism created a demand for the interpretation of both types of attributes.[7]

It was not until the 1980s that formal mechanisms emerged for integrating natural and cultural features in a common preservation enterprise. In 1984, Congress designated the Illinois and Michigan Canal as the first of several National Heritage Areas, a special hybrid classification for extensive corridors that boasted both environmental and historical significance. Completed in 1848, the canal provided a vital transportation link between the fledgling town of Chicago and the Mississippi River through a direct connection to the Illinois River. It was directly responsible for the region's rapid economic growth and Chicago's ascendance as a major urban center. Although the canal was long defunct by the 1980s, historic warehouses, grain elevators, barns, and mansions lined its banks, and remnants of its former lock, aqueduct, and towpath system continued to attract heritage tourists. The 97-mile corridor also supported a rich array of wildlife—birds, foxes, butterflies, and turtles—that drew visitors and added to the area's scenic appeal. Its classification as a National Heritage Area explicitly acknowledged its value as both an environmental and historical resource, and it provided a prototype for the protection of other landscapes with notable historical, scenic, and recreational features elsewhere.[8] Two years later, the National Park Service formally embraced this trend by developing guidelines for the nomination of hybrid landscapes to the national register. As a result, it has become more common for nominations to highlight both environmental and cultural features when making the case for national-register status, and it is now seen as legitimate to consider factors such as vegetation, wildlife, topography, and climate as part of the historical process.[9]

Finally, it should be noted that land trusts have become an important tool for achieving similar ends through private initiative. Originally employed to save precious ecological assets left unprotected by public agencies, land trusts have been used with greater frequency by individuals and groups determined to save properties that also contain important cultural resources such as archaeological remains, battlefields, historic roadways, and industrial sites. Typically land trusts form when a group of individuals pool their resources and form a nonprofit, tax-exempt organization that exists solely to acquire property and take it off the market to prevent development. About two-thirds of all land trusts in existence were created since 1980, and while most are local in their scope, several—such as the Appalachian Trail Lands Trust, the Civil War Trust, the New England Forestry Foundation, and the Southeastern Cave Conservancy—own scattered properties over a large area. Among those that have gone beyond environmental protection to incorporate historic preservation within their mission is the Conservation Trust for North Carolina, which has taken an interest in the old trails and homesteads that lie within its Blue Ridge Parkway corridor.[10]

The Case for Landscape Preservation in Cities

As the examples cited indicate, it was primarily in rural areas that ecological and commemorative impulses came together in comprehensive landscape-conservation schemes. Yet wherever natural spaces and environmental conditions form part of a community's vision for revitalization, there are decisive benefits to be accrued by weaving them into preservation and historical-interpretation programs. In most cases, stabilizing depressed inner-city neighborhoods entails more than finding productive uses for old homes, stores, factories, and warehouses; it also involves beautifying abandoned lots, improving access to recreational space, and ameliorating the deleterious effects of dirty air, soil contamination, and water pollution. Moreover, communities confronting environmental predicaments often lack the historical context with which to explore their origins, assess trends, and learn from past mistakes. Tracing back the interactions between city dwellers and their natural surroundings, including the patterns of thought and perception that guided those interactions, can provide direction for crafting more sustainable and desirable relationships in the future. Thus, environmental history should not be separated from the history that is more commonly interpreted and commemorated. Arriving at a truly useful history of place, one that is aligned with community goals, requires an interlacing of what are, to a large extent, inseparable components of the urban landscape.[11]

For all their idiosyncrasies and claims of uniqueness, many U.S. cities followed a common historical trajectory that accounts for many of the environmental challenges confronting inner-city populations today. The industrial revolution was a major catalyst for urbanization in the nineteenth century.

Cities that grew rapidly during this era pulsated to the rhythms of factory production. Manufacturing typically gravitated to river valleys just beyond central cores in working-class enclaves that form part of today's inner city. These mixed-use areas—mixed in the sense that factories operated side by side or close to shops and residences—were tightly packed with people and buildings. This intense concentration of human activity placed a tremendous strain on air, water, and soil resources and contributed to their degradation and sometimes their depletion. Compact populations also bred deadly diseases. Before the construction of adequate sewer and water systems, cholera and typhoid fever ripped through urban populations in epidemic proportions while airborne germs responsible for tuberculosis and influenza found an abundant supply of human hosts for their propagation. It was these sorts of conditions that motivated families to flee central city neighborhoods for the more sparsely populated and cleaner suburbs when they could afford to do so. The advent of automobiles in the twentieth century facilitated suburban flight, which in turn propelled a pattern of ethnic and racial succession whereby lower-income households and victims of discrimination came to occupy the homes of those who had left.

Contemporary inner-city residents grapple with the legacy of these historical developments. Factories in inner-city neighborhoods continue to operate in proximity to residential populations. Even where firms have abandoned inner-city manufacturing facilities, they have often left behind dangerous amounts of hazardous waste. While the coming of the automobile may have conferred environmental benefits on some segments of the urban population by spurring suburban migration and eliminating the unsanitary by-products of horse-driven transportation technology, it also had an environmental downside. As noted earlier in this book, highway construction was especially extensive in neighborhoods encircling downtown business districts, thereby subjecting residents there to the unhealthful impact of automobile emissions. Although the inner-city dereliction and disinvestment accompanying suburban flight alleviated some of the problems associated with density, it also expanded the habitat for disease-carrying vermin.

The disproportionate impact of ecological degradation on poor, minority populations in inner-city neighborhoods became the basis of an environmental justice movement in the 1990s. Although African Americans, Latinos, and Native Americans had mobilized around issues such as air quality, lead contamination, poor sanitation, and unhealthful working conditions in the past, this movement united disparate local struggles in a national effort to apply environmental laws more fairly and bring attention to the environmental plight of marginalized populations.[12] An underlying premise of the movement was that "environmental racism" was responsible for the uncommonly high levels of pollution and ecological degradation found in neighborhoods inhabited by people of color.[13] Yet few environmental justice initiatives probed very deeply into the past to uncover the precise dynamics of racial discrimination or the historical patterns of environmental abuse that gave rise to present-day inequities. This inattention to history has been unfortunate; at a bare minimum, knowledge about the geography of industrial activity in previous eras can lead communities to sources of contamination they might not otherwise discover. Such a tack proved useful in 1995, when students and scholars at the University of Missouri–St. Louis collaborated with Project HOPE. (Helping Other People Emerge), a grassroots environmental justice organization, to assess environmental risks and develop remediation strategies in three low-income neighborhoods in the St. Louis metropolitan area. Through the inspection of early-twentieth-century fire-insurance maps that showed the former location of manufacturing facilities along with more recent data of industrial emissions gathered from the U. S. Environmental Protection Agency, the project developed systematic plans for environmental testing in places where the probability of contamination was high.

The National Environmental Health and Justice Literacy Project, based in Chicago, represented a much more ambitious attempt to engage citizens in environmental issues through history. In 2002, the Knights of Peter Claver, a black Catholic lay organization, received funding from the National Council of Catholic Bishops to collect and disseminate information about the environmental hazards present in three inner-city Chicago neighborhoods. Under the direction of Sylvia Hood Washington, a scholar then affiliated with Northwestern University, the project relied on historical research and interpretation to identify and explain a wide assortment of environmentally related health problems such as lead poisoning, asthma, and cancer. Its ultimate objective was to spark environmental activism and promote policies that would address the root causes of environmental inequality. In addition to scouring traditional documentary source material in local archives and libraries, project participants tapped the collective memory of target communities through an extensive oral history project. In taped interviews, old-timers recounted tales of negligence and discrimination at the hands of corporations, government officials, banks, realtors, and landlords, all of which fed the steady deterioration of local infrastructure and municipal services over the course of the twentieth century. They also told of previous campaigns to maintain green spaces and fight the siting of waste dumps, thereby placing present-day activism along a continuum of struggle against injustice

within the African American community. By 2007, the project had produced an environmental justice handbook and video documentary that combined oral testimonies with the commentary of public-health professionals
and religious leaders to demonstrate ways that residents could take steps,
individually and collectively, to reduce their exposure to toxic substances and
improve the quality of their surroundings.[14]

Environmental justice represents only one perspective on the ecological
predicament of inner-city neighborhoods; other strands of environmental
activism can likewise benefit from the application of historical research and
public interpretation. In many cities, grassroots organizations have formed
in recent years to resuscitate degraded waterways and restore them as public
amenities. One of the casualties of the late-nineteenth-century sanitary revolution was the conversion of urban rivers into sewers that were used to flush
dangerous wastes from dense population centers. Because urban rivers had
already become receptacles for wastes in many cases, and because they already fed larger bodies of water, they were obvious candidates for integration
into formal sewer systems. In one city after another, these rivers were buried
below ground or otherwise enclosed in permanent channels and removed
from public sight.

This was precisely what happened to the River des Peres in St. Louis (see
Figure 5-1). Often referred to disparagingly by locals as the River "Despair,"
this watercourse meanders across a large swath of the metropolis and was the
object of extensive human engineering between 1924 and 1933. By the turn of
the twenty-first century, most people had observed it only as an ugly concrete
ditch covered with stagnant pools of rainwater and piles of discarded clothes,
soda cans, and shopping carts. Yet, at the dawn of the twenty-first century, a
group of dedicated environmentalists strove to improve water quality, restore
habitats, and establish recreational spaces along the river's edge. To this end,
they formed the River des Peres Headwaters Coalition in 2002 (later renamed
the River des Peres Watershed Coalition) and inaugurated an annual cleanup
drive and a program to install markers at storm-water inlets to discourage
people from throwing trash into storm drains. Subsequently the organization
began work on a River des Peres Watershed Management Plan to guide future
management and development of the river and its tributaries.[15]

In this effort they saw history as an ally. One of the primary obstacles
they faced in generating public support for their ambitions was the persistent impression that the River des Peres, despite its name, was a human-
constructed sewer; and who in their right mind would want to sink resources
into the beautification of a sewer? The Coalition faced a huge public relations
problem, and revising the public's perception of the waterway became a

Figure 5-1. *River des Peres, 2009.* For much of its journey through metropolitan St. Louis, the River des Peres is hidden from public view in a depressed concrete channel. *(Courtesy of the author.)*

prerequisite for further progress. The easiest way to achieve this goal was to reference the river's previous existence as a free-flowing, natural body of water. People had to understand that its transmutation into a sewer was the product of human decisions that could be undone. Historical education thus became an important adjunct to the Coalition's environmental planning and remediation activities. Shortly after the organization formed, it published a glossy brochure on the waterway that traced its history back to 1700, when a group of Kaskaskia Indians settled at its mouth. The brochure narrative then took the river's story into the nineteenth century, when St. Louisans valued it as a "recreational and aesthetic pleasure," and then into the era of floods of urban waste-disposal pressures that led to its reengineering in the twentieth century.[16] In the brochure as well as on its Web site and in public forums, the Coalition hammered home the message that the river's projected future was not some far-fetched pie-in-the-sky imagining of ecolunatics, but simply a return to what it had once been.

In Pittsburgh, an attempt was made to apply historical research to a wider range of environmental issues. In 1993, the Howard Heinz Endowment

funded a study to assess environmental change in the city as a means of identifying the most pressing ecological problems warranting attention. Historians working on the project recommended tracking changes in public access
to hiking and bicycle trails, recreational use of the city's rivers, modes of
public transportation, and the ratio of permeable to paved surfaces. Unfortunately, the research team was hampered by a paucity of relevant data, forc-
ing it to fall back on more conventional environmental measures, such as air
and water quality. The historians concluded that their difficulty measuring
longitudinal change in the original indicators only highlighted the need for
more intensive historical investigation so that Pittsburgh could derive a
fuller sense of where it stood in terms of making environmental progress.[17]

Historicizing the relationship between humans and their natural surroundings raises intriguing possibilities for broadening more conventional
approaches to historic preservation. Built structures that mediated the relationship between humans and the environment in cities warrant recognition
and, wherever possible, should be used to deliver interpretive narration, even
when they have little architectural significance or appeal. As noted in a previous chapter, one of the historic landmarks highlighted in the Old North
St. Louis project was a former bathhouse that served the community between 1937 and 1965. In this particular case, the art deco building did have
some architectural merit. Yet the primary emphasis of the site interpretation
was the challenge of supplying fresh water to working-class households. The
theme of urban waste disposal also lends itself to the preservation of historic
structures, although the controversy over the designation of the Fresno Sanitary Landfill in California to the list of National Historic Landmarks sug-
gests some of the public relations difficulties associated with such unconven-
tional preservation choices.

The Fresno Sanitary Landfill received National Historic Landmark status in August 2001 to commemorate its pioneering role in urban waste disposal. Designed by nationally renowned civil engineer Jean Vincenz, the landfill was the first waste-disposal facility in the nation to employ the practice of
layering, and then compacting, refuse and dirt in trenches. The landfill opened
in 1937, remained in operation for fifty years, and served as the prototype for
hundreds of similar facilities across the nation because it offered a more sanitary alternative to the usual custom of open dumping on vacant land. Scholars and National Park Service officials who spearheaded the campaign for
Landmark designation hoped that official recognition and the landfill's
preservation in the form of a 115-acre sports-and-recreation complex would
contribute to the nation's dialogue about the environmental consequences of

mass consumerism. The government's decision immediately came under a barrage of criticism, and within a day the Secretary of the Interior rescinded the order. Ironically, some of the strongest criticism came from leaders of the green movement who interpreted the celebration of a garbage dump as a reflection of the Bush administration's disregard for the environment. It did not help matters that the property was listed on the Environmental Protection Agency's Superfund list of highly contaminated waste-disposal sites. Others opposed the decision on the grounds that a landfill was not befitting of such an exalted classification and that it did not belong in the company of Mount Vernon, Pearl Harbor, and Martin Luther King's birthplace. Perhaps, in retrospect, a Superfund site was not the best choice for shining a light on the engineering accomplishments of a previous generation. On the other hand, the ultimate shortcomings of what was once considered the best available technology underscores persistent themes in urban environmental history: the elusiveness of pollution control and the unanticipated consequences of reform initiatives. Contemporary populations need to be reminded of past failures as well as triumphs, and as Martin Melosi observed in his analysis of the Fresno Landfill debacle, historical artifacts that provoke discomfort or revulsion can also raise consciousness about very important issues.[18] Moreover, when provocative public interpretation embellishes conservation projects that create more livable cities as was the case with the Fresno landfill, it is well worth the effort.

Urban areas also offer abundant opportunities for interpreting the history of environmental change through the restoration and preservation of natural settings. In a phenomenon unique to the United States, depopulation and dereliction have splattered abandoned lots across inner-city neighborhoods. On some of these plots, the crumbling ruins of houses, tenements, and shops remain visible. On others, remnants of the built landscape have vanished. In the absence of care, many of these lots have been reconquered by nature, commandeered by weeds and wildflowers, and colonized by rats, snakes, feral dogs, and stray cats that thrive amid the tall grasses, piles of trash, and mounds of rubble. In many neighborhoods the reutilization of abandoned lots has been incorporated into preservation-based revitalization strategies. Recognizing that the appeal of beautifully restored homes can be easily undermined by adjoining eyesores and pest hatcheries, neighborhood preservationists have banded together to convert these properties into parks and gardens. In instances when absentee owners have fallen behind on their tax payments, thereby forfeiting their property to local governments, neighborhood organizations have negotiated long-term leases or other maintenance agreements with city officials. Where the abandoned properties have remained in private hands, local citizens have usually had to pool their resources and purchase the parcels outright in the form of a land trust.

As spaces reserved for general community welfare, converted gardens and parks hold tremendous potential for aiding historic preservation in more ways than is afforded by their visual appeal. In Old North St. Louis, for example, local artists have painted historical scenes on the building facades facing several community gardens. One portrays the fountain that once graced Jackson Park, the community's first recreational commons. Another depicts important historical figures related to the neighborhood's development. Projects such as these represent a step toward integrating natural and built landscapes in the branding of neighborhoods as historic and in promoting a historical consciousness among local residents. Incorporating historical interpretation and preservation in the design of natural landscapes, however, requires a larger leap.

That leap may be less daunting if historic preservationists piggyback on the popular native planting movement that has guided landscape design in many parts of the country, including places rife with abandoned and undeveloped urban properties. The cultivation of native plants, as opposed to exotic species, has been touted primarily for its ecological benefits. Trees, shrubs, and flowers indigenous to a region have evolved in the context of local flora and fauna and thus support higher levels of biodiversity. Already attuned to local climatic, hydrological, and soil conditions, they require little maintenance, which means less fertilizer to apply, less pesticide to spray, and in arid areas, less water to import. The cultural advantages of native landscaping have received less attention, although they have not been entirely disregarded. Frederick Law Olmstead, designer of New York's Central Park and chief horticulturist for the 1893 Chicago World's Fair, thought it proper to situate civilization's monuments amid plants, trees, and flowers that were native to the locale. Many of his heirs have likewise recognized that even in urban areas, vegetation, natural topography, and indigenous wildlife all contribute to the essence of place, something that historic preservationists have been just as eager to nurture and protect. Still, the restoration of native habitats has rarely been linked to the promotion of cultural heritage.[19]

Detroit is one of the few urban places where native reforestation has been presented as historic preservation. In the years immediately following World War II, Detroit was sometimes referred to as the City of Trees because of its leafy neighborhood streets. Between 1950 and 1980, however, the city lost half a million trees to Dutch Elm disease. Defoliation exacerbated the blighting of an inner-city landscape victimized in the same years by economic abandonment and infrastructural decay. As historic preservation began to bring investment back to the urban core, a movement arose to replenish the natural environment as well. In 1989, Elizabeth Gordon Sachs mobilized a dedicated core of residents, business persons, and industry professionals under the auspices of The Greening of Detroit to "return the city of Detroit to its former glory" through the replanting of native ash and hackberry trees on vacant lots, parkland, and neighborhood sidewalks. Within fifteen years, the group had added 40,000 trees to the urban landscape, many of them in historic districts undergoing revitalization, including Corktown and Woodbridge. What is both significant and unusual about the initiative The Greening of Detroit is the harnessing of collective memory on behalf of environmental enhancement. Detroit's replanted trees do not merely create a pretty setting for older homes; they help recover a lost aesthetic and, to the extent that shady canopies encourage pedestrians to linger on the street, former patterns of social life.[20]

History and Reconceptualizing the Role of Urban Waterfronts

Urban waterfronts represent an especially exciting opportunity for neighborhoods to tie revitalization schemes to the preservation and historical interpretation of natural landscapes. Because virtually all cities in the United States were founded alongside rivers and bays, older neighborhoods tend to be located in close proximity to waterfront spaces. Throughout most of the nineteenth and twentieth centuries, however, industrial and port development denied urban residents access to these areas. Only after World War II, as older port facilities, warehouses, and factories became obsolete, did cities begin to redevelop their waterfronts as public amenities. In one city after another in the United States, as well as other parts of the industrialized world, these areas were recast as historic districts, places imbued with explicit references to the past. Through the 1980s, however, waterfront redevelopment initiatives rarely aimed to serve the needs of inner-city residents. Refurbished warehouses, old sailing ships, and heritage museums enticed sightseers and shoppers to the waterfront by reminding them that something important had once happened there.[21] Waterfront districts rehabilitated in this fashion, including New York City's South Street Seaport, Boston's Faneuil Hall Marketplace, and Baltimore's Inner Harbor, cultivated a celebratory version of the past that was consistent with their emphasis on tourism and consumption. Typically, references to social conflict were muted and the industrial era was ignored in favor of attention to a more remote preindustrial past.[22] Although many of the mass consumer-oriented waterfront revitalization projects have proved themselves successful from a financial standpoint, they often have compromised the goal of reintegrating the waterfront into the fabric of civic life.[23]

Very recently, however, alternative waterfront development strategies have arisen to accommodate a very different use of history, one oriented less toward tourism and consumption and more toward the needs and agendas of local communities. Continuing population flight to the suburbs and the dissipation of civic identity due to suburban fragmentation and sprawl have legitimized waterfront revitalization strategies that seek to create a sense of place and sites of social engagement for people who live and work in the city. Within the last decade, urban rivers have become the focus of community-building initiatives in a number of major cities, including St. Paul, Memphis, Pittsburgh, Omaha, Los Angeles, and St. Louis. Less preoccupied with central harbor areas close to the downtown business districts, these recent efforts have concentrated on neighborhoods and on portions of the rivers running through them. Along with the shift in geographical emphasis has come a new rhetoric promising to pull waterfronts "into the mainstream of public activity" and claiming that riverfronts are "for everyone." In experimenting with formulas to develop waterfronts as vital community spaces, advocates of the new approach have combined varying mixes of environmental preservation, public history, and economic development. Undoubtedly the most common feature of this new vision is the promotion of active recreation through bike and hiking trails. In many cases, these trails have been enhanced through the restoration of original natural landscapes, including the reintroduction of native flora and fauna, the regeneration of wetlands, and even the removal of floodwalls and embankments to restore rivers to their original meandering channels. The commemoration of historic events has been a less ubiquitous component of recent waterfront revitalization plans, although where history has been incorporated, it has, to a greater extent than ever before, addressed social conflict and brought people of color and members of the working classes to the front and center of narratives.[24]

Los Angeles was among the very first cities to rethink fundamentally the role of rivers in urban life, although historic preservation figured only minimally in the overall conception. In the late 1980s, urban enthusiasts and environmentalists in southern California forged an alliance around the ambitious goals of resurrecting the Los Angeles River and reintegrating it into the fabric of urban life. Although the river snaked a course through some of the city's most densely developed districts, including the downtown, few Angelinos were aware of its existence. Imprisoned in a concrete channel in the early part cf the twentieth century, the river had been gradually removed from public view by chain-link fences, barbed wire, and freeways. Those who knew that Los Angeles had a river generally considered it as nothing more than a sewer, much like the River des Peres in St. Louis and not an unreasonable contention given that its primary function was to guide the city's wastewater out to the Pacific Ocean. Friends of the Los Angeles River, however, envisioned the waterway as a continuous 51-mile corridor of parks, trails, and wetlands. Its plan also entails reconstruction of the river itself, breaking up the concrete in places and replanting vegetation. Because of the coalition's success in lobbying local and state governments for funds, parts of the plan have been implemented, including the creation of more than twenty new riverside parks.[25]

Elsewhere, cities have embarked on slightly less ambitious river rehabilitation projects but have employed history more systematically to increase citizen involvement in river-based revitalization initiatives and to strengthen local attachment to place. Place in History was founded in 1997 to "use history as a foundation to build communication among diverse local constituencies" and to provide a point of departure for community planning. It has sponsored numerous projects in the New York City area, including one that sought to engage local residents in the process of redeveloping properties along the banks of Newtown Creek, a neglected industrial waterway separating Brooklyn and Queens. A series of workshops held in 2000 enabled local residents to meet with city officials, share their memories of the creek, and consider the lessons of history for future actions. The process culminated in a landscape design for one of the major streets terminating at the creek.[26] Pittsburgh's Riverfront Development Plan, published in 1998, pledged to protect and enhance environmental quality through controls on land use at the water's edge and the preservation of natural buffers, but it also aimed to bolster public use of the riverfront through historical exhibition. A proposed Three Rivers Heritage Trail for bikers and hikers featured historical markers linking the waterfront interpretively with adjoining neighborhoods. Since the plan's release, the north and south banks of the Allegheny River have attracted more than $2 billion in private and public investment. A new housing development has arisen on an island that once held a slaughterhouse and tannery, and several abandoned railroad bridges have been preserved and integrated into the Heritage Trail.[27]

St. Louis's counterpart to the L.A. River Greenway and Three Rivers Heritage Trail is Confluence Greenway, a 40-mile heritage, recreation, and conservation corridor that hugs the Mississippi River. Confluence Greenway features a 9-mile bike trail that begins in downtown St. Louis and follows the river north to the city limits. Future plans include a major interpretive center, expansion of a community native plant nursery, habitat restoration, and nature observation stations. According to promotional literature, "rediscovering heritage" constitutes a major thrust of its "plan to reunite people with our rivers" and to "restore the Mississippi River as the focal point of the St. Louis region's ecological, economic, and social vitality."[28] To draw attention to the rich history of the waterfront and garner some national support, the project's organizers, a coalition of local social service, conservation, and civic groups are exploring the possibility of securing a "National Heritage Corridor" designation from the National Park Service. More impressive, they have encouraged and supported grassroots initiatives that incorporate the Riverfront Trail into neighborhood revitalization schemes.

Reestablishing a Riverfront Connection in North St. Louis

In twenty-first-century St. Louis, more than ever before, reconnecting urban residents to the Mississippi River requires a direct appeal to and the active engagement of the city's African American community. African Americans constitute roughly 50 percent of the city's population, and in the wards through which the Riverfront Trail passes the percentage is even higher. Yet the orbit of neighborhood life rarely extends to the waterfront on the north side of St. Louis, largely because of a series of physical obstructions that include a highway, an industrial corridor, and a floodwall. The goal of the Mary Meachum Freedom Crossing is to transform the northern waterfront into both a community asset for nearby residents and a major tourist destination by highlighting the special historical relationship between African Americans and the Mississippi River. Still under development, the project has pursued this goal by bringing previously unknown stories from the city's past to public light and locating them in a compelling counternarrative. It also provides an outstanding model for interpreting social history through the preservation and interpretation of a natural landscape (see Figure 5-2).

The Mary Meachum Freedom Crossing commemorates the attempt of nine slaves to gain their freedom by poling across the Mississippi River to Illinois on the night of May 21, 1855. They were assisted by Mary Meachum, a prominent free woman of color and widow of John Berry Meachum, a nationally renowned clergyman and abolitionist. From Meachum's house downtown, the entourage made its way to a remote location on the river just north of the city limits. There, they boarded a skiff and set off across the rushing water to Illinois. Whereas most Underground Railroad episodes are lost to

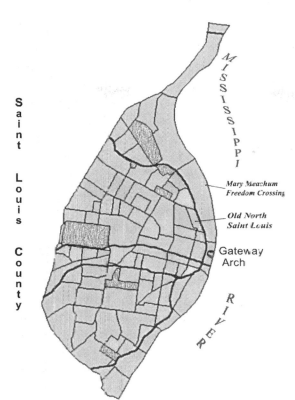

MISSISSIPPI

Mary Meachum
Freedom Crossing

Old North
Saint Louis

Gateway
Arch

RIVER

Figure 5-2. *Map of St.
Louis Neighborhoods.
(Illustrated by Kathryn
Hurley.)*

Saint Louis County

the historical record because of their clandestine nature, this one left a trail of newspaper accounts and court documents because it went awry. Unbeknownst to the fugitives, a posse awaited them on the Illinois shore. On landing, the runaways and their conductors encountered a barrage of gunfire. One abolitionist escort was shot, five slaves were apprehended, and Meachum was arrested for operating an "underground railroad depot." At least one of the captured slaves, a woman named Esther, was separated from her children and "sold downriver" as punishment by her owner.[29]

In 2001, the Mary Meachum Freedom Crossing received National Park Service certification and a historical marker at the spot where the skiff was launched. Two years later, local residents began commemorating the anniversary of the event with a reenactment of the tragedy on the banks of the Mississippi River. During the fall of 2003 and the spring of 2004, north St. Louis residents collaborated with professional designers to plan a much more elaborate memorial, one that would magnify the gravity of the tragedy for both local and national audiences and establish this parcel of riverfront property as a sacred landscape, a kind of holy ground that stood front and center of the national struggle for freedom and racial justice.

The campaign to establish and enhance the Freedom Crossing was spearheaded by the Grace Hill Settlement House, a local social-service agency. Founded in 1903, Grace Hill Settlement House has dedicated itself to the mission of assisting needy families on the north side of St. Louis through a variety of programs for youth, the unemployed, the homeless, and the infirm. Beginning with Lyndon Johnson's War on Poverty, Grace Hill took on the responsibility for administering a wide range of social programs funded by the federal government, including Head Start, VISTA, and, more recently, AmeriCorps. Today it operates several inner-city health clinics and offers transitional housing for homeless women, adult literacy courses, job training programs, and a resource-exchange service.[30]

Grace Hill's interest in historic preservation flowed from its commitment to create resilient and healthy inner-city communities. With the creation of Confluence Greenway's bicycle trail, Grace Hill recognized an opportunity to draw interest, investment, and resources not just to the waterfront but to the adjacent neighborhoods, where it maintained an active presence. Public history emerged as an ideal mechanism for leveraging the appeal of the riverfront trail into a broader strategy for neighborhood revitalization. Heritage tourism became a central part of that strategy because it promised to enhance the riverfront as community asset by providing jobs, recreational opportunities, and a sense of inclusion in broader civic initiatives among the low-income, largely African American population served by the agency. In this respect, historical commemoration on the riverfront dovetailed with Grace Hill's efforts to hire local youth as trail rangers and to replant native flowers along the trail under the federally funded AmeriCorps program.

To ensure that development of the Mary Meachum Freedom Crossing coincided with local needs, Grace Hill engaged surrounding communities in the planning process. During the summer of 2003, Grace Hill convened a community advisory board consisting of representatives from neighborhood associations, churches, schools, and the mayor's office, along with local scholars and preservationists. Over the course of nine months, the Board endorsed the selection of a professional design team for further development of the Freedom Crossing site and then consulted directly with the chosen team. Its most important duty, however, was to solicit the participation of the wider public in a series of community workshops at which the site design was developed and refined. Well over a hundred residents, children as well as adults, attended each of these workshops, which were held at north-side schools on three separate weekends in early 2004. Through breakout sessions and small group presentations, the local community relayed to the designers its views on such matters as the physical configuration of the site, historical interpretation, neighborhood access to the waterfront, and how the site might incorporate amenities for north-side residents such as fishing piers, food concessions, and swimming facilities.[31] The final plan, unveiled at a Juneteenth celebration on the waterfront, was very much a product of the conversations and feedback generated at the community and advisory board meetings.

While the goal of making the site a national tourist destination demanded a compelling national framework for the story, the community called for elaboration of the local context as well. By the 1850s, the nation's destiny hinged on events occurring in places like St. Louis. Missouri was a border state, evenly divided over the issue of slavery that was threatening to split the nation. St. Louis thus became an intense battleground between proponents and opponents of the peculiar institution, and the outcome of local events reverberated far and wide. It was in St. Louis that lawyers first argued the Dred Scott case, which ultimately made its way to the United States Supreme Court and became a major catalyst for the Civil War. The Mississippi River at St. Louis was also a major junction on the Underground Railroad as slaves sought to make the passage from bondage in the Deep South to freedom in Canada. Mary Meachum's crossing was thus part of a dramatic story that unfolded on a national canvas; to ignore its national scope would not only diminish its tourist appeal but also minimize its true significance.

Yet, for the people living in the vicinity of the historic site, commemoration also offered the possibility of publicizing local history—not just the tension between slavery and abolition as it developed in antebellum St. Louis, but a thorough account of neighborhood development over two centuries. At the first community workshop, participants expressed a keen desire to showcase the rich heritage of the north side of St. Louis, including the Native American mound builders that flourished before the arrival of European settlers, the teeming immigrant quarters of the late nineteenth century, and the struggle of African Americans to break the barriers to integrated housing in the twentieth century. Although most of those in attendance already knew something about these subjects, they wanted to know more and saw the Mary Meachum initiative as an opportunity to conduct further research on a part of the city that had received scant attention from historians.[32]

Weaving together the local and national stories required the design team to ask why an event of national proportions occurred where it did, a question that could be answered only by investigating local history. In 1855, when Mary Meachum set out on her perilous journey, the crossing site was just beyond the northern boundary of the City of St. Louis in a kind of no-man's land, wedged between the working-class neighborhood of Bremen on the south and the fledgling municipality of Lowell on the north. It was part of a much larger estate once owned by Captain Lewis Bissell, who had served his country during the War of 1812 and eventually returned to the St. Louis area to build a country estate on a bluff overlooking the Mississippi River. Although Bissell gradually sold off a substantial portion of his property to other speculative investors and subdividers, the parcel along the river-front remained unsuitable for development because it was subject to periodic flooding. Isolated from nearby municipal jurisdictions, it was an ideal place to evade the law. It was also a place where crossing the river, always a treacherous endeavor, was made slightly more difficult by the Mississippi's narrow width at that point. Indeed, the relatively short crossing inspired Lewis Bissell to establish a ferry service to Illinois in 1850 just south of the location where Meachum launched her skiff. Several decades later, in 1889, railroad companies built a bridge across the river, connecting the same points as the ferry.[33] The natural characteristics of the Mississippi River and the spatial relationship to downtown St. Louis were factors that influenced Mary Meachum's decision just as they influenced the development of north-side neighborhoods. Thus, the geography underlying the Meachum tragedy opened a window onto a very different story, one with the potential to satisfy the yearning among residents to have their local history acknowledged and told.

The proposed site design for the Mary Meachum Freedom Crossing employs the natural environment in an unusually imaginative way, creating meaning directly from the site's topography and viewshed. To this day, the land on the river side of the massive concrete floodwall remains undeveloped and appears much as it did in Meachum's period. Ironically, continuity in the contours of the landscape over time is in part due to the success of human engineering in securing a permanent channel for navigation purposes. The most likely change in the appearance of the landscape is the abundance of trees on the contemporary riverbank as the practice of wooding contributed to deforestation along the shoreline during much of the steamboat era.[34] Thus, standing at the spot where Meachum launched the skiff, visitors can gaze eastward onto a relatively unaltered landscape and appreciate the river's role as a boundary and the land beyond it as a horizon of hope. Because there are no structures on the site that pertain to the event, the natural landscape has emerged as the major object of preservation. To communicate the story to visitors, some new construction is planned; a "Wall of Remembrance" arcing around the site will constitute a canvass for text and images, while a barge located in the river will be used for further interpretation and a visitor center. Nine light towers rising behind the curving steel wall will symbolize each of the runaway slaves. A beacon on the opposite shore will symbolize the goal of freedom by allusion to the North Star, which fugitive slaves used as a navigation aid. Rather than intruding on the landscape, however, the site design is intended to draw attention to it. In particular, the steep slope down to the river will be utilized to convey both literally and metaphorically the precarious and dangerous nature of the escape endeavor. Under the nine U-shaped towers visitors will read about and stand in the shoes of the fugitives. Steep grooves will be cut in the embankment to lead visitors to the river where they can visualize and reexperience the tension between the dangerous and unruly Mississippi at their feet and beacon of freedom beckoning on the opposite shore. Although this design is currently undergoing further refinement to ensure its compliance with U.S. Army Corps of Engineers regulations, the power of interpretation will reside in the natural landscape and its preservation on both sides of the river remains critical to the fulfillment of the community's vision (see Figure 5-3).

The innovative design approach at the Mary Meachum Freedom Crossing points to yet another advantage of considering the natural environment as an interpretive canvas: the ability to recover the collective memories of

Figure 5-3. *Mary Meachum Freedom Crossing Design Sketch. (Courtesy of H3Studios.)*

marginalized social groups. One of the major challenges faced by public historians intent on highlighting people of color, the poor, transient populations, and Native Americans is finding remnants of past activity through which to tell their stories. People of meager means and status were the least likely to have a direct connection to the homes, churches, and workplaces that have withstood the test of time. In the absence of extant structures, some projects, such as the Power of Place in Los Angeles, have turned to public art as a substitute. An equally inviting alternative, one employed much less frequently, is to interpret remnants of the natural environment that shaped, and were shaped by, the lives of ordinary urban dwellers. Even where no buildings remain to retrieve and showcase collective memories, there may be wind, rocks, plants, rainfall, wildlife, and soil.

A mile downstream from the Freedom Crossing, the goal of reestablishing a relationship between community and waterfront also animated the Old North St. Louis history project, described more fully in Chapter 3. Unlike the architects of the Freedom Crossing, residents of Old North St. Louis harbored no illusions of converting their portion of the riverfront into a national tourist destination. Rather, they hoped to use the rich history of the waterfront to brand their neighborhood as a historic district. The waterfront represented an obvious target for special attention, given the proximity and popularity of the Confluence Greenway bike trail. Not only did the trail promise a steady supply of potential visitors but it also offered an amenity that could enhance the quality of life for Old North St. Louis residents.

To obtain a clearer sense of the river's past role in community life, the subject was raised in many of the oral history interviews conducted during the duration of the project. The interviews revealed that until the construction of the interstate highway in the late 1950s, the river remained an active and compelling social space. Several residents claimed that proximity to the river was one of the most appealing features of the neighborhood. Born in 1950, John Vignali claimed that he "grew up on the river," spending countless hours watching the river boats and yachts.[35] Ruth Gannaway remembered taking walks along the river as a young girl in the 1940s.[36] Mike Genovese and his friends routinely rode their bicycles to the waterfront near the sewer outfalls and played in the sand bars until they sank down to their knees.[37] Even people who rarely ventured to the river themselves recalled others who did. Anna Garamella moved into her home on North Market Street in 1940. On warm summer evenings she often sat on her front steps, watching the parade of fishermen returning home with their daily catches tied on a string.[38]

Not all recollections about the riverfront were uplifting. With its fast current and unpredictable channel migrations, the Mississippi River could be quite dangerous, and many parents forbade their children from going near it. James Reid, who attended Dessalines School in the 1920s, was among those who were cautioned to stay away from the river; for the most part, he obeyed his mother's warnings. Not all of his classmates did likewise. Reid recalled the riverfront as a favorite destination for children playing hooky from school, one of whom drowned in the river.[39]

Taken together, the stories testified to the neighborhood's determination to preserve the waterfront as a social space, even in the face of an official policy that sought to convert the northern river corridor into an exclusive zone of industrial production and cargo transfer. When the city decided to modernize and expand St. Louis's port facilities during World War I, it chose the northern riverfront as the location for a new public terminal.[40] Plans to strengthen the city's manufacturing base after World War II similarly targeted northern waterfront property. At that time, however, frequent flooding dimmed the prospect of fresh industrial investment. To overcome this problem, city leaders secured federal funding for the construction of a 52-foot flood wall that promised to protect riverfront property from inundation and reclaim land for manufacturing plants and freight transfer stations.[41] Before construction could commence, however, the city had to evict several dozen families that made their home. The riverfront was not just a place where people of Old North St. Louis strolled, fished, and played; it was a place where people lived, albeit illegally. In 1950, Louise Thompson moved into a home just a few blocks from the Mississippi River. When asked about her memories of the waterfront, the first image that came to mind was the "cardboard huts" constructed by transient families that camped on the river. She explained that many of them roamed the neighborhood, going door to door requesting food and part-time work. John Vignali also referred to the "bums" that inhabited the waterfront district in the 1950s.[42] These "bums" belonged to a squatter settlement that dated back to the Great Depression. Cobbling crude shelters out of orange crates and tar paper, dozens of families established a shantytown alongside the river. They remained a notable presence in the neighborhood until 1959, when city officials evicted them.[43]

The riverfront stories captured in oral interviews, along with information culled from newspaper accounts and archival sources, were delivered to the public as part of the overall interpretation of the neighborhood's history. For example, the evolving relationship between Old North St. Louis and the river was highlighted in the brochure for a self-guided history trail that began at the river and extended into the heart of the neighborhood. Because it intersected with the Confluence Greenway bicycle trail, cyclists were invited to detour into the neighborhood, just as local residents were directed from the neighborhood down to the river. Along the way they learned about sites once occupied by ancient burial mounds built by Indians who conducted an extensive river trade, old woodworking factories that relied on lumber hauled from the river, streets that were used to carry goods to and from the river, and the interstate highway that ultimately made the river difficult to reach. Confluence Greenway viewed this history tour as a prototype for other neighborhood detours that would allow St. Louisans to rediscover one another and develop a sense of ownership for a shared landscape. For current residents of Old North St. Louis, most of whom had lived there less than thirty years, the rich history of waterfront activity through the 1950s was somewhat of a revelation. By demonstrating that the riverfront was such a vital part of the neighborhood's fabric, it was hoped that people would begin to reclaim it as a birthright. Although the exposition of riverfront history did not lead the community to embark on any natural-restoration initiatives, it strengthened the community's resolve to restore and preserve a historical relationship between the community and the waterfront.

The history that surfaced along the north St. Louis riverfront departed markedly from the uncontroversial tales of conquest and civilization celebrated in downtown tourist-oriented landscapes. Although the Mary Meachum Freedom Crossing and the Old North St. Louis public-history project were not developed exclusively for local audiences, the imperative of making history relevant to local residents required a full reckoning of some disturbing aspects of the past, such as slavery and homelessness. It was a history designed not only to help the largely African American population better understand how they arrived at their present situation but also to provide an agenda for the future.

Indeed, in the riverfront wards of north St. Louis a new historical consciousness inspired residents to political action and coalition building in defense of public access to the river. Toward the end of 2003, north-side residents learned that the St. Louis mayor's office had endorsed a plan to expand a wholesale-produce-market complex across Branch Street, the only public thoroughfare leading directly from north-side neighborhoods to the riverfront. Since 1953, the region's major fruit and vegetable wholesalers had occupied a strip of warehouses and loading docks just one block from the Mississippi River, stretching from North Market Street to a point near Branch Street. While "Produce Row" had flourished over the past fifty years, other nearby companies had abandoned their multistoried manufacturing plants in favor of sprawling horizontal facilities in suburban areas that facilitated the movement of materials and the assembly of products. In June 2002, the St. Louis Development Corporation—the city's economic development agency—hired a planning firm to devise a strategy for reviving economic activity in an 1,100-acre tract of land along the northern riverfront. In its final report, completed in December 2003 with the input of local business leaders, the planning firm recommended the creation of the "Produce Row Business Campus," which would build on existing economic strengths and target new opportunities in food-related commerce, specifically value-added packaging. Crucial to the success of the business park, however, was the construction of large, horizontal buildings for light manufacturing and storage. According to the final master plan, the ideal setting for new construction lay just north of the existing Produce Row, covering Branch Street and thus interrupting pedestrian and vehicular traffic between the waterfront and the residential neighborhoods further west.[44]

The news was a devastating blow to sponsors of the Mary Meachum Freedom Crossing and the Old North St. Louis history trail because both projects relied on Branch Street as the primary point of public access to the waterfront. In contrast to previous eras, when industrial and commercial expansion along the riverfront north and south of downtown elicited little formal resistance, the fall of 2003 saw citizens mobilize to oppose the plan. Indeed, groups that had little previous history of cooperation found themselves aligned on the issue of saving Branch Street. Armed with letters of support from the Old North St. Louis Restoration Group and other northside neighborhood associations representing the predominantly low-income African American population in the area, Doug Eller of the Grace Hill Settlement House took the case to City Hall. At meetings with representatives from the mayor's office and the St. Louis Development Corporation, Eller, along with Grace Hill's Executive Director, Theresa Mayberry Dunn, explained how the expansion of Produce Row would further sever the riverfront from the community and jeopardize two well-supported historic-preservation projects. The campaign to save Branch Street also received vocal support from Trail Net, the largely white, middle-class organization that spearheaded the riverfront bike trail. Over the course of the spring and summer of 2004, the informal coalition continued its work by trying to woo local aldermanic representatives and prominent business leaders.[45]

At the time of this writing, the fate of Branch Street remains undetermined. Regardless of the outcome, the struggle to preserve access to the river testifies to the power of history to mobilize citizens on behalf of alternative priorities for waterfront land use. North St. Louisans have reimagined their relationship to the Mississippi River, seeing it once again as a vital part of their communities. In the process, they have rediscovered one another.

Toward a Systems Approach to Landscape Preservation

The possibility of rediscovery on a metropolitan and even a regional level is precisely what makes landscape preservation and interpretation such a powerful revitalization and community-building tool. Events of the last half-century have clearly demonstrated that the fate of inner-city neighborhoods is tied directly to larger-scale metropolitan developments. Because environmental dynamics rarely correspond to neighborhood or political boundaries, their interpretation illuminates the relationships between different strands of the metropolitan fabric. As historian Hugh Gorman observed, "The urban demand for water, efforts to protect watersheds supplying that water, efforts to preserve greenfields by making better use of brownfields, and debates over how to expand a city's infrastructure without destroying an area's character all highlight the need to treat cities and their suburbs as a single interconnected entity."[46] By exploring these environmental struggles in historical perspective, urban inhabitants may acquire a better understanding of metropolitan interdependencies and a greater appreciation of unfamiliar people and places.

Furthermore, preservation efforts that foster metropolitan-wide feelings of attachment to inner-city environments can serve as an antidote to what is perhaps the most ecologically destructive aspect of contemporary urban development: sprawl. The intrusion of urban development into the countryside has disrupted wetlands, forests, and other robust habitats while exacerbating the strain on natural resources, especially those related to energy production. Historic preservation is too infrequently advertised as a recycling program, but that is precisely what it is. If the restoration, conservation, and public interpretation of river systems, park systems, and habitat networks help more people appreciate inner-city environments and consider them as viable alternatives to suburban subdivisions, it will contribute to more-sustainable environmental practices.[47]

Sustainable relationships between the constituent parts of the metropolis—city and suburb as well as natural and humanized—are what urban practitioners in the field of landscape preservation are groping toward, unwittingly or not. Viewed from this perspective, it makes little sense to concentrate preservation efforts on built structures or natural settings independently of one another. The challenge that lies ahead is finding effective ways to link the preservation of built and natural landscape more coherently in terms of interpretation and comprehensive urban planning. Some of the basic principles of the approach have already been articulated, and some of the mechanisms are already in place. In 1991, at a conference of historic-preservation professionals, a consensus emerged on the need to integrate preservation into comprehensive land-use planning and zoning ordinances rather than to maintain the traditional emphasis on landmark and historic-district designation processes. Likewise, the National Park Service has gone a long way toward developing systematic procedures for inventorying the important cultural and natural elements that complement one another in defining the essence of a place.[48]

One can glimpse the possibilities for urban neighborhoods in the redevelopment of Portland, Oregon's South Waterfront district. This area was once known for its shipyards and lumber mills, but toward the end of the twentieth century, the City of Portland slated it for redevelopment as a high-density, mixed-use residential district. With 3,000 residential units, retail shops, public plazas, offices, and parks, the South Waterfront project would fulfill the broader metropolitan mission of bringing people back to the Willamette River and linking waterside neighborhoods by way of a pedestrian and bicycle-friendly greenway. To maintain continuity with the past and facilitate historical interpretation, the design for the South Waterfront Greenway called for the incorporation of industrial artifacts—the bow of a Liberty Ship, gantry cranes, construction debris—into displays of public art. What made the plan especially innovative were provisions for the restoration of migratory-bird and salmon habitats along the river's edge. In constructing and implementing a coherent urban vision, South Portland's citizens and planners found inspiration in both natural and cultural antecedents.[49]

The difficulties involved in expanding this model to urban neighborhoods elsewhere are not trivial. River settings undoubtedly represent the most promising terrain for experimentation because they are almost always in the public domain. Where private property is involved, things become complicated. It is often unfeasible to take large chunks of urban property off the market for preservation purposes, and the sort of financial incentives that have induced property owners to restore buildings to vintage condition simply do not exist for natural landscape elements. For these reasons, communities may have to develop innovative zoning tools. Truly effective implementation of landscape-conservation principles may yet require a fundamental revision of protectionist laws, which to some degree still bear the legacy of divergent legalistic approaches to preservation. Widely scattered small-scale initiatives that employ a holistic approach, however, represent an important step toward the real prize of preserving desirable and sustainable patterns of urban life that flow organically from the past.

6

≒⊣⊢

Scholars in the Asphalt Jungle

The Dilemmas of Sharing Authority in
Urban University-Community Partnerships

The public-history movement of the 1970s was premised on the conviction that academic scholarship could enrich civic life and instigate progressive social change. Since that time, numerous university-community partnerships have put this hypothesis to the test. Some of the most successful have followed a truly collaborative model in which scholars "share authority" with their public partners by defining research agendas, interpreting data, and publicizing findings collectively. Arguably, communities seeking to investigate local history with greater depth and sophistication have benefited from the resulting infusion of critical perspectives and university resources. Likewise, meaningful public participation and frank dialogue have produced versions of history capable of addressing contemporary concerns. Yet, for all the virtues of this model in terms of democratizing history and making it relevant, sharing authority remains a tricky proposition. The construction of viable and equitable partnerships requires project participants to reconcile very different ways of understanding the past and acquiring historical knowledge. Academic scholars seeking to make an impact beyond university gates invariably face the predicament of adapting professional standards of research and interpretation to the needs and objectives of nonacademic partners. They also confront the challenge of convincing those with little or no academic training that there is some value added in attaching local stories to broader narratives, moving beyond history as mere celebration, and adopting more rigorous methods for extracting and analyzing data.

These dilemmas have assumed particularly sharp edges in urban communities where class and racial divisions reinforce the bifurcation between professional and popular cultures. Urban residents may harbor suspicions about the motives of academic interlopers or feel intimidated by their presence. Within diverse neighborhoods, fear of opening or aggravating social wounds may mitigate against serious historical investigation. Likewise, the high priority accorded to economic revitalization in many historic districts creates additional pressures to produce distorted depictions of the past. To confront these issues is to ask how epistemological differences can be reconciled without sacrificing the professional integrity of scholars or the good faith of local communities.

The question yields no simple answer, but we can make significant headway by examining how public historians in urban settings have sought to turn divergent perspectives into a constructive tension through open dialogue, compromise, and painstaking negotiation. As Dolores Hayden, a veteran of community-based public-history projects, has remarked, successful collaborations require participants to leave their comfort zones and dispose themselves to alien worldviews and ways of doing things.[1] For professional scholars, this means ceding some of the intellectual authority over the production of knowledge and acknowledging that they are no longer the sole source of expertise. Yet professional historians also have a responsibility to proselytize the advantages of employing academic protocols. If public history is to play a role in supporting community agendas, there is much to be gained by striving for consensus in the construction of historical interpretations. As we shall see, one of the most valuable tools scholars can offer is a set of ground rules for assessing evidence and drawing conclusions.

Museums and Civic Engagement

Although this chapter focuses on university-community partnerships, it is worthwhile acknowledging a parallel trend toward greater levels of civic engagement among museums and historical societies. In urban areas, this impulse has resulted in formal collaborations with schools, neighborhood groups, and community organizationsrepresenting a range of specialized constituencies. The commitment among urban museums and historical societies to give ordinary citizens more opportunity for input should not be terribly surprising, given their mission to serve broad public audiences. Nonetheless, the concept of steering historical interpretation toward contemporary concerns is of relatively recent vintage. In 1998 the American Association of Museums inaugurated its Museums and Community Initiative to "explore the potential for dynamic engagement between American communities and their museums."[2] To generate discussion and ideas, the sponsoring organization established a national task force and assembled professionals and community leaders in six regional forums. Robert Archibald, president of the Missouri Historical Society and a fierce advocate for broadening the civic mission of museums, was selected to chair the new task force. Archibald viewed more strategic intervention in the public life of cities and towns as an imperative for twenty-first-century museums because of the larger democratizing forces sweeping across society. "Once considered closed circles of authority," he explained in a recent book on the subject, "our institutions now seek to interact with our communities in more meaningful ways, to apply innovative technologies and educate our constituencies by methods that more clearly reflect the increasingly dispersed authority and power within our communities and nation."[3]

For some museums and historical societies pursuing this path, civic engagement simply took the form of cultivating more socially inclusive audiences. In forging partnerships with local African American and Arab American arts organizations, for example, the Henry Ford Museum in Dearborn, Michigan sought to create "a more welcome place for underserved audiences."[4] Other institutions took the concept further by creating a safe space for dialogue on divisive issues. Following an outbreak of civil unrest in the Over-the-Rhine district, the Cincinnati Museum Center made a bold decision to mount an exhibit on the disorder that featured recorded comments from politicians, police officers, protestors, and business owners. A notebook and a graffiti board positioned near the exhibit's exit invited visitors to express their own views on the recent civil disturbance.[5] Along similar lines, the Japanese American National Museum in Los Angeles sponsored a town hall discussion comparing the discrimination faced by Japanese Americans during World War II with the prejudices encountered by the city's Muslim population in the wake of 9/11.[6] In the pursuit of social relevance, many professionals in the field discovered an effective model in Historic Weeksville. This interpretive project began as a grassroots campaign to save four dilapidated wood-frame houses that once formed part of a free black community in Brooklyn, New York. Subsequent educational and cultural programming at the site made the restored homes a source of hope for the surrounding African American community and an agent of social change. House tours conducted by the Weeksville Heritage Center offered the legacy of the self-sufficient, pre-Civil war village as an inspiration for visitors confronting unemployment, crime, poor housing, and limited educational opportunities in their own lives; oral history projects, performances, social gatherings, and a community-driven instructional curriculum facilitated public conversations about "racism, oppression, and discrimination."[7]

Equally noteworthy were those institutions that extended their programming beyond museum walls. An unusual example of civic intervention occurred in the late 1990s when the Ybor City Museum Society spearheaded a campaign to protect historic homes endangered by highway construction and convert them into residential units.[8] Not surprisingly, given the inclinations of its president who headed the AAM's Museums and Community Initiative, the Missouri Historical Society exemplified the new paradigm with programs such as "Exploring the Hood." In partnership with the St. Louis Archdiocese and the St. Louis Public School system, the Historical Society recruited students and teachers from several predominantly African American neighborhoods in St. Louis. Through a series of structured exercises, students surveyed the areas around their homes and identified the physical assets of their neighborhoods. They then reflected on the challenges involved in improving the places where they lived. The final segment of the project educated participants about government mechanisms so that they could become familiar with the appropriate avenues for enacting political change.[9]

University-Community Partnerships

Academic historians confront many of the same dilemmas as museum professionals in developing fruitful partnerships with community organizations. Yet the peculiar environment of academe presents distinct challenges as well as opportunities. That many of the pioneering public-history projects described herein emerged from university settings—for example, the Power of Place (University of California–Los Angeles), Philadelphia's Moving Past (University of Pennsylvania), and Archaeology in Annapolis (University of Maryland–College Park)—testifies to the creative propensities of academic culture. In particular, the doctrine of academic freedom gives university faculty more latitude to experiment and innovate than their counterparts in museums and historical societies. At the same time, other institutional constraints inhibit the sort of community collaboration that flows more naturally out of the culture of museums.

For historians employed by institutions of higher learning, community-building activity represents more of a stretch in fulfilling their primary responsibilities, and for this reason, universities have been slower to contribute their expertise to public-history projects. The internal reward structure governing faculty behavior presents a daunting obstacle. Tenure and promotion guidelines oblige faculty to publish their research in scholarly journals and in books printed by academic presses. Through these outlets, scholars communicate primarily with their peers. Heavily referenced and couched in abstruse theoretical frameworks, much of this work remains inaccessible to lay audiences and thus does little to help urban communities expand their self-knowledge. Faculty contact with the "masses" occurs largely in the realm of teaching, where the incentives for doing local public history are equally weak. The traditional format of classroom instruction that requires students to meet regularly in a campus lecture hall or seminar room is ill suited to engagement with actors who operate outside the college or university. The trend toward online instruction offers few advantages in this regard. Perhaps even more germane are the curricular constraints imposed by the accreditation process and the pressure to make completed credits and terminal degrees portable. Although history instructors have more flexibility at the postsecondary level than do their counterparts who teach elementary, middle, and high school, most college courses still emphasize national themes, thereby giving faculty little opportunity to apply their expertise to local peculiarities. In cases where scholars have marched to the public-history banner, they have usually done so independently of their research and teaching duties, often at the direct expense of career advancement.

Militating against these disincentives, shifting political and pedagogical currents appear to be opening a wedge for integrating community development with more traditional forms of research and teaching. Increasingly, institutions of higher learning are taking on community development as part of their mission. Universities relying on state funding face political pressure to broaden their constituencies and demonstrate good citizenship. Many have responded by bolstering extension programs through which they provide services to communities in nontraditional formats. Courses taught through extension services do not apply to degree programs and generally emphasize practical skills. Moreover, they are open to all citizens regardless of whether they meet a university's admissions standards for academic programs. Private universities have their own reasons to adopt the role of good neighbor. During the 1960s and 1970s, many private institutions in central city areas became embroiled in bitter squabbles with surrounding populations over campus expansion schemes. As those populations became more empowered, university administrators came to recognize the importance of improved community relations. Over the past thirty years, many schools have worked strenuously to foster goodwill, and in some cases to atone for past transgressions, by sponsoring applied research initiatives. Loyola University, located on Chicago's North Side, launched its Center for Urban Research and

Learning in 1996 for the explicit purpose of involving faculty and students in research directly related to the needs of local populations. Through partnerships with community organizations, the Center has investigated a wide range of urban issues, including welfare reform and affordable housing.[10]

Ultimately, the extent to which universities and colleges direct their resources toward community development depends on how easily those activities can be leveraged to enhance institutional prestige. In this regard there are encouraging signs. In recent years, the Carnegie Classification of Institutions of Higher Education, the most widely recognized yardstick by which research universities calibrate their hierarchical position with respect to their peers, has incorporated community engagement into its calculations. Moreover, accrediting agencies have begun to recognize community-based teaching and learning as appropriate endeavors for institutions of higher learning.[11]

Perhaps the most promising development in terms of directing university resources to the cause of urban rehabilitation has been the embrace of pedagogical approaches that fuse community activism and instruction. Under the banner of "service learning," many schools have begun to experiment with programs that coordinate traditional classroom instruction with related activities in external social environments. Learning, in this model, takes place in the context of real-life experiences. A few examples may clarify the concept. In the early 1990s, architecture and urban planning students at the University of Illinois collaborated with a neighborhood organization to operate a farmer's market for low-income residents in East St. Louis, Illinois.[12] At Franklin and Marshall College in Lancaster, Pennsylvania, undergraduates enrolled in a political science course prepared legal documents for detained immigrants in the York County prison seeking asylum.[13] As part of their service-learning project, engineering students at Howard University mingled with homeless populations in Washington, DC and put their technical skills to use inventing an inflatable sleeping bag.[14] Advocates of the pedagogy maintain that student immersion in "real world" situations not only enhances intellectual development but also fosters responsible citizenship. Ideally, the work performed by students also brings tangible benefits to host communities.[15]

Although this departure from the standard academic curriculum has met a certain amount of resistance from students and teachers, it is fast becoming standard pedagogical practice at all levels of education, from the elementary to the postsecondary level. For colleges and universities, the potential for service learning is especially rich given the maturity and independence of students; over the last decade many have incorporated it into their curriculum.

As of 2005, nearly 1,000 postsecondary institutions had formalized their commitment to service learning through membership in the national Campus Compact coalition. Some of these, including Rutgers University, Providence College, and Portland State University, have even made service learning a graduation requirement.[16]

Historical research has not occupied a particularly prominent place in the service-learning experiment, although it is well suited to the enterprise because, as Ira Harkavy and Bill Donavan observed, "the complex, interrelated real-world problems of real communities are, of course, historical problems—problems that are profoundly shaped by past events and experience." [17] These authors also advance a case for making urban problems "a primary focus for service-learning courses and research projects." For universities situated in cities, the social ills of poverty, unemployment, inadequate housing, and alienation are hard to ignore and often manifest themselves just beyond campus gates. Moreover, these urban maladies demand the sort of comprehensive, structural solutions that historical analysis can illuminate. Examples of history courses structured around service learning include a class on poverty at Stanford University that required students to volunteer their time at a homeless shelter and another on American character at the University of Pennsylvania that brought undergraduates into a mentoring relationship with pupils at a West Philadelphia middle school.[18]

Service learning has both benefits and drawbacks, as Community History Research and Design Services (CHRDS) discovered when it employed the model in Old North St. Louis. Graduate students in a course on public history made important contributions to the project by conducting archival research on topics of interest to the community and also by conducting oral histories. Service learning at the undergraduate level was less successful. In an urban-history class, students researched the history of particular buildings that the neighborhood had targeted for adaptive reuse. Unfortunately, the process of exposing students to general historical themes and grounding them in the specifics of one neighborhood left little time for meaningful research, and the submitted work was uneven in quality. This problem was less acute in the graduate seminar because of higher workload expectations among students. Nonetheless, the one-semester time frame proved to be limiting in both cases. For this reason, CHRDS has preferred to hire students as research assistants so they can work on community projects more intensively over an extended period, sometimes as long as two academic years. Research assistants putting in as much as twenty hours per week have compiled vast amounts of primary historical documentation for each of our St. Louis projects, relieving community residents of the tedious chores of tracking changes in property ownership, transcribing oral interviews, extracting relevant data from census manuscripts and city directories, and determining the vintage of objects recovered in archaeological excavations.

In addition to student labor, universities provide the interdisciplinary resources that enable communities to address problems from multiple directions. Our project in Old North St. Louis—in which public history complemented public health, political leadership, and personal-finance training initiatives—exemplified a multipronged approach to revitalization. An earlier environmental justice project administered by the Public Policy Research Center at the University of Missouri–St. Louis provides yet another example of applied interdisciplinary research directed toward community development. In 1996, the university partnered with community activists in Project HOPE to alleviate environmental hazards in three low-income African American neighborhoods in the St. Louis metropolitan area. Historians helped residents investigate hazards associated with the improper disposal of toxic wastes in the past, faculty and students from the political science department guided residents through the bureaucracy of government agencies, and engineers at the University of Missouri–Rolla contributed a scheme for strategic soil and air testing.

Heritage and History

Whether employed by museums or universities, personnel with academic training contribute a critical perspective that has often been cited as a necessary ingredient for good public history. The literature on public history often trumpets the ability of professional historians to place local events in broader theoretical and geographical contexts and to insist on rigorous standards for assessing and employing evidence. Linda Shopes, a leading authority on the practice of oral history, notes that lacking professional schooling, amateur historians have trouble stringing fragments of historical information into meaningful narratives and comprehending the past in anything but purely personal terms.[19] Similarly, Shelley Bookspan has argued that "rigorous schooling in the art of historical methods and criticism" sharpens a facility for "explaining seemingly random facts" and imposing "order on chaos."[20] If writers such as Shopes and Bookspan are correct in asserting that academic perspectives produce better history, the question of why urban communities should *want* "better history" is still left open. If urban historic districts often portray the past in terms that trouble academic historians, it is worthwhile to inquire why they do so. Only by understanding why scholars and communities approach the past differently can we determine what more rigorous forms of inquiry have to offer to communities that want to capitalize on their historical assets for the purposes of revitalization.

The two approaches to understanding the past are often framed in terms of the distinction between heritage and history. In his book *Possessed by the Past: The Heritage Crusade and the Spoils of History*, David Lowenthal expounds on the difference. History, he argues, is the attempt to understand the past on its own terms. Its methods and goals belong to academe; its practitioners are professionally trained scholars. Heritage, on the other hand, enlists the past for purposes related to the present and is manifested primarily in the realm of popular and commercial culture. Whereas history aims to explain the past, the purpose of heritage is to justify or motivate present-day actions and stances. Most commonly, heritage operates to solidify group identity on the basis of a shared legacy. In this guise, heritage also services claims of superiority.[21] Frans Schouten offers a more stark definition when he writes that "heritage is history processed through mythology, ideology, nationalism, local pride, romantic ideas or just plain marketing, into a commodity."[22]

For Lowenthal, at least, the point of distinguishing between these two brands of interpretation is not to vilify heritage and sanctify history, but rather to better appreciate the distinct virtues and dangers of the former. At its best, heritage promotes stewardship over that which is precious. At its worst, "it signals an eclipse of reason and a regression to embattled tribalism."[23] Groups may invoke heritage to substantiate declarations of superiority and ownership, thereby fomenting conflict with rival claimants. In transitional urban districts, this dynamic frequently inflames tensions between existing residents and those seeking gentrification through the rehabilitation of historic housing. Here, heritage is not associated with traits carried through bloodlines but rather with architectural traditions passed down through successive property owners. In lovingly restoring older homes to their former beauty and grace, rehabbers anoint themselves as the only legitimate custodians of neighborhood tradition. In this formulation, lower-income tenants and property owners become demonized as destroyers of the local patrimony when financial constraints prevent them from keeping seasoned structures in pristine condition. Heritage claims thus serve as justification for eviction and displacement. Therein lays the danger of interpreting local history solely in terms of architectural aesthetics.

Although it may be useful for purposes of discussion to present heritage and history as oppositional paradigms, in practice the line is not so hard and fast. Academic history, no matter how pure, is animated by contemporary concerns. To address readers in the present, scholars necessarily filter their view of the past through all that has happened since. The relatively new fields of women's, gender, environmental, and social history testify to the influence of contemporary social and political movements on scholarly currents. In the selective presentation of themes and topics, professional historians act on their subjective assessment of what is and is not worthy of study. Such assessments are closely tethered to the interests and curiosities of those living in the present, including the historian authors. Moreover, on any given topic, professional scholars must work within the constraints of available evidence. Thus, knowledge of the past is never complete.

If present-day bias always seeps into analysis of the past one way or another, a fundamental difference nonetheless remains in how the two interpretive modes manufacture narratives. Again quoting Lowenthal, "history differs from heritage not, as people generally suppose, in *telling* the truth, but in *trying* to do so despite being aware that truth is a chameleon and its chroniclers fallible beings."[24] A key distinction, in this regard, pertains to how practitioners arrive at their conclusions. Professional strictures require scholars to ground their conclusions in recorded evidence that can be verified by peers. Heritage enforces no such constraint. Historical interpretations gain legitimacy through logical persuasion. Heritage commands loyalty through acts of faith. Freed from any expectations of objectivity, heritage is susceptible to errors of distortion, omission, and overglorification.

Urban communities gravitate toward the heritage end of the spectrum to the extent that they perceive the past as a means of marketing their location to outsiders, attracting investment, and stimulating tourism. When economic motivations drive public history, creating the right impression frequently trumps the quest for accuracy. To distinguish themselves from the competition, historic districts strive to project a coherent set of visual cues that proclaim a definable identity within clearly marked territorial boundaries. Indeed, in residential neighborhoods, the most effective selling point may not be the historic ambience per se, but rather the evident dedication among homeowners to the creation and maintenance of that ambience. Moreover, the act of rebranding a neighborhood represents an attempt to break from the past. Thus, a distancing from history becomes embedded in the process of historic-district creation. Troubling aspects of the past, periods of urban decay, and the previous presence of poor or minority population are likely to get expunged from the historical record under these conditions.[25] When urban regeneration strategies combine the pursuit of fresh investment with the quest for tourist dollars—which they nearly always do, to some extent—the pressures to suspend rigorous analysis and present history selectively are intensified.

Lowell, Massachusetts was one of the first urban areas in the United States to pursue a revitalization strategy based on a total image makeover, and its struggle to manufacture a marketable past illuminates the collision of heritage and history. In the early nineteenth century it was a center of textile production, famous worldwide for its advanced level of mechanization and the "Lowell girls" who operated the machinery. Later in the century, when a more docile immigrant labor force replaced the native-born females, Lowell assumed the characteristics common to industrial cities of the Northeast and Midwest. The relocation of many mills to the South in the early twentieth century ushered in a prolonged period of economic decline. By the 1960s, Lowell was a ragtag poster child for industrial abandonment and urban decay. Among its assets, however, were remnants of the early-nineteenth-century mills, boardinghouses, and canals that had once made Lowell the industrial showplace of the world. It also boasted a local citizenry inspired by an unprecedented vision of cultural and economic generation. In the early 1970s, a coalition of educators, preservationists, politicians, planners, and civic leaders spearheaded a campaign to designate the entire city as a cultural park celebrating Lowell's industrial and ethnic heritage. Under the auspices of the National Park Service, professional historians were invited to craft a public interpretation that would simultaneously reflect the latest currents in academic scholarship and repackage the aged mill town as a national tourist attraction. Within six years of its dedication as a national park, Lowell bragged a vibrant tourist industry and a burst of private investment.[26]

In her recent book on the "Lowell experiment," Cathy Stanton questions the integrity of public history in the service of culture-based revitalization schemes. Stanton concludes that in such contexts, the pressure to tell an uplifting story and achieve community consensus severely compromises the spirit of critical inquiry so central to scholarly analysis. The professional historians employed at Lowell managed to interpret the city's remote industrial past as a symptom of capitalist development and thus clarify the forces that contributed to labor exploitation. Yet they faced tremendous local resistance to carrying the theme of capitalism's social consequences into the twentieth century. Instead, community leaders insisted on presenting the recent history of Lowell as a celebration of ethnic diversity. The result was a fractured storyline where the past bore little relation to the present. The struggle to make the past relevant in Lowell convinced Stanton that "culture-led strategies . . . often disguise the workings of history and power rather than rendering them legible."[27] The professional historians at Lowell did not escape condemnation either. Indeed, Stanton charged that much of what passed for history at Lowell could best be understood as a performance ritual in which both public historians and their audiences attached themselves to a tale of progress—from exploitative industrialization to heritage-based regeneration, from ethnic and working class roots to middle-class assimilation—so as to anchor themselves comfortably amid the uncertainties of the global postindustrial economy.

Economic motivations need not be paramount for communities to veer toward a heritage orientation. The urge to swell pride, for example, inclines communities toward selective commemoration and celebration. To strengthen people's attachment to place and make people feel good about the places they live in, local histories will accentuate the positive. Favorite sons and daughters who went on to gain fame and fortune are placed on a pedestal, acts of aesthetic accomplishment attain renown, and uplifting tales of the downtrodden managing to eke out respectable lives in the face of adversity resound in community lore. In neighborhoods known for the predominance of a particular ethnic or racial group, local history often becomes a template for the inscription of ethnic and racial achievement.

Archaeologist Paul Mullins found this to be the case when he embarked on a project to recover the lost of history of Indianapolis's near-Westside. Local residents, who were overwhelmingly African American, wanted to highlight stories of success. As part of their preservation effort they had drawn attention to two longstanding sources of neighborhood pride: the Walker Theater and Crispus Attucks High School. The Walker Theater was built in 1927 to commemorate Madame C. J. Walker, the Indianapolis entrepreneur who made a fortune in the hair care business. The high school, which opened in the same year, provided an avenue of mobility for the African American students who signed up for its rigorous academic programs. Local residents hoped that archaeological research would reinforce existing narratives of racial solidarity and achievement. Yet the remains of material culture told a far more complicated story. On the one hand, in the nineteenth century the neighborhood was ethnically and racially mixed and there was evidence of considerable intermingling. Moreover, the lives of descendant African Americans revealed through the archaeological evidence rarely showed the sort of dramatic mobility suggested by Madame C. J. Walker and Crispus Attacks High School. What troubled Mullins most of all was that the prevailing historical interpretation, articulated powerfully by these two landmarks, had little explanatory power with regard to the subsequent developments that led to the neighborhood's abandonment and destruction in the following decades. Residents, however, remained resistant to counternarratives.[28]

Cities, towns, and neighborhoods may go to perverse lengths to blot out stains on their reputation. Robert Weyeneth has described how Centralia,

Washington erased the hanging of a labor activist from civic memory in the years after 1919. The hanging victim had been a member of the radical union, the International Workers of the World, also known as the Wobblies. The act of vigilante justice was executed in reprisal for the union's role in the shooting death of four legionnaires earlier that day. The fiercely antilabor war veterans had used an Armistice Day parade as an opportunity to attack the Wobblies' meeting hall in the Roderick Hotel. In the course of the armed defense, four legionnaires lost their lives. Although the Wobbly perpetrators received stiff prison sentences for their crimes, the citizens who dragged the presumed ringleader from the city jail and hanged him from a bridge were never arrested or brought to trial. In the heated climate of the Red Scare, these events split the local population into hostile camps. Yet, rather than attempt reconciliation, the city chose to forget. The shootings and the hangings became Centralia's dirty little secret, something that future generations swept under the rug. In subsequent decades, the local library collected no information on the incident and the county historical society refused to reference it in any of its museum exhibits. When an outsider tried to raise local consciousness on the topic by nominating two related sites to the National Register of Historic Places in the 1990s, he encountered a mixed response. While some citizens welcomed the opportunity to give history its due, others feared that it would only reignite tensions and make for bad publicity. Perhaps most tellingly, those civic elites who have chosen in recent years to resuscitate the event as a means of stimulating heritage tourism have thoroughly depoliticized the conflict and have gone so far as to depict the Wobblies as a mainstream labor organization rather than the radicals they truly were.[29]

All of the proclivities described here steer public history away from critical analysis and toward the creation and perpetuation of celebratory myth. When urban communities deploy history as propaganda, they tend to adopt research methods and interpretive strategies that try the scholar's sense of professional propriety. In flaunting their best side, avoiding controversy, and burying unflattering aspects of the past, what gets presented to the public is anything but the full story—and a flagrant violation of the professional historians' commitment to objective truth.

So the conundrum for scholars operating in the public realm boils down to determining what constitutes an acceptable level of distortion. If, as this book contends, history can play a constructive role in the creation of vital urban neighborhoods, the past is necessarily placed in the service of the present. To some extent, then, heritage goals are appropriate. On the other hand, it is important to recognize that there is a heavy price to pay for the uncircumscribed reconstruction of past events for present-day purposes. Gross distortions and easily refutable assertions undermine credibility. A flawed understanding of the past is unlikely to provide much guidance on how to grapple with pressing problems and issues. The public historian has an obligation to alert communities to these dangers and to communicate the benefits of employing professional standards of research and analysis. Between the poles of a dogmatic academic approach and pure propaganda is a fertile middle ground where rigorous historical inquiry can meet the needs of living communities. It is a middle ground that permits the foregrounding of historical characteristics that speak to contemporary concerns and yet draws a line at outright fabrication. Unfortunately this middle ground is not a destination that can be located by means of some universally applicable set of directions. Rather it is one best arrived at through flexible negotiation between professionals and community representatives. The fluidity of the concept demands that we explore its utility through concrete cases rather than abstract discussion.

In every local-history project organized by CHRDS, research unearthed some aspect of the past that clashed with the community's desired public image. Whenever we stumbled across one of these inconvenient truths, we carefully considered the implications of public revelation as well as our obligation to portray the past accurately. Case by case, professional historians and community activists struggled to reconcile the evidence with project goals. Spirited discussions usually resulted in some compromise between absolute censorship and full exposure. The most successful resolutions, however, twisted the meaning of unflattering discoveries in ways that advanced neighborhood agendas.

More often than not, discussions of this nature were connected to the topics of violence and crime. Recall how residents of Old North St. Louis balked at any references to crime for fear of perpetuating negative stereotypes about inner-city danger. Yet it was precisely because crime loomed so large in the public's perception of the area that some of us on the project thought it worth addressing directly. Besides, it was not a subject that could be easily avoided. Without our prompting, many oral history informants raised the issue of public safety. External audiences inquired about it as well. Perhaps there was something to be gained by exploring the issue honestly and systematically in a historical context. Interestingly, our investigation uncovered abundant evidence that contradicted the popular perception of the neighborhood's linear descent from safe haven to menacing slum. Rather, oral histories and the archival record showed that crime was a persistent hazard. Gang warfare plagued the neighborhood during the 1930s;

juvenile delinquency was a major concern in the 1960s and 1970s. At various times in the twentieth century, shooting rampages and grisly murders crystallized neighborhood concern and anxiety. If our evidence strongly indicated that crime was an enduring feature of life in Old North St. Louis, it also suggested that persistent threats to public safety did not undermine a general satisfaction with urban living or the development of rich community support networks. The matter came to a head in the making of a video documentary on the neighborhood's history. Some members of the steering committee wanted to exclude clips in which on-camera informants spoke of murders and gunfights, while they simultaneously endorsed the use of an interview with a former resident who recalled a time when neighbors felt secure enough to leave their doors unlocked at night. After a lengthy discussion about historical accuracy and how the crime segments contributed to or detracted from larger interpretive themes, the committee reached a consensus. A colorful story about a domestic dispute that ended in murder was cut from the video, but a recounting of gang activity during the Depression was embedded in a section on the varied expressions of ethnic identity.

Negotiations elsewhere produced a range of outcomes. Members of the Forest Park Southeast history committee chose to acknowledge in their brochure text that an abandoned service station on its History Trail once operated as a front for a gambling den. Another local-history committee decided that the cache of spent ammunition unearthed behind the Scott Joplin House did not belong in its museum exhibit. After considering the possible explanations for this unusual concentration of bullets, historians and residents settled on a scenario in which the building on the property was used as a shooting range just before its demolition. Because the bullets did not illuminate any of the main exhibit themes—cultural innovation, political activism, and community-building mechanisms—their exclusion did not seem to distort the historical record.

One of the more interesting cases of this nature arose in conjunction with an after- school program at an inner-city high school. In this particular extracurricular activity, students were asked to photograph buildings of historical or architectural significance in their neighborhood. Taken together, the images were supposed to paint a flattering portrait that confounded popular perceptions of urban decay and degeneracy. After shooting several rolls of film, each student chose a few images for display in a public exhibition and conducted historical research for the purposes of writing accompanying text. Among the pictures submitted was an unusual roadside motel that lay partially hidden behind a brick wall on a main thoroughfare. The only information about the property gleaned from local newspapers, however, involved a string of robberies and murders. Students in the class were understandably reluctant to include this material in the public exhibit. Yet, rather than expunge the photo, the class decided to dig a little deeper in search of some alternative interpretation. Further investigation revealed that Robert Riggins, one of the motel's previous owners, was a successful entrepreneur whose business empire included a renowned nightclub and the only African-American-owned radio station in East St Louis.[30] By juxtaposing these stories in the photo caption, the image turned out to be among the most effective at showing how easily surface impressions, especially those created by the media, could mask more uplifting narratives.

When social and cultural rifts overlay the schism between professionals and amateurs, further complications and obstacles arise. Generally, academics come from more privileged backgrounds than those who inhabit distressed urban neighborhoods. University-community partnerships forged in the context of racial and class differences may suffer the weight of historic antagonisms and mutual suspicions regarding intent and integrity. Racial and ethnic minorities remain resentful of having been written out of much of the history presented in school textbooks and public venues. Moreover, a long record of oppression renders racial and ethnic minorities particularly susceptible to suspicions of exploitation at the hands of outsiders. Prior experiences with academics specifically or with outside experts more generally predispose members of marginalized communities to doubt the sincerity of faculty and student intentions as well as their willingness to undertake anything but short-term commitments. It requires considerable persuasion to convince communities that community engagement is not simply a mechanism for career advancement on the part of students and university faculty. On the other side of the equation, academics are prone to discount culturally specific modes of historical understanding that depart from academic protocols. Cultures that ground collective memory in nontangible vestiges of the past or unverifiable claims are likely to elicit skepticism, if not scorn, from professionally trained historians and archaeologists. Despite the best of intentions, collaborative ventures that cross cultural divides may collapse as a result of seemingly irreconcilable methods of assessing truth and interpreting evidence. Needless to say, successfully bridging these divides requires tremendous sensitivity.

The perils of cultural arrogance have been quite evident in clashes between public historians and archaeologists, on the one hand, and Native American communities, on the other. The wanton desecration and destruction of relict Native American sites in the nineteenth century fostered a legacy of resentment toward Euro-American investigators. Those remnants of the Indian past deemed worthy of protection tended to be associated with white history—for example, the sites of massacres and battles.[31] Even as professional scholars adopted more respectful practices in the late twentieth century, conflicts erupted over divergent ways of establishing historical truths. Academic scholars place much greater emphasis on tangible evidence, discounting the oral traditions and religious rituals that sustain and validate collective memory within Native American communities. That which constitutes historical evidence for scholars may take on an entirely different meaning in the context of Native American culture.[32]

Few controversies have exposed this dissonance more explosively than the one that erupted over the remains of the Kennewick man in the state of Washington in 1996. The discovery of a nearly intact human skeleton with unusual features immediately aroused the curiosity of scientifically trained archaeologists. Presumed to be between 5,000 and 9,000 years old, the skeleton's unusual dental and bone features defied prevailing theories about the human settlement of the Americas. Because the bones were found on federal land that was claimed as an ancestral home by the Umatilla tribe, authorities were required by law to turn them over to the Native American community for reburial. A group of scientists challenged this mandate, and for nearly a decade the Kennewick man became the object of a tug-of-war between distinct and conflicting epistemological systems. To the scientists, the bones constituted archaeological evidence critical to the construction of scientifically based knowledge. To the Umatilla, they were the sacred remains of an ancestor who deserved the dignity of peaceful interment. The issue was eventually resolved in favor of the scientific community, but not without hard feelings on both sides.[33]

In diverse urban districts, the potential for cultural conflict extends across a wide array of ethnic, religious, and racial configurations. The legacy of slavery—along with more recent racist practices in the provision of housing, education and public services—continues to cast a pall over relations between African Americans and white people in many urban areas. Given the record of interaction with white figures of authority, African Americans, like Native Americans, have good reason to be suspicious of historical inquiries conducted under the auspices of academic institutions. Although not directly related to historical research, the notorious Tuskegee experiment, in which nearly 400 black syphilis patients between 1932 and 1972 were allowed to degenerate for the sake of advancing medical knowledge, lingers in the collective memory of African Americans as a reminder of the potentially harmful repercussions of engagement with professional investigators.[34] Such heinous injustices are compounded by persistent examples of insensitivity in the public interpretation of historical topics such as slavery. When the curators of Colonial Williamsburg reenacted a slave auction on the basis of academically grounded research in 1994, they encountered a barrage of protests from civil rights activists who charged that the exhibition trivialized the cruelty of slavery by conflating history with entertainment. Subsequently, several black actors refused to don their slave costumes for the grand opening of a Colonial Williamsburg retail store in a Cleveland shopping mall because they believed the venue was inappropriate for the presentation of such serious and flammable content.[35] For white scholars working in partnership with African American communities, failure to address racially charged themes directly, sensitively, and preemptively can easily result in a fatal cascade of misunderstandings and offenses.

Public historians can expect communities of color to take exception to academic critiques that undermine sources of racial pride. Like Native American tribes, African American communities have long relied on the spoken word, ritual performance, and song to transmit collective memory across generations.[36] Dismissal of these nonwritten sources can easily be interpreted as a sign of disrespect for cultural traditions. When charges of evidentiary inadequacy challenge the veracity of cherished narratives or squelch treatment of key themes in African American history, disputes can become quite bitter. In the community project to restore St. Augustine's church in New York City, historians and community preservationists became embroiled in a tense debate over the use of the term "slave galleries" to describe the upper-level pews reserved for African American worshippers. African American members of the community favored the term because it drew attention to the odious institution of forced bondage that existed not only in the South but in northern cities like New York. Professional historians working on the project objected to the term because there was no hard evidence indicating that any of the African American worshippers were slaves. Moreover, given the fact that slavery was abolished in New York City one year before the church was constructed, at least one historian averred that use of the term "slave galleries" was "irresponsible." Meanwhile, several community representatives argued that abandoning the term constituted an act of racism.[37]

A similar if somewhat less heated quarrel arose during the design phase of the Mary Meachum Freedom Crossing in north St. Louis. Project designers proposed to house the site's educational center on a floating barge, moored to the bank of the Mississippi River. The barge recalled the floating schoolhouse that Mary Meachum's husband, John Berry Meachum, purportedly anchored in the Mississippi River in the 1840s to evade state laws forbidding the provision of education to free blacks. Commemorating this act of courage and resistance lent direct support to the project's goal of portraying the Meachums as inspirational figures and role models for the present-day African American tourists expected to visit the site. Unfortunately, the professional historians working on the project found no documentary evidence to verify the story, which had become part of local lore. Tracing back the tale in published accounts hit a dead end in 1964.[38] Some members of the advisory committee counseled against any reference to the steamboat schoolhouse on the grounds that it would undermine the project's credibility. Yet the issue was settled in favor of integrating the story into the site interpretation.

Clandestine acts, such as the one supposedly perpetrated by Meachum, rarely left paper trails for future scholars to follow, and therein lies a dilemma for public historians. Strict adherence to academic protocols would seem to exclude many acts of illegal resistance from public exposition. On the other hand, presenting information to the public on the basis of anecdotal evidence clearly violates scholarly canons of evidence. No historical topic has generated more controversy in this regard than the Underground Railroad. There is no dispute about the existence of the Underground Railroad; there are enough primary sources to provide historians with a general understanding of its geography and mode of operation. Yet the documentary record is slim because of the severe consequences of discovery, especially after passage of the Fugitive Slave Act in 1850. Filling the vacuum of archival sources, local lore has manufactured history out of rumors regarding tunnels that led from one safe house to another, hideouts that masqueraded as root cellars, and distant relatives who came to the aid of fleeing captives. The inspirational quality of Underground Railroad legends creates an overpowering temptation to eschew rigorous academic scrutiny, not only among African Americans but among whites eager to highlight examples of interracial opposition to a disgraceful form of servitude. After all, white people as well as black people assisted runaway slaves. Motivations such as these account for the recent spate of history trails and tourist attractions marking Underground Railroad activity across the country. For some professionally trained public historians, however, the satisfaction derived from greater public awareness about this aspect of the nation's past has been tempered by the perpetuation and propagation of historical falsehoods.[39]

One can go a long way toward bridging the divide between academically trained scholars and inner-city populations by reflecting neighborhood diversity in the social composition of professionally trained project personnel. Oral historians have noted the benefits of pairing interview informants with interrogators who have similar social and cultural backgrounds. June

Manning Thomas, for example, observed that a shared African American heritage helped interviewers and narrators develop an immediate rapport in her Detroit oral history project. With respect to the field of historic preservation, Antoinette Lee recently called for recruiting more people of color into the ranks of professionals employed in the field, arguing that it would expand the terrain of preservation.[40] Certainly, greater efforts in this direction will make it easier for professionals to gain community trust when working in inner-city neighborhoods.

Negotiating Consensus

Yet the simple addition of racial and ethnic minorities to project staff will not automatically solve the problems that derive from cultural divergence. Thus far, this chapter has presented the dilemma of sharing authority in terms of a cultural gap between external experts and community-based amateurs. In diverse inner-city neighborhoods, however, the division is rarely so stark. More commonly, inner-city residents are located along a spectrum of methodological bents that do not neatly correspond to racial, ethnic, or class configurations. Hence, the lines of debate over evidentiary standards and interpretation are just as likely to be drawn within communities as between them and external professionals. It is tempting to circumvent these tensions entirely by tolerating conflicting accounts of the past. Indeed, it has become fashionable in recent years to present history to the public through multiple lenses, eschewing authoritative narratives in favor of parallel versions of reality. The intellectual justification for this approach flows out of a postmodern rejection of objective truth as well as a multiculturalist emphasis on tolerance and diversity. Examples of this brand of public history abound. During the 1990s, the National Park Service developed new programs to interpret its preserved landscapes from multiple points of view. The history of its fur trapping sites, for example, was presented from the perspective of the trapper, the Indian, and the beaver that was nearly driven to extinction.[41] Crossing the Boulevard, a public-history project in the urban setting of Queens, New York adopted a similar tack. A book, mobile story booth, audio CD, and Web site detailed the borough's recent history through the voices of its immigrant population. In the resulting compilation of oral histories, no attempt was made to force the disparate stories into any sort of unified narrative or even to verify the authenticity of narrator claims. From the start, project organizers decided to let each account stand on its own, even if it contradicted other sources.[42]

The plural-perspectives model has limited utility, however. Airing alternative reconstructions of the past may well serve a constructive purpose by fostering mutual understanding and jump-starting dialogue across social and cultural boundaries. As the culmination of research and analysis, however, it falls short because it does little to advance communities toward specific goals. At some point, the agreement to disagree becomes a conversation stopper and thus a poor catalyst for decisive action. Left alone, discordant histories cannot possibly unite communities behind a common agenda or bring closure to festering social wounds. To direct history toward these salutary ends, it is more profitable to engage in the messy and time-consuming pursuit of singular narratives through consensus. For all the difficulties of negotiating a commonly agreed-on representation of the past, there are instructive examples of communities that have done so in the most acrimonious of social environments.

Richmond, Virginia provides a case in point. Over two centuries of slavery and racial segregation produced deep and lasting social wounds that persist to this day and account for two diametrically opposed accounts of past events. In this former capital of the Confederacy, no topic has been more contentious and subject to differing interpretations than the Civil War. In the "Lost Cause" version, upheld by many whites, the war was a noble defense of states' rights and a benign system of slavery. Among Africans Americans, the war ended the vile practice of forced labor and inspired a longer-term struggle to overcome the injustices of racial discrimination. Given the sharp disparity in interpretation, it should not have been terribly surprising when members of the local African American community objected to the prominent display of Robert E. Lee's likeness at the newly opened Canal Walk festival marketplace in 1999. Canal Walk represented an attempt by local business and civic leaders, Civil War buffs, and the National Park service to use history as a lure in the creation of a vibrant district for tourists and shoppers along the James River. The plan revolved around the creation of a waterside promenade, a historically oriented visitor's center to be housed in a defunct iron works, and a park. Lee's portrait, one of thirteen historical murals hung alongside the Canal Walk, provoked an immediate rebuke from local African American leaders. City councilman Sa'ad El-Amin charged that the heroic depiction of the Confederate General was insulting to the city's African American residents and he promptly called for a boycott of Canal Walk. When the Richmond Historic Riverfront Foundation responded by removing the offending panel, it incited an equally venomous reaction from white southern heritage groups that threatened to organize their own protests.

Despite the hard feelings on both sides, business owners and civic boosters understood that the canal walk and hence the entire downtown revitalization scheme required agreement on some version of the city's history—not simply agreement on what happened, but what it meant. By the 1970s, the twin blows of suburbanization and industrial decline had sapped the vitality of the downtown commercial district, thereby convincing white and black community leaders that it was in their mutual interest to work together on a revitalization plan. After a few failed initiatives, they pinned their hopes on heritage tourism. Because this particular strategy presumed a multiracial base of tourists and consumers, it demanded a reconciliation of the two racially charged historical perspectives. Canal Walk designers mistakenly believed they had struck a reasonable balance between the two versions of history in their selection of images for the floodwall mural. When it became apparent that they had not, project developers wisely chose to revise the entire process. Rather than send the design firm back to the drawing board, they turned the matter over to a multiracial citizens' committee. A compromise solution retained a spot for Lee on the floodwall but altered the context considerably. Lee, dressed in civilian clothes rather than military garb, would be flanked by two additional figures: a black Union soldier and Abraham Lincoln. The committee proposed additional changes for other panels as well. The image of dancer Bill "Bojangles" Robinson was removed on the grounds that it fed unflattering African American stereotypes, and more space was devoted to local civil rights activists.

Finally, and perhaps most significantly, the theme of reconciliation was directly incorporated into the amended interpretation, primarily through the placement of a statue of Abraham Lincoln in the visitor center. With the words "to bind up the nation's wounds" inscribed at its base, the statue articulated the supposition that Lincoln intended to treat the South leniently after the Civil War. Although Lincoln's actual intentions remain open to debate, offering up the Great Emancipator as a friend to the defeated South served Richmond's need to resolve contradictory versions of the past through a unifying figure. Although the final exhibit design elicited some criticism, opinion polls indicated that a majority of African Americans and whites found it acceptable; no protests or indecorous incidents accompanied its installation. Among the most notable repercussions of the controversy was a commitment among white Canal Walk developers to pursue a biracial commercial investment model that included aggressive recruitment of African American shareholders.[43]

Somewhat further afield, the recent experience of South Africa provides another example of consensus history in the service of social reconciliation and reconstruction. As this embattled country made the precarious transition from a racially oppressive apartheid regime to democratic rule after 1994, its political leaders invoked history to rally a bitterly divided people around a commonly held identity. A rewriting of history to include the experiences and struggles of previously misrepresented racial and ethnic groups promised to resolve difficult but vital questions about who would be included in the postapartheid nation, under what terms, and according to what principles. The public history endorsed by the new national unity government emphasized a shared heritage and laid the basis for a stable and inclusive "Rainbow Nation." In seeking consensus around the national goals of democracy and social justice, the new government recognized that its biggest challenge involved coming to terms with the brutality of the preceding apartheid regime. The primary responsibility for executing this task fell to the Truth and Reconciliation Commission (TRC), which was established by an act of Parliament in 1995.[44]

In the latter half of the twentieth century, more than a dozen countries have established truth commissions to document human rights abuses and foster social healing. None have been as ambitious as South Africa in expecting such a body to set the tone and direction for nation building. As indicated in the commission's title, the concept of truth lay at the heart of its method; its work was premised on the existence of a truth capable of garnering widespread assent. To reach this truth, the TRC solicited testimony from thousands of individuals who either suffered or perpetrated human rights abuses during the nearly five decades of apartheid rule. A key provision in the law guaranteed legal amnesty to those who confessed their crimes, thereby rewarding honest disclosure. Recognizing the unreliability of oral testimony based on human memory, the TRC sought to corroborate all information through other witness accounts and documentary evidence. Part of the TRC's work thus involved an exhaustive examination of archival records. The emphasis on factual verification was designed to ensure the legitimacy of broader conclusions. Indeed, the TRC aimed to do more than simply compile stories; integral to its mission was arriving at an explanation for the rise and maintenance of apartheid. The founding act stipulated that the commission would undertake to uncover the "antecedents, circumstances, factors, and context" that gave rise to human rights atrocities.[45] Although the final TRC report lacked a full-blown disquisition on historical causality, it did offer something of an overarching narrative structure and "official" explanation: systematic brutality was the product of a morally corrupt apartheid regime that was itself rooted in a much longer history of racism.[46]

Neither the methodology employed by the TRC nor its historical conclusions met with universal acceptance or praise. Academic scholars from a variety of disciplines took particular exception to its claims of "truth." In addition to contesting the very notion of a singular truth, scholars identified specific flaws in the TRC's analysis and findings. An economist, reviewing the final report in *African Affairs*, chided its authors for attributing the evils of apartheid to a generic version of racism that remained more or less unchanged from 1652 through the twentieth century. A more accurate assessment of racism's impact, he averred, would have probed the specific variant that emerged out of misguided scientific theories of the mid-nineteenth century.[47] Mahmood Mamdani, Director of the Institute for African Studies at Columbia University, castigated the TRC for limiting its scope to political crimes against individuals, thereby omitting from its historical account injustices—such as land dispossession—that were perpetrated against entire communities.[48] Similarly, feminist scholars were quick to criticize the narrowly circumscribed definition of human rights abuse that excluded the routine, pervasive, and often violent violations of women's rights committed under the patriarchal apartheid system.[49] The repackaging of history in postapartheid monuments, museums, documentaries, plaques, and tours likewise elicited scholarly denunciation. Ciraj Rassool, a distinguished South African historian, argued that the impulse to expose the multicultural roots of the "Rainbow Nation" in heritage tourist sites had the effect of reducing the nation to a "kaleidoscope of frozen ethnic stereotypes."[50] The urgent need to create a new pantheon of national heroes in the mold of "tolerance and understanding" likewise deformed historical memory. To take a particularly egregious example, national leaders invoked the martyrdom of Stephen Biko, a founder of South Africa's Black Consciousness movement, to sanction the cause of racial conciliation.[51]

If public history produced in the service of national unity fell short of academic standards, there was nonetheless widespread agreement, among scholars and nonscholars alike, that postapartheid historical revisionism and the TRC report in particular served a "positive function."[52] To its credit, the TRC recognized that the truth it exposed was only partial, providing only "a perspective on the truth about the past" and not the "whole story."[53] Yet it supplied enough truth there to imbue the process and product with the credibility needed to legitimize a precarious state, even if in time a majority of South Africans became disillusioned with the ideals of the Rainbow Nation and rejected it in favor of alternative paradigms.[54] Moreover, it bears noting that despite their misgivings, South African scholars remain optimistic that rigorously conducted public history can play a constructive social role;

debates hinge less on its potential utility than on finding the proper formula for bringing critical inquiry in line with progressive social agendas.

If South Africa offers a lesson for practitioners of public history in the United States, it is that the concept of truth, with all its slipperiness, offers an imperfect but nonetheless useful tool for building consensus around social and political goals, at least in the short term if not in the long run. Transferred to inner-city settings, a nation-building strategy becomes one of community building. Although there is no singular methodology capable of unifying communities around revitalization agendas, protocols of inquiry based on the pursuit of truth have surprising resonance among inner-city inhabitants. Many, if not most, urban residents cling to a belief in the truth and are comforted by a methodology that promises to at least approach it if not actually deliver it. In this respect, they do not differ substantially from their suburban or rural counterparts. The idea of deliverance through the recovery of truth, however, is especially strong among marginalized populations that believe they have been shortchanged in previous accounts of the past.

What professional historians can offer in this regard is a road map to the truth based on empirical analysis. The key to making this enterprise work is distinguishing between different orders of truth, much as South Africa's TRC did as it worked out its own methodology. A crucial distinction must be made between forensic truth and what the TRC termed "social" or "dialogue" truth. The first pertains to the evaluation of facts, and the second pertains to the meaning attached to those facts and the narratives constructed through their combination. The first invites definitive verdicts, while the second promises no more than partial or tentative resolution. Moreover, the two versions of truth are reached by way of very different protocols. Forensic truths demand corroboration, and this is where the academic tradition becomes especially valuable. Dialogue truth, on the other hand, emerges from "interaction, discussion, and debate."[55] Because the latter concept does not seek truth objectively, it can more accurately be described as the pursuit of authoritative narrative. Separating out the tasks of determining forensic truth and constructing authoritative narrative and drawing a hard line between them often go a long way toward reconciling the type of tensions outlined earlier in this chapter. Moreover, it allows scholars to retain their professional integrity while conferring a measure of credibility on the work produced by communities. The tricky part in executing this strategy involves shifting discussions so that debates take place within appropriate frameworks. To illustrate, let us turn to a specific example.

The Case of Scott Joplin's Toilet

Determined to repair tattered relations with nearby African American residents, the Scott Joplin House State Historic Site in St. Louis invited a community activist to deliver a public talk in January 2007 about the grassroots campaign to save the famed musician's house from demolition. Well over fifty members of the local community turned out to learn about the speaker's role in preserving the house and then shepherding its conversion to a museum in the 1980s and 1990s. As she explained to a rapt audience, her tenure as site administrator in the early 1980s was marked by incessant wrangling with her superior at the Missouri Department of Natural Resources (DNR). A major issue of contention involved Scott Joplin's bathroom habits. The state official was eager to excavate the backyard area in hopes that the discovery of a buried privy would yield a rich trove of archaeological artifacts. The afternoon's speaker described her reaction at the time:

> I kept telling . . . [him], "This was the city. There was indoor plumbing. There was no privy." We'd argue, "Yes there was. No there wasn't. Yes there was." So, while wandering around in the building alone one day, I went over to this one little room and I began to look at the walls and it was bead-board. It's board that's lined up vertically. Looking at the bead-board, which was original construction . . . I saw clearly outlined what was the bathtub and the toilet tank, the old pull chain toilet tank. You could see the toilet tank. You could see the drain. You could see the whole outline that proved my point that this house had indoor plumbing. Scott Joplin wasn't some down at the heels vagabond. The time Joplin lived here, he may not have been rich, but he was a person of some substance, and if you could afford a flat or apartment with indoor plumbing, you were doing okay. I was able to prove that just by wandering around, looking at things, and listening to what the building had to say.[56]

As she spoke these words, DNR staff members currently employed at the site became visibly disturbed, although they refused to challenge the speaker openly. The speaker's position had not weakened since the early 1980s and had indeed become the source of visitor exhortations to open Joplin's bathroom for public display. Yet, based on what they knew about sanitation practices in the City of St. Louis at the turn of the twentieth century when Joplin occupied the house, the ragtime composer surely would have relieved himself outdoors. Moreover, they were anxious to proceed with the backyard archaeological investigation that had remained on hold for over two decades.

Clearly, there was more at stake here than the precise location of Scott Joplin's bodily eliminations. The disagreement exposed divergent systems of assessing evidence and constructing historical interpretations. The former site administrator saw it as her mission to portray Joplin as a "man of taste and culture,"[57] and people of taste and culture presumably did their daily business inside the house. Discovery of the shadow markings merely confirmed her original supposition. To further accentuate her characterization of Joplin, she decorated the house interior with artifacts of high Victorian culture—globe lamps, fancy divans, and clawfoot bathtubs—even though there was no direct evidence that Joplin ever owned such items or could even afford them. At the risk of reading too much into the situation, there appears to have been an issue of racial, or at least local, pride at work here. The campaign to save Joplin's house had galvanized the struggling neighborhood. In the throes of physical dereliction and deterioration, it had few assets with which to broadcast a positive identity. The Joplin house was a tangible reminder of the neighborhood's glory days, and its restoration embodied hopes for a broader revitalization. Moreover, as the state's only designated African American heritage site, the property carried the full burden of communicating black America's cultural contribution to a general audience. To portray African American historical figures in anything less than a dignified manner invited the perpetuation of negative stereotypes. For the community activist turned administrator, protecting and enhancing the reputation of the neighborhood, and of African Americans more generally, meant uncovering, or perhaps inventing, a local heritage of middle-class gentility. For employees of DNR, on the other hand, it was important to "get the story right" and present an accurate version of Joplin's life to the public.

Our formal partnership with the Scott Joplin House State Historic Site thrust CHRDS into the middle of this delicate situation. On reflection, we envisioned two possible courses of action. The first was to do nothing and hope that the disagreement would not impair the site's community-building initiative. The site administrator at the Scott Joplin House was predisposed toward this strategy, believing it the safer option. The last thing she wanted was an uncomfortable showdown with the former administrator, who remained active in civic affairs. In a worst-case scenario, a direct confrontation might spill over into the wider community, foment discord, and even jeopardize the backyard dig. For the time being, curators and administrators at the Scott Joplin House were content to let the former site administrator make whatever claims she wanted in public forums while they stuck to their contradictory script during site tours.

Our position, on the other hand, was that, left unresolved, the disagreement was more likely to widen the rift between the community and the site, especially if the State proceeded with the backyard excavation. An archaeological dig on the property across the alley from the Joplin house already had uncovered the remains of an outdoor flush toilet. Releasing this information to the public would inevitably raise questions about sanitary facilities on the Joplin site. Respectful of the staff's reluctance to force a showdown with the former administrator on the issue, we suggested an alternative: turning the question over to our neighborhood history committee for resolution. We proposed to explain the controversy, present relevant evidence, consider the larger implications, and reach a decision about public interpretation by consensus. To facilitate this process, we found it extremely useful to separate the discussion into two distinct questions: first, what does the weight of empirical evidence suggest about the state of sanitary facilities at the time of Joplin's residency, and second, how should those conclusions be interpreted and communicated to the public?

To begin this exercise we collected documentary and oral evidence pertinent to the subject. Among the most important sources was a fire-insurance map from 1897, three years before Joplin's occupancy, that showed the outline of a water closet in the rear of the property. According to the map, about a dozen water closets existed at various locations on Joplin's block. Another revealing document was a U.S. census report from 1940 indicating that eighty-three of 119 housing units on the block lacked indoor plumbing. A 1947 survey of sanitary facilities conducted by the St. Louis City Planning Commission calculated the percentage of households relying on outdoor toilets in the vicinity of the Joplin House at under 50 percent, a figure that was consistent with usage in much of the City of St. Louis. We were fortunate to have oral testimony from a mother and daughter who had lived four addresses to the east of the Joplin house in the 1950s. Both women recalled the removal of the outdoor privy from their backyard sometime around 1953. Finally, the group was shown a fragment of the outdoor toilet found in the recent archaeological excavation across the alley. The fragment bore a maker's mark from 1948. The documents and artifacts sparked considerable debate. One perplexing issue was that the number of water closets shown on the 1897 map seemed low in relation to the number of households on the block. Did this mean that there was tremendous congestion at the water closets? Perhaps the map makers did not represent every outhouse on the block.

Or did it suggest that in fact many houses had already acquired indoor plumbing? As the conversation progressed, several older members of the local-history committee shared their own memories of using outdoor privies in the neighborhood during the 1940s and 1950s.

In the end, the committee concluded that in all likelihood Joplin did not have indoor plumbing. When it came to ascertaining the meaning of this fact, however, local residents rejected the former site administrator's assumption that outdoor privy use connoted lower-class status, either for Joplin or his African American neighbors. A discussion about sanitary habits quickly shifted to the larger question of how to measure socioeconomic status. Census records revealed that Joplin's neighbors included several teachers, a doctor, a bookkeeper, a grocer, and a chemist, although most labored in blue-collar service occupations such as laundress, barber, janitor, and porter. The neighborhood may not have been wealthy or even middle class, but neither was it impoverished, and given the recent construction of much of the buildings it could hardly have been considered a slum. That sanitary conditions in the neighborhood were by no means atypical for the city further refuted a correspondence between outdoor plumbing and slum conditions. The committee had reached agreement about the existence of an outdoor privy, but it also insisted that this information be placed in its proper context. In other words, yes, Scott Joplin most likely relieved himself outdoors, but so did many people in working and middle-class neighborhoods at that time. Framed in this way, the committee felt comfortable assenting to the excavation of the backyard privy. Although this process did not accomplish any rapprochement with the former site administrator, it did produce solid community support and a credible evidentiary basis for public interpretation. Moreover, it demonstrated how controversies over specific facts can be resolved by massaging the historical context and diverting energy and attention to what South Africa's TRC termed "dialogue truth."

The Messy Middle Ground

It should be clear by now that democratizing the interpretation of urban landscapes in the pursuit of consensus requires patience, diplomacy, and willingness among all participants to compromise. For scholars, it means relinquishing the monopoly on authority that they typically enjoy within university settings. To work productively in inner-city neighborhoods, scholars must be prepared to set aside their academic research agendas in favor of those that emerge directly from communities. Likewise, they must respect a community's desire to suppress or deemphasize topics that feed negative stereotypes. Explicit value judgments and prescriptions for future action that might otherwise undercut academic professionalism may be entirely appropriate in the arena of public history. Incidentally, it is not always scholarly recalcitrance that accounts for the failure to democratize expertise. Whether out of respect or intimidation, community representatives sometimes display *too much* deference toward their academic partners. Communities divided on matters of historical interpretation may expect professional historians to referee their disputes. Depending on the predilections of those involved in a project, it may require some coaxing to invest nonprofessionals with the confidence and sense of entitlement to assert themselves in deliberations with their academically trained partners.

At the same time, professional scholars have an obligation to alert communities to the benefits of open-ended inquiry and verifiable evidence. Academic protocols can play a constructive role in building community consensus around both historical interpretation and developmental goals. Adopting rigorous standards of evidence and striving for objectivity provide a framework for adjudicating disputes over what actually happened in the past. At the very least, an emphasis on verifiable evidence establishes parameters for what are within and beyond the bounds of admissibility, thereby circumscribing the field of potential disagreement and debate. Grounded in the particularities of place and time and subject to moral interrogation, empirical analysis need not affirm the status quo or repressive political doctrines, as some suggest.[58] Moreover, an insistence on high standards of evidence does not rule out the use of less traditional sources of information such as storytelling, myth, and ritual.[59] Nonetheless, it bears emphasizing that a common set of ground rules based on academic precepts resonates with diverse publics because they command respect even among those who do not accept it as the sole basis of knowledge production. Indeed, because empirically based analysis retains tremendous credibility across multiple cultures, its adoption as a methodology assures wider credibility, something struggling communities care a great deal about. Of course, agreement on methodological procedures is not always possible, and even when achieved it may not produce consensus on larger interpretive issues or neighborhood priorities. Moreover, rigid adherence to academic rules is not the only possible basis for community accord or even the optimum formula. What seems reasonable to assert, reflecting on the examples cited in this chapter, is that giving considerable weight to verifiable evidence may provide a framework for the resolution of culturally and socially driven disagreements. Indeed, in deploying the scientific method to separate fact from fiction, the brand of truth espoused here works against one of the worst aspects of heritage, dogmatic allegiance to a particular belief system. If we are committed to getting the story right, we also have to admit the possibility of getting it wrong.[60]

Although it may appear contradictory to the previous set of statements, another virtue of the scientific perspective—in terms of its capacity for building consensus—is its assurance that ultimate historical truth will remain forever elusive. Because the evidence available to historians is always fragmentary, past events can never be reconstructed perfectly; they are always subject to revised interpretation as additional evidence surfaces. Thus, all historical interpretations based on verifiable evidence have a provisional status. Moreover, the open-endedness of critical inquiry, with all conclusions subject to further testing, leaves a door eternally open to alternative versions of the past. Consensus in this context does not mean "case closed." Rather, it represents a temporary accord subject to further debate and revision. Releasing interpreters from the obligation of a permanent commitment lowers the stakes associated with any negotiated settlement.

Finally, and perhaps most important, rigorous modes of analysis and interpretation imbue history with the power to animate social and political change. A fluid historical consciousness invites continuous reevaluation of our present-day assumptions and our planning prescriptions for the future. Confronting the past through open-ended inquiry permits the past to shape and refine contemporary agendas rather than rubber stamp them. If we accept the existence of material reality, however far it may lie beyond our intellectual grasp, a methodology based on empirical data promises more assistance in meeting the challenges of an ever-changing world or neighborhood than one that does not. The more we base our actions on a plausible account of past events, the less likely we are to be betrayed by false expectations or enslaved by the strictures of destiny. The closer we get to unanimous agreement on what happened in the past, the more decisively we can act on behalf of the health and welfare of our urban communities.

Returning to the categories of heritage and history, it should now be apparent that for the purposes of urban revitalization this chapter espouses an approach that combines the virtues of each. In contradistinction to those who would enforce a separation between heritage and history, it urges diverse communities and scholars to negotiate a middle ground. Heritage and good history are not mutually exclusive. Indeed, the worst traits of heritage—assigning immutable characteristics to certain groups and places, and interpreting the past to fit preconceived outcomes—are mitigated by a scientific perspective. At the same time, an activist brand of history demands explicit consideration of its political and moral implications. Finding the right balance between the two poles of inquiry is a messy but worthwhile endeavor, especially when pursued democratically. The concept of shared authority, as invoked by public historians, often takes on the aura of a warm and harmonious fuzzy love-fest in which everyone emerges as a winner. In practice, however, the exposure and engagement of conflicting viewpoints can spark as much acrimony as their suppression. Yet, rather than elide conflict by treading lightly over points of contention, it is preferable to strive for a history forged out of a constructive tension between popular heritage and scholarly history in which the past exists in perpetual dialogue with the present.

7

Conclusion

An Agenda for Urban Preservation

The preceding chapters of this book have insisted on a role for public history as well as public archaeology in preserving inner-city landscapes and cultivating a shared sense of purpose and belonging. When urban districts capitalize on their historical assets to attract residents and fresh investment, they acquire the capacity to stabilize social relations, articulate community values, and plan more intelligently for the future. Achieving these ends, however, requires that communities activate an explicit dialogue between past and present. Ironically and sadly, serious public engagement with historical content has rarely accompanied the metamorphosis of inner-city slums into historic districts. Too often history has served as mere window dressing for the purposes of establishing a neighborhood's historic credentials so it can receive tax credits, attract visitors, and gain some cachet within a metropolitan context. In such cases, it matters little *what* happened in the past, only *that* it happened in the past. Fully unleashing the constructive power of history requires attention to interpretation, the "what happened" of history. Many examples presented in this book demonstrate that rigorous historical investigation can help communities refine their vision of the future and generate support for a locally determined path of development. The key to success lies in identifying and illuminating aspects of the past that have direct relevance for the type of places communities wish to create and the ends to which they wish to guide historic preservation.

There was a time when commemoration of past events and personages lay at the core of the historic-preservation movement. Then, in the latter half of the twentieth century, an emphasis on economic revitalization and the associated practice of adaptive reuse muted the didactic aspect of preservation. No longer were old buildings restored and maintained as house museums with an educational mission; rather, they acquired new life as trendy consumer venues and modern housing. Although preservation's contribution to the late-twentieth-century urban renaissance is undisputed, there is much to be gained by reviving the practice of fabricating meaning from the evolving urban landscape.

A return to the patriotic and celebratory mode of interpretation that prevailed at the beginning of the last century, however, is unwarranted. An interpretive thrust that merely transfers allegiance from the nation to the locality is similarly deficient. Building neighborhood pride is certainly a worthy endeavor, and if members of a community find inspiration in the deeds of their predecessors, that is all well and good. Yet a single-minded quest for resuscitating past glory, whether expressed as military triumph or architectural virtuosity, will be of limited utility in terms of assisting specific redevelopment and revitalization goals.

Pursuing preservation as public enlightenment need not conflict with the popular convention of recycling vintage structures for contemporary purposes. There are many good reasons for endorsing the practice of adaptive reuse. Historic preservation, prosecuted in this fashion, can play a valuable and desirable role in restoring the economic vitality of inner-city districts. Heritage tourism, for all its shortcomings, can inject badly needed revenue into struggling local economies and also generate new business activity. When investors convert obsolete warehouses, factories, and transportation terminals into restaurants, bookstores, and shops, they create exciting and commercially viable urban spaces. Undeniably, housing rehabilitation for modern-day living is preferable to dereliction. While citizens have good reason to worry about the destabilizing consequences of rapid neighborhood transformations, market-driven preservation does not inevitably produce exclusive residential enclaves or consumer emporiums that masquerade as historic districts. Nor does it preclude serious history. Wherever communities retain control over redevelopment processes, they have an opportunity to put old buildings to new symbolic and functional uses that compensate and gratify local residents.

Adaptive reuse also reinforces the idea that history is not dead weight, but rather a dynamic asset to contemporary society. The practice of freezing landscapes in time for the purposes of exhibition, as in a Colonial Williamsburg, is dangerous because it chops time into discrete and seemingly unrelated segments; there is no connection between past and present except by way of comparison. Without proper interpretive intervention, the house-museum approach to preservation can make history quaint and irrelevant. If, however, communities embrace the past as a foundation for prospective development, the reuse of historic structures becomes a starting point for broader consideration of a future infused by the past. Of course, preservation also serves a more basic function: the presence of aged landscapes reminds us that there was a yesterday. Just as we inherited our world from previous generations, our legacy is the world we leave to our descendants. Putting the matter more eloquently, Stewart Brand, author of *How Buildings Learn: What Happens after They're Built*,[1] remarked, "One of the attractions of being in a building more than 100 years old is that it represents a longer frame of reference than your own lifetime. And as you get comfortable taking hold of that much time past, you become more comfortable with thinking of at least that much time forward—and the consequences of your own actions."[2]

This book offers a blueprint for interpreting elements of preserved urban landscapes in a manner that directly advances community objectives. Thus far, it has devoted a great deal of attention to the narrative themes and strategies that neighborhoods might consider in the public interpretation of urban environments. This chapter will conclude the discussion by summing up some of the book's core arguments and elaborating on some of the practical mechanisms communities might adopt to harness the power of history. As in earlier chapters, many suggestions flow from work conducted in cities around the country, including St. Louis. Hence, the following pages sketch, if not quite a step-by-step guide to conducting public history in inner cities, then a set of considerations that should benefit any such undertaking.

Some Basic Principles: Broadening the Concept of Shared Authority

Because all communities have distinctive needs and concerns, public-history programs that work splendidly in one place may not translate well to others. Still, there are certain guiding principles that tend to promote a unified sense of identity and purpose wherever they are applied. Foremost among them is social inclusivity. Urban neighborhoods, particularly those undergoing fresh cycles of investment, typically comprise populations that have little in common with one another aside from a postal code. The overlapping categories of race, ethnicity, and class configure a diverse mosaic of cultures, ambitions, and financial capabilities. If not taken into account and managed sensitively, the suspicions and animosities arising from these differences can derail the most passionate efforts to make history usable. Thus, public-history programs should always seek broad community engagement and buy-in.

Interpreting history in a socially inclusive manner impels us to expand our notion of sharing authority. Whereas the ideal of shared authority is usually applied to the relationship between public-history professionals and their nonacademic audiences, it is also worth pursuing with respect to the social and cultural hierarchies that occur within urban neighborhoods. For communities undergoing the transition from bedraggled inner-city neighborhood to reenergized historic district, the stakes involved in the allocation of intellectual authority are especially high. The question of who gets to interpret local history invariably becomes intertwined with the question of who gets to direct the path of redevelopment. When one faction within a community seizes the mantle of local heritage to advance its own material interests, it breeds the most socially disruptive tendencies of urban revitalization. The successful negotiation of social and cultural difference in the interpretation of the past on the other hand, can help neighborhoods evolve more gently toward mutually desired ends and ensure that the fruits of preservation-based regeneration are widely distributed.

Selecting historical themes and topics that resonate with diverse urban audiences certainly facilitates broad engagement. The mere presentation of compelling content, however, may not, in and of itself, invest an entire community in a public-history project. In the end, there is no getting around the importance of involving different elements of the community directly in the process of research, interpretation, and dissemination. It is tempting, when organizing local public-history initiatives, to rely on the small set of joiners who dominate formal neighborhood associations. If those associations do not reflect the social profile of the community-at-large, however, the project may elicit hostility among those who feel excluded, and any revitalization plans that emerge from the program may further divide a community. To be certain, there is no guarantee that a socially inclusive public-history program will produce unanimity on planning goals, but it can aid in moving a neighborhood in a direction that has the support of diverse segments of the population. Public history, in this capacity, can also serve a bridge-building function.

A second principle advanced here is that project agendas must be constructed at the grass roots. Unquestionably, professional expertise adds a valuable dimension to local-history projects. Neighborhood residents benefit from exposure to the research methodologies, theoretical insights, and analytical strategies employed by academic historians, archaeologists, and museum administrators. Professionally trained scholars can play an especially constructive role by steering communities away from shallow or skewed representations of the past. More practically, museums, libraries, and universities enjoy access to computer technology, exhibit space, recording equipment, and print information, all of which can expand a project's resource base. Ideally, then, grassroots community groups and professionals should seek collaborative opportunities. Indeed, that is the model we have adopted at Community History Research and Design Services (CHRDS) at the University of Missouri-St. Louis. Outside experts and institutions, however, are in no position to speak for the needs and interests of a community. If public history is to serve as a catalyst for preservation-based revitalization, a large measure of project authority must rest with those responsible for guiding the path of redevelopment and those who will live with the results.

Not only should research questions and narrative structures germinate from the community itself, but they should reflect consensus. Implicit in the ideal of shared authorship is the production of an intellectually coherent text or account. The unified narrative, however, is not embraced by all scholars and public-history professionals. In recent years, the postmodern rejection of objective truth combined with a multiculturalist devotion to the full expression of viewpoints has convinced some practitioners that the past is best presented in a fragmented manner through multiple lenses. That is, instead of one story, many stories.[3] Extending this framework to neighborhood history offers an enticing strategy for evading the contradictions arising from different standards of historical accuracy and evaluating past actions. Grassroots history should open space for people to tell stories from their own point of view. At the same time, those of us involved in CHRDS have come to appreciate the utility of a consensus version of history, one behind which a neighborhood can stand and one that rises above the many perspectives of its constituent elements. Especially if a project aims to galvanize community support around a concrete set of goals, a coherent narrative may be of more value than competing versions of the past. A community may not reach accord on every aspect of its past, and it is often necessary to accommodate uncertainty on particularly contentious topics. With regard to the core messages and values that emerge from rigorous analysis, however, agreement on basic historical story lines can help communities negotiate a consensus outlook on the future. Moreover, the search for agreement on matters of interpretation can help communities surmount factional hostilities, especially those that are deeply rooted in the past. Places as distinct as South Africa and Richmond, Virginia have learned that reconciling conflicting perspectives on the past can facilitate the reparation of social relationships. The model is worth applying to urban neighborhoods in the United States.

The principles just outlined are not likely to strike anyone as overly controversial. The real difficulty comes in translating those principles into a public-history program that can be completed with modest resources in a timely manner. Again, there is no magic formula guaranteed to produce successful results wherever it is adopted. Instead, what follows are reflections on specific techniques that have been tested by CHRDS in various St. Louis neighborhoods

Toward a Research Methodology

An effective local-history project requires the imposition of parameters. Once the present is understood as the culmination of all preceding actions and events, history assumes the dimensions of a bottomless pit. Without a clear plan of research, information retrieval becomes an exercise in caprice. Although random inquiries into the historical record may yield fascinating tidbits of information, they will rarely raise the accumulated data above the category of trivia. The arbitrary constraint of research tasks is just as likely to produce meaningless history. The past can speak to the present only when queried appropriately. Tailoring historical research to contemporary needs demands a careful calculation of what is to be investigated and how to gather the relevant evidence. Working with communities in the St. Louis area, we have found it useful to organize research around themes that speak directly to contemporary challenges, cover broad chronological periods, and resonate with diverse elements of the local population. They have included race relations, business development, artistic innovation, and environmental change. Other candidates for investigation might include transportation, park development, political organization, and public safety. Preservation of the built environment frequently elicits curiosity about the history of architectural styles. As a means of instilling pride and anchoring current residents in local tradition, it may be entirely appropriate to highlight the skills and backgrounds of those who initially developed a neighborhood. In pursuit of narratives that embrace a multitude of social groups and a full chronological sweep, we have found it useful to move beyond an exclusive preoccupation with architectural aesthetics by exploring the ways that built space conditioned social relationships over time and how building occupants continuously modified the built landscape to achieve particular social objectives.

One of the obstacles confronting those who research the history of inner-city neighborhoods is the paucity of conventional source material. Historians trad[.]tionally rely on the written record to reconstruct the past, but the diaries, letters, monographs, and official reports collected by libraries and archives rarely document the mundane characteristics of everyday living that shaped most inner-city neighborhoods, particularly the working-class variety. Newspapers are the functional equivalent of personal diaries for cities and neighborhoods; they can be accessed at local libraries and historical societies. Few newspapers, however, indexed their content before the 1970s, and extracting information on specific historical themes and subjects often devolves into a needle-in-a-haystack endeavor. Public historians underutilize court records, but again, discovery veers toward the serendipitous unless researchers can pinpoint specific cases and litigants. The fine-grained data found in census manuscripts, city directories, birth registries, burial records, marriage certificates, tax assessment rolls, fire-insurance atlases, plat maps, and building permits are invaluable for compiling social portraits of an entire neighborhood, but go only so far in exposing the rich texture of life.

To compensate for a dearth of easily accessible primary sources, many communities have turned to two alternative research methodologies: oral history and archaeology. Both offer a means of filling voids in the historical record, particularly with respect to the activities of ordinary people. Archaeological excavations in residential neighborhoods are especially useful for probing the lives of women because they tend to highlight domestic material culture.[4] Oral history also has the capacity to redress the male bias in written historical records because of the control researchers exert over their sources. Oral historians, after all, choose their informants. Indeed, there is probably an inadvertent bias in oral history toward female perspectives because projects often target elderly populations in which women outnumber men.

In recovering the voices and material culture of nonelite groups, archaeology and oral history facilitate the construction of counternarratives that decouple the concepts of inner city and slum. Much of what we know about inner-city neighborhoods comes to us through the eyes of middle- and upper-class observers who often associated lower-class habits with deviance and depravity. Even reformers sympathetic to the plight of the urban masses sensationalized and caricatured the more brutal aspects of inner-city life to publicize their cause and validate their own agendas. By the twentieth century, the inner city's unsavory reputation was invoked by policymakers to justify massive clearance and displacement. Even today, neighborhoods unable to shake the slum stereotype remain vulnerable to the sort of urban redevelopment that wipes out tangible references to the past and erodes identity. It is no coincidence that, at least through the 1980s, urban preservation initiatives flourished in districts that escaped the taint of slum designation by virtue of their upper- or middle-class origins.[5] Alan Mayne and Tim Murray have argued that archaeology acts as a powerful antidote to the "imagined slum" by revealing a more complex and human story. Viewed from the inside out, inner-city life was rarely as horrific as outsiders portrayed it. Through the material remnants of daily life—decorated plates, clay pipes, toys, and cleaning brushes—it becomes possible to reconstruct a more realistic representation in which neighborhood and ethnic pride, aspirations for social mobility, and accomplishment coexisted with material deprivation and squalor.[6]

Rebecca Yamin's research on the notorious Five Points district of New York City offers a concrete demonstration of Mayne and Murray's contention. Few neighborhoods in history have suffered a reputation worse than Five Points did in the mid-nineteenth century. In most accounts, past and present, it is portrayed as the epitome of social disintegration, poverty, vice, crime, and filth; it was the quintessential slum. An archaeological dig conducted in the 1990s, however, turned up abundant contradictory evidence. Decorative items and flowerpots suggested that living spaces were subject to aesthetic alterations. Figurines and fashionable tea and tableware sets indicated an engagement with consumer culture and at least some concern about status mobility. Food remains revealed a diet heavy in meat.[7] In the case of Five Points, the research came too late; the district was razed and redeveloped in the 1880s. Yet neighborhoods that continue to suffer negative stereotypes remain vulnerable to freeway extension schemes, new stadium construction, and suburban-style redevelopment. In these neighborhoods, oral history can complement archaeology by humanizing and complicating more recent historical periods.

Both archaeology and oral history have the capacity to carry narratives up to the present, another attribute in their favor. If one of the shortcomings of preservation is the propensity to freeze time in some remote era and discard all that followed as irrelevant, archaeology and oral history offer a remedy. Even oral histories that span the full chronology of an individual life will emphasize developments that occurred within the previous one hundred years, at most. Archaeology generally reaches much further into the past but, like oral history, can also expose changes along a continuum that extends to the present. Perhaps most valuable of all are the ways that these research methods can be employed to stimulate broad community engagement and guide analysis of the past toward contemporary goals. The following sections sketch some considerations for designing archaeology and oral history projects in service of these ends.

Oral History

Since the 1970s, oral history has not only gained legitimacy in academic circles as a means of gathering evidence but has become a widely used technique for communicating history to the public in museums, publications, and video documentaries as well as on Internet Web sites. There are some obvious reasons why many communities that embark on local-history projects are eager to incorporate oral history into their research design. For many people, the prospect of sitting down for a conversation with a neighbor seems much less formidable than trying to navigate an unfamiliar archive or research library. The tasks of finding suitable informants and asking appropriate questions undoubtedly strike most people as more or less intuitive. Moreover, the personal memories of those who lived through historic events have an intrinsic appeal to nonspecialized audiences. Despite the seemingly low threshold of professional and technical expertise required, a modicum of professional training and preparation can go a long way toward maximizing the yield of an oral history project. Fortunately, there are excellent manuals and books that cover the essentials: tips for interviewing, recording techniques, transcription protocols, and the ethics of doing research with human subjects.[8] Presented here are a few suggestions for tailoring oral history projects to the goals of neighborhood stabilization and revitalization. In particular, they call attention to some of the benefits that can be accrued by thinking of oral history as more than simply a way to extract fugitive historical data.

Use Oral History as a Means of Involving Diverse Segments of a Community

People who avoid formal participation in civic affairs are among the hardest to reach in public-history projects. Because sitting for a recorded interview requires a minimal commitment of time, it can be an effective mechanism for eliciting participation among those outside the usual cadre of joiners and for deepening their interest in a project by giving them a sense of personal investment. For similar reasons, it can be an effective way to engage populations that are underrepresented in formal neighborhood-oriented organizations. Recruiting interview subjects at senior citizen centers, apartment complexes, street festivals, social-service agencies, and houses of worship help a project cast a broad net across a community and ensure that a diversity of perspectives are brought to bear on historical themes.

Invite Interview Subjects to Reflect on Their Past Experiences in the Context of the Present

While oral histories provide an opportunity to fill gaps in the historical record, they are just as valuable as a means of democratizing the interpretation of history. Much of the excitement that attended the proliferation of oral history projects after 1970 stemmed from the medium's potential for removing historical interpretation from the exclusive purview of scholars and giving ordinary people a platform to infuse meditations of the past with a healthy dose of local wisdom.[9] Yet the appropriation of history by local communities for their own purposes is not something that magically emerges from a series of interviews. Rather, it requires that interrogators move beyond questions of what happened and when and direct conversation to matters of interpretation and analysis. To get informants to reflect on the relevance of their memories, we often conclude with a series of questions that explicitly turn the conversation toward contemporary times: How can a historical perspective help us better understand the challenges we face today? What is it about your own experiences that you think is important to pass on to today's younger generation? How can local historical organizations and institutions better serve their communities? The responses to these sorts of queries are extremely useful for arriving at and refining project narratives.

Do Not Restrict Your Pool of Interview Subjects to the Elderly

If an important goal of oral history is to supplement the historical record, it makes a certain amount of sense to begin by recording the memories of those who have been around the longest. Not only can old-timers reach back furthest into the past but their mortality makes the capture of their recollections a matter of some urgency. On the other hand, an exclusive focus on the aged may deprive a community of valuable perspectives that derive from passing through life's cycles in different historical eras. Moreover, when one sees oral history as a way to elicit commentary about how history speaks to contemporary concerns, one generation's insights are no more worthwhile than another's.

Turn Projects over to the Community

Many oral history projects accentuate hierarchies of authority by relying on professionally trained personnel to conduct interviews. As noted earlier, training in oral history techniques can be extremely valuable. Moreover, the involvement of professional historians can help oral history projects avoid what Linda Shopes has called "the life history" approach, whereby interview subjects view the past from the narrow perspective of their own lives. Narratives that frame the past solely in terms of personal characteristics can hardly provide guidance for collective action. Historians can provide valuable assistance in terms of encouraging interview subjects to connect their subjective experiences to wider economic, political, and social structures.[10] Nonetheless, these skills and approaches can be transferred to members of the community through a series of workshops or presentations. It does not take lengthy training to produce qualified oral historians. By having members of a community interview one another, the tensions flowing from the clash of professional and nonprofessional cultures are mitigated and communities take fuller control and responsibility over the production of local knowledge.

Archaeology

Archaeological excavations require considerably more expert guidance than oral history projects, if only to prevent mishaps that might impair the validity of accumulated data. Nonetheless, there are ways to actively involve communities in the retrieval and interpretation of archaeological evidence that will enhance the democratic potential of public-history projects.

Incorporate Public Visibility into Site Selection Criteria

When choosing sites for archaeological digs, it is crucial to consider the relevance to research themes, the integrity of the terrain, and the legal implications of property ownership. Conducting an excavation in a place that offers high visibility, however, can benefit a project by stimulating greater community interest and demystifying the process of knowledge construction. Archaeologists digging on the near-Westside of Indianapolis concluded that the mere act of watching artifacts emerge from the ground enhanced local residents' psychological attachment to place. Especially when the exhumed relics once belonged to populations with whom current inhabitants identify by virtue of a shared racial or ethnic background, as was the case in Indianapolis, open-access excavation sites can give marginalized populations a sense of proprietorship over their neighborhood.[11] To enhance the experience for spectators, it is advisable to make formal interpretive material available in the form of printed matter or, better yet, by way of site tours led by practicing archaeologists. On-site interpretation invariably adds to the cost of excavation, sometimes by more than 25 percent. Yet giving visitors the opportunity to interact with researchers and inquire about the artifacts establishes an impromptu and casual mechanism for active citizen participation in projects.[12]

Involve the Community in Excavations

Communities should always be involved in drafting the research design for an archaeological excavation. In addition, with proper supervision and a limited amount of training, many tasks can be assigned to those with minimal or no previous background in archaeology. School groups, Boy Scout and Girl Scout troops, church congregations, senior citizen clubs, and local residents represent volunteer pools that can be mobilized through field schools to assist in hand digging operations, soil screening, and bagging on site. Off site, volunteers can be employed to help perform the laboratory tasks of washing, drying, sorting, labeling, analysis, and data entry.

Use Archaeological Evidence in Conjunction with Oral Histories

The artifacts routinely exhumed in urban excavations—bottles, dishware, coins, toys—are memory triggers and can thus be used profitably in conjunction with oral histories. By attaching stories to recovered artifacts, community members play a critical role in the interpretation of archaeological evidence. Indeed, interview subjects can often clarify the identity of objects that would otherwise remain shrouded in mystery.

Working with Community Organizations

Earlier chapters in this book stressed the importance of building projects around grassroots organizations that are directly involved in the redevelopment process as well as those that can represent the full range of social diversity within targeted areas. It is quite possible that one neighborhood association alone, particularly if it functions as a community-development corporation, will meet both criteria. In other cases it may be necessary to amass a coalition of groups. Project organizers should not overlook churches, libraries, social-service agencies, political clubs, and cultural associations in the search for partners. Participating stakeholders need not share equal status; it may make more sense for one organization to assume a lead role while others adopt ancillary positions.

With respect to assigning responsibilities among project participants, CHRDS generally employs a two-tiered structure of community engagement consisting of a small committee that makes crucial decisions and performs most of the work and a wider community forum for periodic input and feedback. The smaller committee should include representatives from partner organizations and those volunteers or paid staff members charged with executing the most important tasks. We have observed that neighborhood organizations often wish to give committee assignments to members who have lived in the area for many years and have direct knowledge about local historic events. What we try to emphasize is that it is even more important to fill the committee with people who are actively engaged in civic affairs. A committee that cannot articulate a local planning agenda is one that is poorly positioned to use history as a tool for revitalization. Size makes a difference as well. A group that is too small may not adequately represent the various constituencies within a neighborhood. A group that is too large may have trouble reaching consensus and may also find it hard to sustain regular commitments on the part of individual members. Nonetheless, there are cases where local-history committees have functioned effectively with as few as three members and as many as thirty.

There is nothing particularly novel about the idea of setting up a citizen advisory committee to provide input on public-history projects, but that is not exactly what is being proposed here. This model calls for a community *steering* committee, one that establishes project goals and serves as the final arbiter on all major decisions regarding the analysis of data and its dissemination to the broader public. The steering committee is thus the appropriate venue for seeking and achieving consensus on matters of interpretation. It is also among these participants that a project must set the ground rules for assessing evidence and handling differences of opinion.

In our work in St. Louis we have found public community workshops to be the ideal mechanism for soliciting broad community input and securing broad community involvement. These workshops are always part informational and part activity based. They can be built, for example, around the surveying of community needs, preservation priorities, research into archival documents, oral history, or exhibit design, among other things. They are also an ideal mechanism for presenting final products to a community.

Balancing Objectives

Community organizations tend to see public history as a platform for advertising their cultural assets to outsiders, particularly those with the financial wherewithal to raise depressed neighborhoods out of their economic doldrums. They may be slower to grasp the benefits of nurturing an appreciation for history among existing residents for the purposes of improving mutual understanding, fostering a shared sense of stewardship over built and natural landscapes, and constructing a coherent local identity and vision. As a result, glossy brochures, house tours, street festivals, and informational booklets typically target visitors eager to patronize local businesses, families in the market for historic homes, and investors looking to rehabilitate disused properties for commercial gain. Public history can be an effective marketing tool, so it is easy to understand the magnetism of heritage tourism. Certainly, if communities hope to avoid the disruptive and exploitative aspects of heritage tourism, it is absolutely essential that any related activities remain under local control. Preoccupation with the visitor experience, however, can easily alienate current residents, generate sugarcoated history, and preclude opportunities for serious and sustained analysis. The two paradigms are not mutually exclusive, and so, when feasible, pitching history to local and peripheral audiences simultaneously makes sense. Given the proclivities of many neighborhood associations, however, finding the proper balance between these orientations may demand more thought and energy in the direction of improving internal dissemination and engagement.

To make historical interpretation a permanent adjunct of community stabilization and planning, organizations should craft projects that build internal capacity for investigation and analysis. Training workshops and "how-to" manuals are excellent instruments for transferring research skills from professionals or a small group of local "experts" to a much wider base. The productive life of a history initiative can be extended considerably through the methodical collection of historical resources and the provision of widespread public access. To this end, it is advisable to catalogue and archive source materials gathered over the course of a project with a local institution that can accommodate future researchers. Possible depositories include neighborhood association offices, libraries, museums, and community centers. Here again, the question of balance must be addressed thoughtfully. The long-term benefits of skill and resource development must be weighed against the short-term payoff from visible results. Communities derive a tremendous amount of pleasure and pride from seeing the fruits of their labor exhibited in a public venue. Producing something tangible (a video documentary, a set of building markers) or staging a public-history event (a tour of local landmarks, a heritage festival) invariably produces a sense of accomplishment and can indeed provide the impetus for additional projects and deeper exploration. Ideally, then, a public-history project should combine both capacity-building and result-oriented activities (see Figure 7-1).

Figure 7-1. Portable local-history display for the Beckett Park neighborhood, created by Caleb Carter, a graduate student at the University of Missouri–St. Louis. *(Photo by Caleb Carter.)*

Preservation without Displacement

Democratic mechanisms for community participation and inclusive interpretive narratives can go a long way toward strengthening the bonds of community solidarity and finding consensus on local planning goals. By themselves, however, they may not shield neighborhoods from the destabilizing effects of revaluation that typically accompany successful preservation initiatives. It is one thing to assert a commitment to social diversity through preservation and public interpretation, quite another to prevent soaring property values from displacing existing residents or at least imposing hardship on those with meager financial resources. For legitimate reasons, historic preservation continues to get a bad rap for its elitist implications. Decades after neighborhoods like Society Hill in Philadelphia and Georgetown in Washington, DC exposed historic preservation as a catalyst for gentrification and the displacement of low-income populations, extensive rehabilitation of inner-city property has continued to erode social diversity in many places around the country. In Milwaukee, for instance, increasing property values, higher tax assessments, and rising rental rates in the early 2000s threatened to make the Brewer's Hill district just north of downtown an exclusive enclave for affluent urban professionals. In Memphis, City Council members worried about where working-class households would find housing because of the conversion of older downtown apartment buildings into condominiums. And in Los Angeles, the downtown real estate boom left the elderly and disabled occupants of residential hotels victims of condominium redevelopment projects.[13]

The negative publicity generated by these logical consequences of preservation-based revitalization obscures the contribution that preservation can make, and in many cases has made, to the provision of affordable housing in the United States. Escalating housing costs over the last several decades have made it increasingly difficult for moderate-income wage earners to find decent accommodations, especially in urban areas. Yet virtually every city in the United States contains acres of vacant and underutilized houses, apartment buildings, churches, schools, and warehouses that—with varying amounts of repair and restoration work—can be reclaimed as viable living quarters for moderate- and low-income families. Preservation need not be the handmaiden of displacement. Where profit motives alone govern the process of urban regeneration, however, there is no way to safeguard the interests of existing poorer residents or ensure the maintenance of racial and economic diversity. Engineering the social consequences of preservation-based revitalization requires proactive intervention.

Fortunately, many communities are willing to intervene. It would be erroneous to assume that the occupants of newly rehabilitated historic homes desire social exclusivity. Although one has to be careful about taking people's comments at face value, those who move into transitional neighborhoods often cite the rich mix of classes, ethnicities, racial groups, and household configurations as a motivating factor. Moreover, the prospect of skyrocketing property values is not appealing to those who purchase their homes for residential rather than speculative purposes. Thus, the pursuit of affordable housing in conjunction with preservation generally aligns with the wishes and values of communities undergoing fresh cycles of investment. Where preservationists and community organizations intercede in the market process on behalf of social and economic diversity, the results can diverge sharply from the more commonly publicized outcome of gentrification, and the transformation of inner-city neighborhoods can advance more harmoniously. For all the examples of disruptive displacement and thorough socioeconomic transformation, there are others that testify to the possibilities of more stable and just transitions.

In many cities, affordable housing advocates have taken the lead in chan-neling preservation practices toward the needs of the poor. The rehabilitation of Seattle's Pacific Hotel as a residential facility for destitute and low-income individuals in 1995 grew out of a protest staged by a homeless advocacy or-ganization. Constructed in 1916 and located in downtown Seattle, the hotel had longed served a transient population. After it closed in the early 1980s, it was occupied by homeless men and women. When learning of the build-ing's imminent sale to an office developer, the homeless occupants called at-tention to their dire need for shelter. In the aftermath of this demonstration, a local nonprofit housing developer pledged to rehabilitate the decaying structure and rent thirty-seven studio and one-bedroom apartments at mod-est rates while operating another seventy-five-units as a single-room-occupancy facility. To complete the restoration, the Plymouth Housing Group secured low-interest loans from private lending institutions and both municipal and state housing agencies. The developer raised equity for the project through the syndication of the federal government's Historic Preservation Tax Credit and its Low-Income Housing Tax Credit. These two federal programs also proved crucial to the conversion of a downtown Sioux City library into an affordable housing apartment complex two years later. As in the Seattle example, a nonprofit housing developer took the lead on the project and car-ried it through to completion. Because the Sioux City owned the library and chose to donate it to the developer, there were no acquisition costs. Without the pressure of producing a profit or the need to raise funds for purchasing the property, the tax credits—along with low-interest loans—were sufficient to build and operate an apartment facility for a mix of elderly, disabled, and low-income households and simultaneously save an architectural landmark that had graced the city's downtown since 1912.[14]

While these laudable projects demonstrate the compatibility of preserva-tion and affordable housing on the scale of individual buildings and high-light the utility of several public incentives, they do not represent the type of interventions required to forestall gentrification at the neighborhood level. Fortunately, there are models to emulate in this regard as well. Beginning in the 1960s, when preservation first gained notoriety for its disruptive social effects, several standout communities made it a matter of principle to orches-trate a more orderly and socially inclusive transition from slum to historic district. In particular, the early successes of Pittsburgh and Savannah paved the way for an evolving set of mechanisms and policies that have been em-ployed over the years by communities with similar goals.

In the years after World War II, Pittsburgh experienced the quintessen-tial urban-redevelopment makeover; bulldozers razed hundreds of homes and businesses in the poor, African American districts close to downtown; federally subsidized highways split neighborhoods; and modernistic glass and chrome architecture obscured an older landscape of church spires, brick homes, stately civic buildings, and steel factories. It was in response to these destructive developments that Arthur Ziegler, an English professor, and James Van Trump, an architectural historian, formed the Pittsburgh History and Landmarks Foundation in 1964. Almost immediately, the organization set its sights on several north-side neighborhoods where the slow process of urban decay enticed slumlords and threatened to destroy beautiful Victorian row houses. Ziegler, Van Trump, and other like-minded preservationists desperately wanted to save the homes—but not at the expense of existing residents. Indeed, maintaining community cohesion stood alongside the physical rehabilitation of historic properties as a paramount goal. The key to the organization's success was its direct involvement in the rehabilitation of endangered homes. Through the establishment of a revolving fund, local residents were able to cycle a limited amount of investment capital through a series of preservation projects, thereby retaining control of the process and ensuring that it met community needs and desires. The Landmarks Foundation was fortunate to receive a private donation of $100,000 with which to begin the work of restoring old houses on its own terms. It selected some of the most dilapidated homes north of the Allegheny River, fixed them up, and then worked out an arrangement with the city's Urban Redevelopment Authority to lease the homes to low-income tenants. Through additional grants from private foundations and a commitment of funds from the city, it managed to set up a program of low-interest loans for homeowners who agreed to rehabilitate their homes. At the organization's urging, the city also agreed to pay for façade restoration in return for guarantees of continued maintenance on the part of homeowners. As a result of these inventive mechanisms, housing rehabilitation proceeded without the eviction of long-term residents.[15]

The Historic Savannah Foundation was also one of the first organizations to retain local control over the inner-city investment process through the establishment of a revolving fund for housing rehabilitation. With seed money provided by civic-minded businesses and bankers, the Foundation purchased dilapidated properties and resold them to buyers who pledged to restore them according to strict architectural guidelines. Through the incremental purchase and resale of homes, the Historic Savannah Foundation sparked the revival of the city's downtown core as a major tourist destination in the 1960s. As preservation fever veered toward the adjacent Victorian District, some members of the Foundation perceived the influx of fresh investment as a mixed blessing. Although they were pleased to see more of

Savannah's beautiful homes restored, they worried that speculators and affluent urban pioneers would drive out the neighborhood's poorer African American inhabitants. Foundation President Leo Adler decided to take preemptive action. In 1974, he founded a second organization, the Savannah Landmark Rehabilitation Project, to concentrate exclusively on preserving both old homes and social diversity in the Victorian District. A twenty-three-person board composed of local residents governed its activities. Cobbling together private grants and public funds, the Rehabilitation Project amassed enough money to purchase 400 rundown rental properties before outsiders had a chance to get their hands on them. After making the necessary repairs, it rented out the units to low-income tenants from the neighborhood. When the expected influx of middle-class residents arrived, the Rehabilitation Project had already secured enough properties for low-income use to prevent wholesale gentrification.[16]

Within national preservation circles, Pittsburgh and Savannah were held up as shining examples of preservation-based revitalization that successfully balanced the goals of economic vitality and community cohesion. Many of the techniques pioneered in those cities were subsequently adopted and refined by preservationists elsewhere. In 1975, Ziegler and Adler, along with a third author, attempted to disseminate the Pittsburgh and Savannah approaches more widely with the publication of "Revolving Funds for Historic Preservation: A Manual of Practice." The booklet, which explained the revolving-fund concept and various ways to employ it, became a bible for community-based preservationists. Over the next several decades, Boston, Providence, and New Orleans joined the roster of cities where revolving funds allowed preservationists to make sizable dents in local housing markets in the pursuit of neighborhood stabilization. The National Trust for Historic Preservation also championed the technique and publicized it on its Web site and in its various publications. [17]

Another idea that has begun to gain currency and allow local residents to maintain control of the reinvestment process for progressive social ends is the community land trust. In this procedure, local residents form a private nonprofit corporation for the purpose of buying, rehabbing, and reselling old homes to low-income families. A distinctive feature of the community land trust is that it separates the cost of the land from the cost of the building: buildings are sold to residential occupants but the trust retains ownership of the land in perpetuity. This device accomplishes two things. First, it reduces the cost of acquisition for the home buyer, thereby making housing available for low- and moderate-income buyers. Second, by taking land off the speculative market, it dampens inflationary pressures on neighborhood properties more generally. When those who purchase their homes from the land trust are ready to move on, they can resell the built structures to either the land trust or another low-income household. Like most other locally generated development-oriented preservation initiatives, land trusts must secure start-up capital from lenders or donors to ignite the process. Once they do, they retain collateral by holding on to the land while the resale of housing stock replenishes their liquid capital.

As the preceding discussion makes clear, there are a variety of strategies available for communities that wish to engineer the social consequences of inner-city preservation initiatives. What they share is some sort of direct engagement in the housing market, or at least the exertion of influence over those who engage in the redevelopment process. Community organizations that partner with private investors, for example, may be able to set conditions prescribing the percentage of rehabilitated units that must be reserved for low-income households. Letting neighborhoods evolve according to the logic of capital investment and speculation makes it difficult for communities to control their own destiny. Development-oriented preservation, left to its own devices, will not always result in widespread social dislocation, but the chances of undesirable outcomes diminish when communities involve themselves proactively. Although community intercession cannot guarantee the elimination of financial hardships associated with rising property values, it can go a long way toward minimizing them. Through instruments such as revolving preservation funds and land trusts, communities can achieve some degree of control over the pace, character, and social costs of urban regeneration in historic districts.

The examples presented here also highlight the critical importance of public policy. Federal and state tax credits have not only aided preservation by making it profitable but have reduced the pressure on property owners to charge high rents to recoup costs or attain a decent return on investments. Few pieces of federal legislation have been as instrumental in freeing up the flow of capital to inner-city areas as the Community Reinvestment Act of 1977. Under the provisions of this law, banks located in cities were required to make a significant portion of their loans in low-income areas. Compliance with this regulation opened a credit spigot for all sorts of projects, including those that involved the rehabilitation of old housing for low-income families. Without the compunction of law, many banks would be reluctant to sink money in projects that did not promise a high rate of return. Local governments have also contributed to a more socially inclusive preservation-based revitalization process through the liberation of credit. Many cities offer low- or no-interest loans to low-income homeowners who wish to make repairs on their properties. Some cities have utilized federal Community Development Block Grant money for this purpose. Typically, local governments contract with nonprofit organizations, such as Catholic Charities, to administer the loan programs. One of the most ambitious programs of this kind operates in Grand Rapids, Michigan. A subsidiary of Catholic Charities, Home Repair Service, has used Community Development Block Grant funds to create a tool library where financially strapped property owners can borrow wheelbarrows, saws, carpet stretchers, and many other items to assist with basic and advanced home maintenance. Using more coercive means, other cities have passed laws requiring new housing developments, including those that involve the rehabilitation of older structures, to reserve a certain percentage of units for low-income buyers.[18]

Aligning public-history narratives with preservation practices along an axis of social diversity and community cohesion may require individuals to make forays into unfamiliar terrain. Public historians may feel uncomfortable meddling in the mechanics of the housing market just as rehabbers may be unaccustomed to thinking too deeply about historic interpretation. The best way to combine the multiple components of socially responsible preservation is through partnerships that bring to the table those with relevant expertise and skills in development, community organizing, and historical interpretation. If the translation of local values and desires into a viable neighborhood is a central goal, community-based organizations must stand at the center of initiatives.

Finale: The Historic District and Urban Revitalization

The arguments presented in this book are rooted in the premise that inner cities are worth renewed investment and that the application of historical knowledge to revitalization efforts will produce socially desirable outcomes. Restoring the vitality of residential neighborhoods close to the historic core allows a metropolis to reap the benefits of concentration and centralization. Among them are the informational exchanges that derive from the sort of random encounters likely to occur in dense urban settings. Centrality also maximizes access to other parts of the metropolis. In the past, one of the most important advantages of residing close to downtown was proximity to major transportation routes. Because most transportation systems, from the streetcar lines of late nineteenth century to the superhighways of the twentieth century, were designed to connect downtown to peripheral nodes, inner-city areas enjoyed the densest array of transportation options. This configuration was particular helpful to households with multiple wage earners and those who anticipated frequent job changes. In today's economy, the rise of dual-income families and the mobility of capital continue to make this factor relevant. To the extent that repopulated inner-city neighborhoods support mass transport systems, they reinforce the benefits of centrality and serve as a counterforce to the destructive tendencies of centrifugal development. The phenomenon of urban sprawl has been indicted for despoiling natural habitats on the fringes of cities, creating costly inefficiencies in the provision of public services, draining vital resources from the urban core, and depriving metropolitan inhabitants of the opportunity to establish intellectual and emotional attachments to the places in which they live and work. While it is important to resist the facile notion that suburbs have less depth of character than do inner cities, a vital urban core makes a unique contribution to the goal of a more ecologically and socially sustainable metropolis. When considering the environmental virtues of inner-city preservation, one should also keep in mind that buildings constructed before the advent of air conditioning and central heating tend to be far more energy efficient than the post-World War II suburban prototypes.

Public-history programs tied to the commercial reuse of preserved inner-city buildings will not always be successful in jump-starting moribund economies. To the extent that highly interpretive preservation programs operate in conjunction with comprehensive renewal initiatives that address housing, economic growth, public health, and political capacity, however, the prospects of tangible results are enhanced. Nonetheless, the fortunes of any urban neighborhood always depend, to a large extent, on forces beyond the control of local actors. Whether or not a preservation-based revitalization strategy will pay economic dividends depends on how actions at the local level intersect with metropolitan, regional, and global patterns of investment, population movement, and social change. Indeed, when considering long-term trends in urban property values and family structure, we discover that inner cities are primed for fresh cycles of capital investment regardless of what public historians and preservationists do.

Whatever the limitations of preservation and public history in acting as catalysts for economic growth, they have tremendous potential to influence the manner in which redevelopment unfolds. Disparate urban design models vie for the attention of planners, developers, and homeowners. Certain archetypes have fallen out of favor over the past half-century, most notably high-rise public housing, which became widely derided as a social disaster by the 1970s. On the other hand, the suburban ideal continues to inform much inner-city redevelopment. In almost every part of the country, one can find newly built ranch-style homes with 40-foot setbacks, aluminum siding, and garage-dominated facades stretched across acres of inner-city terrain or incongruously interspersed among older brick row houses and two-story wood-frame homes. The tenacity of the suburban model is likewise revealed in the profusion of urban mini-malls, with shops arrayed around parking lots rather than alongside pedestrian walkways. The ubiquity of suburban inspired design is not hard to understand given its close association with the beloved automobile and the cultural cachet derived from its middle-class connotations. For all its advantages and appeal, however, it fails to build upon the distinct infrastructural and landscape features that have accumulated over time in inner-city settings. What the conjoining of public history and preservation offers is the opportunity to consider the already existing physical infrastructure and set of sociospatial relations when making choices about the future. Using place to establish continuity with the past not only fosters stewardship of a shared landscape but also minimizes the social disruptions that invariably accompany the physical annihilation of neighborhoods. Through critical reflection on the meanings and social implications of an evolving natural and built environment, historic preservation becomes more than just an aesthetic ideal; it becomes the basis for a mode of urban life.

Readers should harbor no illusions about a return to some mythic golden age when streets were safe, everybody got along, and people were poor but happy. The benefits of density and centrality were offset by a lack of privacy, cramped living quarters, high levels of pollution, poor sanitation, and conditions that bred contagious diseases. To avoid a full accounting of urban ills is to create a false basis of comparison with the present and to establish unreasonable standards of emulation. Because the scenario will not stand up to scrutiny, it lacks credibility. Because it severely distorts the past, it cannot possibly promote an understanding of how inner cities arrived at their current predicaments. These are the dangers associated with a brand of public history concerned exclusively with celebrating local heritage and bolstering local pride.

Nor does this book endorse selecting some past incarnation of the inner city, sores and all, as a blueprint for contemporary planning. The cities and neighborhoods of today cannot be reconstructed as they once were. Building intelligently from a historical foundation does not require us to forsake electricity, indoor plumbing, or even our automobiles. It does, however, demand that we devise innovative ways of adapting existing infrastructures to new conditions so as not to create a rupture between past and present. It requires us to think of redevelopment as an evolutionary rather than a revolutionary process. Such a perspective encourages social as well as material stability by promoting respect for those individuals and groups that contributed to the community's development in preceding generations up to the present. It is also empowering. We live in world where forces beyond our control buffet and blindside us from all directions and all parts of the planet. One way to gain some semblance of control over our lives is to take command of the places in which we live. The ability to position a neighborhood in the flow of time—to know what worked and what failed, to arrive at a consensus about what was admirable and what was reprehensible, to understand how the present emerged out of the past—enhances a community's potential to direct change toward desirable outcomes. How ironic, or perhaps how appropriate, if through public engagement with history the urban historic district were to find itself on the cutting edge of revising the politics of place.

Notes

PREFACE

1. Rebecca Conard, "Spading Common Ground: Reconciling the Built and Natural Environments," *Public History and the Environment*, eds. Martin V. Melosi and Philip Scarpino (Malabar, FL: Krieger, 2004), 11.

CHAPTER 1. PRESERVATION IN THE INNER CITY

1. Diane Lea, "America's Preservationist Ethos: A Tribute to Enduring Ideals," *A Richer Heritage: Historic Preservation in the Twenty-First Century*, ed. Robert E. Stipe (Chapel Hill: University of North Carolina Press, 2003), 1–3. Michael Holleran, "Roots in Boston Branches in Planning and Parks," *Giving Preservation a History: Histories of Historic Preservation in the United States*, eds. Max Page and Randall Mason (New York: Routledge, 2004), 81–106. Charles Hosmer, Jr., *Presence of the Past: A History of the Preservation Movement in the United States before Williamsburg* (New York: G. P. Putnam's Sons, 1965), 29–101. Randall Mason, "Historic Preservation, Public Memory and the Making of Modern New York City," *Giving Preservation a History*, 131–162. William Murtagh, *Keeping Time: The History and Theory of Preservation in America* (Pittstown, NJ: Main Street Press, 1988), 25–38

2. Cited in Norman Tyler, *Historic Preservation: An Introduction to Its History, Principles and Practice* (New York: W.W. Norton, 2000), 38.

3. Robert R. Weyeneth, *Historic Preservation for a Living City: Historic Charleston Foundation, 1947–1997* (Columbia: University of South Carolina Press, 2000), 1–22.

4. Tyler, *Historic Preservation*, 60.

5. Michael Wallace, *Mickey Mouse History and Other Essays on American Memory* (Philadelphia: Temple University Press, 1996), 177–246. Holleran, "Roots in Boston,

Branches in Planning and Parks," 81–106. Mason, "Historic Preservation, Public Memory, and the Making of Modern New York City," 131–162.

6. Chris Wilson, *The Myth of Santa Fe: Creating a Modern Regional Tradition* (Albuquerque: University of New Mexico Press, 1997).

7. Nathan Weinberg, *Preservation in American Towns and Cities* (Boulder, CO: Westview, 1979), 42–51. Anthony J. Stanonis, *Creating the Big Easy: New Orleans and the Emergence of Modern Tourism, 1918–1945* (Athens: University of Georgia Press, 2006), 141–169, 235–244. Christine M. Boyer, *The City of Collective Memory: Its Historical Imagery and Architectural Entertainments* (Cambridge, MA: MIT Press, 1994), 325.

8. Briann Greenfield, "Marketing the Past: Historic Preservation in Providence, Rhode Island," *Giving Preservation a History*, 163–184.

9. Kathleen Maxa, "Georgetown," *American Preservation* 3:2 (1980): 42–57. Linda Wheeler, "A Block-Long Walk into Georgetown's Past," *Washington Post* (November 20, 1999): G1. William A. Kinney, "Washington's Historic Georgetown," *National Geographic* 103 (April 1953): 513–544.

10 What most critics meant when they used the term "urban renewal" was really "urban redevelopment." The latter term was used in the Federal Housing Act of 1949 to describe the practice of comprehensive clearance and rebuilding. The term "urban renewal" eclipsed "urban redevelopment" with the 1954 amendments to the National Housing Act. Ironically, the 1954 law was much more sympathetic to the practice of preservation and rehabilitation. Because it retained the clearance provisions of the original law, however, the term "renewal" came to stand for "redevelopment" in common parlance. See Howard Chudacoff and Judith E. Smith, *The Evolution of American Urban Society* (Englewood Cliffs, NJ: Prentice Hall, 1994), 267.

11. Jon C. Teaford, *The Rough Road to Renaissance: Urban Revitalization in America, 1940–1985* (Baltimore, MD: Johns Hopkins University Press, 1990), 10–43, 122–136. Kenneth Jackson, *Crabgrass Frontier: The Suburbanization of the United States* (New York: Oxford University Press, 1985), 231–245. John F. Kain, "The Distribution and Movement of Jobs and Industry," *The Metropolitan Enigma: Inquiries into the Nature and Dimensions of America's Urban Crisis*, ed. James Q. Wilson (Washington, DC: Task Force on Economic Growth and Opportunity, Chamber of Commerce of the United States, 1967), 1–30. Kenneth Fox, *Metropolitan America: Urban Life and Urban Policy in the United States, 1940–1980* (Jackson: University Press of Mississippi, 1986), 50–78.

12. Mark H. Rose, *Interstate: Express Highway Politics, 1941–1956* (Lawrence: Regents Press of Kansas City, 1979), 55–94. Robert Fogelson, *Downtown: Its Rise and Fall* (New Haven: Yale University Press, 2001), 383. Teaford, *Rough Road to Renaissance*, 93–105.

13. Examples of this dynamic at work in particular cities can be found in Andrew Feffer, "Show Down in Center City: Staging Redevelopment and Citizenship in Bicentennial Philadelphia, 1974–1977," *Journal of Urban History* 6 (September 2004): 791–825; Joseph Heathcott and Máire Agnes Murphy, "Corridors of Flight, Zones of Renewal: Industry, Planning, and Policy in the Making of Metropolitan St. Louis, 1940–1980," *Journal of Urban History* 6 (January 2005): 151–189; June Manning Thomas, *Redevelopment and Race: Planning a Finer City in Postwar Detroit* (Baltimore,

MD: Johns Hopkins University Press, 1997); Roy Lubove, *Twentieth Century Pittsburgh, Volume Two: The Post-Steel Era* (Pittsburgh, PA: University of Pittsburgh Press, 1996).

14. John A. Jakle and David Wilson, *Derelict Landscapes: The Wasting of America's Built Environment* (Savage, MD: Rowman and Littlefield, 1992), 132. Teaford, *Rough Road to Renaissance*, 105–20, 136–162. Fox, *Metropolitan America*, 79–106. Chudacoff and Smith, *Evolution of American Urban Society*, 265–270.

15. Chudacoff and Smith, *Evolution of American Urban Society*, 265–270.

16. Raymond A. Mohl, "Stop the Road: Freeway Revolts in American Cities," *Journal of Urban History* 30 (July 2004): 674–706.

17. Audrey G. McFarlane, "When Inclusion Leads to Exclusion: The Uncharted Terrain of Community Participation in Economic Development," *Brooklyn Law Review* 66 (Winter 2000/Spring 2001): 867. Thomas H. Jenkins, "The 1960s—A Watershed of Urban Planning and Renewal," *The Planning Partnership: Participants' Views of Urban Renewal*, eds. Zane L. Miller and Thomas H. Jenkins (Beverly Hills, CA: Sage, 1982), 35.

18. Jane Jacobs, *The Death and Life of Great American Cities* (New York: Vintage, 1961).

19 Herbert J. Gans, *The Urban Villagers: Group and Class in the Life of Italian-Americans.* (New York: Free Press of Glencoe, 1962).

20. Charles Abrams, *The City is the Frontier* (New York: Harper & Row, 1965).

21. Martin Anderson, "Fiasco of Urban Renewal," *Urban Renewal: The Record and the Controversy*, ed. James Q. Wilson (Cambridge, MA: MIT Press, 1966), 491–508.

22. National Historic Preservation Act of 1966, section 1(b)(2).

23. Tyler, *Historic Preservation*, 192–193.

24. David Hamer, *History in Urban Places: The Historic Districts of the United States* (Columbus: Ohio State University Press, 1998), vii. Tyler, *Historic Preservation*, 192.

25. Ann Markusen, "City Spatial Structure, Women's Household Work, and National Urban Policy," *Women and the City*, eds. C. Stimpson et al. (Chicago: University of Chicago Press, 1981), 31. Jakle and Wilson, *Derelict Landscapes*, 227–232.

26. Neil Smith, *The New Urban Frontier: Gentrification and the Revanchist City* (London: Routledge, 1996), 61–74.

27. Dennis R. Judd, "Constructing the Tourist Bubble," *The Tourist City*, eds. Dennis R. Judd and Susan S. Fainstein (New Haven, CT: Yale University Press, 1999), 35–53. Alison Isenberg, *Downtown America: A History of the Place and the People Who Made It* (Chicago: University of Chicago Press, 2004), 255–311. Peter H. Brink, "Heritage Tourism in the U.S.A.: Grassroots Efforts to Combine Preservation and Tourism," *APT Bulletin* (Association for Preservation Technology International) 29:3/4 (1998): 59–63.

28. Larry R. Ford, *Cities and Buildings: Skyscrapers, Skid Rows, and Suburbs* (Baltimore, MD: Johns Hopkins University Press, 1994), 115–119. Roberta Brandes Gratz, *The Living City* (New York: Simon & Schuster, 1989), 285–288, 316–330. Robert Campbell, "The Lure of the Marketplace: Real-Life Theater," *Historic Preservation* 32 (January/February 1980): 46–49. Bernard J. Frieden and Lynne B. Sagalyn, *Downtown, Inc.: How America Rebuilds Cities* (Cambridge, MA: MIT Press, 1989).

29. Karolin Frank and Patricia Petersen, eds., *Historic Preservation in the USA* (Berlin: Springer, 2002), 132–135. William Purcell, "News of History," *American Heritage* 6 (June 1955): 110. Smith, *New Urban Frontier*, 119–139.

30. Wallace, *Mickey Mouse History*, 224–229. William J. Murtagh, "Historic Preservation and Urban Neighborhoods," *Monumentum* 13 (1976): 61–70.

31. Jakle and Wilson, *Derelict Landscapes*, 242.

32. Hamer, *History in Urban Places*, 21.

33. Lawrence Hurley, "Sharing the Pain," *Preservation* 52 (November/December 2002): 15–16. Yanni Tsipis, "History and the Housing Crisis," *Boston Globe* (September 15, 2004): A15. Michael Corkery, "Historic Tax Credit Helps R. I. Economy," *Providence Journal* (April 8, 2005): F1. Arnold Burke, "Trust Me," *Preservation* 56 (July/August 2004): 10.

34. Thomas A. Horan, Hank Dittmar, and Daniel R. Jordan, "ISTEA and the New Era in Transportation Policy: Sustainable Communities from a Federal Initiative," *Toward Sustainable Communities: Transition and Transformation in Environmental Policy*, eds. Daniel A. Mazmanian and Michael E. Kraft (Cambridge, MA: MIT Press, 1999), 217–245. Richard Moe, "From the President," *Preservation* 49 (March/April 1997): 6.

35. Richard Moe, "Triumph for the Trust," *Preservation* 55 (March/April 2003): 4. Hap Connors, "The Good Work," *Preservation* 54 (September/October 2002): 91–93.

36. Lea, "America's Preservation Ethos," 15.

37. Gratz, *The Living City*, 12.

38. Richard Moe and Carter Wilkie, *Changing Places: Rebuilding Community in the Age of Sprawl* (New York: Henry Holt, 1997), 239.

39. Evelyn Gonzalez, *The Bronx* (New York: Columbia University Press, 204), 133.

40. Wallace, *Mickey Mouse History*, 206. Daniel J. Levi, "Does History Matter? Perceptions and Attitudes toward Fake Historical Architecture and Historic Preservation," *Journal of Architectural and Planning Research* 22 (Summer 2005): 148–159. Ada Louise Huxtable, *The Unreal America: Architecture and Illusion* (New York: New Press, 1997). Michael Sorkin, "Introduction: Variations on a Theme Park," *Variations on a Theme Park*, ed. Michael Sorkin (New York: Hill and Wang), xi–xv.

41. R. Timothy Sieber, "Waterfront Revitalization in Postindustrial Port Cities of North America," *City and Society* 5:2 (1991): 120–136. J. Goss, "Disquiet on the Waterfront: Reflections on Nostalgia and Utopia in the Urban Archetypes of Festival Marketplaces," *Urban Geography* 17 (1996): 221–247. John Hannigan, *Fantasy City: Pleasure and Profit in the Postmodern Metropolis* (London: Routledge, 1998), 195–197.

42. James Oliver Horton and Lois E. Horton, eds., *Slavery and Public History: The Tough Stuff of American Memory* (New York: New Press, 2006). Angela DaSilva, "African American Heritage Tourism," *Preservation Issues* (Missouri Department of Natural Resources) 7 (September/October, 1997), available at http://law.wustl.edu/staff/taylor/preserv/v7n3/afamtour.htm, accessed December 12, 2009. Polly Welts Kaufman, "Who Walked before Me? Creating Women's History Trails," *Her Past around Us: Interpreting Sites for Women's History*, eds. Polly Welts Kaufman and Katharine T. Corbett (Malabar, FL: Krieger, 2003), 11–30. Gail Lee Dubrow, "Restoring Women's History through Historic Preservation: Recent Developments in

Scholarship and Public Historical Practice," *Restoring Women's History through Historic Preservation*, eds. Gail Lee Dubrow and Jennifer B. Goodman (Baltimore, MD: Johns Hopkins University Press, 2003), 1–14.

43. Hamer, *History in Urban Places*, 121–122. Smith, *New Urban Frontier*, 122. Brink, "Heritage Tourism in the U.S.A.," 59–63. For an account of heritage tourism's disruptive impact on Albuquerque, see Judy Mattivi Morley, *Historic Preservation and the Imagined West: Albuquerque, Denver, and Seattle* (Lawrence: University of Kansas Press, 2006), 21–42.

44. Robert McGregor, "Historic Preservation in New York State," *Public Historian 7* (Fall 1985): 72.

45. Hamer, *History in Urban Places*, 25–53.

46 Hamer, *History in Urban Places*, 95.

47. McGregor, "Historic Preservation in New York State," 76.

48 Hamer, *History in Urban Places*, 67–72.

49 Robert R. Archibald, *A Place to Remember: Using History to Build Community* (Walnut Creek, CA: Alta Mira Press, 1999), 17–18. Ray Oldenburg, *The Great Good Place* (New York: Marlowe, 1989); Hamer, *History in Urban Places*, 79.

50. Jakle and Wilson, *Derelict Landscapes*, 227–232, 245–252.

51. Smith, *New Urban Frontier*, 4–164. Antoinette J. Lee, "Discovering Old Cultures in the New World: The Role of Ethnicity," *The American Mosaic: Preserving the Nation's Heritage*, eds. Robert E. Stipe and Antoinette J. Lee (Washington, DC: U.S. Committee International Council on Monuments and Sites, 1987), 199. Frank F. DeGiovanni,' An Examination of Selected Consequences of Revitalization in Six US Cities," *Urban Studies* 21 (August 1984): 245–259.

52. Jakle and Wilson, *Derelict Landscapes*, 245–252. Ford, *Cities and Buildings*, 174.

53. W. Dennis Keating, "Federal Policy and Poor Urban Neighborhoods," *Rebuilding Urban Neighborhoods: Achievements, Opportunities, and Limits*, eds. W. Dennis Keating and Norman Krumholz (Thousand Oaks, CA: Sage, 1999), 18–21.

54. Jakle and Wilson, *Derelict Landscapes*, 252

55. Zane L. Miller and Bruce Tucker, *Changing Plans for America's Inner-Cities: Cincinnati's Over-the-Rhine and Twentieth-Century Urbanism* (Columbus: Ohio State University Press, 1998), 96–137. For other examples of low-income opposition to preservation initiatives, see Robin Elisabeth Datel, "Preservation and Urban Orientation," *Geographical Review* 75 (April 1985), 138. On Seattle's moderately successful efforts to balance the needs of its Skid Row constituency with entrepreneurial preservation, see Morley, *Historic Preservation and the Imagined West*, 67–90.

56. Jakle and Wilson, *Derelict Landscapes*, 248–250. Gratz, *The Living City*, 62–81. Edward N. Coulson and Robin M. Leichenko, "Historic Preservation and Neighborhood Change," *Urban Studies* 41 (July 2004): 1587–1600.

CHAPTER 2. TAKING IT TO THE STREETS

1. Terrence O'Donnell, "Pitfalls along the Path of Public History," *Presenting the Past: Essays on History and the Public*, eds. Susan Porter Benson, Stephen Brier, and Roy Rosenzweig (Philadelphia: Temple University Press, 1986), 239. John Higham,

History (Englewood Cliffs, NJ: Prentice-Hall, 1965), 1–25. Michael Kraus, *A History of American History* (New York: Farrar & Rinehart, 1937), 291–320. Peter Novick, *That Noble Dream: The "Objectivity Question" and the American Historical Profession* (Cambridge, UK: Cambridge University Press, 1988), 40–46. Leslie Fishel, Jr., "Public History and the Academy," *Public History: An Introduction*, eds. Barbara J. Howe and Emory L. Kemp (Malabar, FL: Krieger, 1986), 8–19.

2. James W. Loewen, *Lies across America: What Our Historic Sites Get Wrong* (New York: W.W. Norton, 1999), 31.

3. Loewen , *Lies across America*, 46.

4. Sanford Levinson, *Written in Stone: Public Monuments in Changing Societies* (Durham, NC: Duke University Press, 1999), 45–48. Loewen, *Lies across America*, 16, 170–172, 214–219.

5. Loewen, *Lies across America*, 25. Donald P. Baker, "A Final Triumph: Ashe Statue Takes Its Place on Va.'s Monument Avenue," *Washington Post* (July 11, 1996): B01. Eileen Eagan, "Immortalizing Women: Finding Meaning in Public Sculpture," *Her Past Around Us: Interpreting Sites for Women's History*, eds. Polly Welts Kaufman and Katharine T. Corbett (Malabar, FL: Krieger, 2003), 32, 56–57.

6. James Green, "Engaging in People's History: The Massachusetts History Workshop," *Presenting the Past*, 341–342.

7. Joyce Appleby, Lynn Hunt, and Margaret Jacob, *Telling the Truth about History* (New York: W. W. Norton, 1994), 146–159. Novick, *That Noble Dream*, 512.

8. Novick, *That Noble Dream*, 512–513. Green, "Engaging in People's History," 339–356.

9. Jeremy Brecher, "A Report on Doing History from Below: The Brass Workers History Project," *Presenting the Past*, 267–277.

10. Cathy Stanton, *The Lowell Experiment: Public History in a Postindustrial City* (Amherst: University of Massachusetts Press, 2006), 8–16.

11. Michael Frisch, *A Shared Authority: Essays on the Craft and Meaning of Oral and Public History* (Albany: State University Press of New York, 1990), xxi–xxii, 225–238.

12. Linda Shopes, "Oral History and Community Involvement: The Baltimore Neighborhood Heritage Project," *Presenting the Past*, 249–263.

13. Jill Levey, "Historical Societies as Agents of Social Change: The Crown Heights History Project," *History News* 49 (May/June 1994): 19. Kate F. Stover, "Neighborhoods Forging Their Own History," *History News* 49 (May/June 1994): 14–17. Barbara Franco, "The History Museum Curator of the 21st Century," *History News* 51 (Summer 1996): 9.

14. Henri Lefebvre, *Production of Space* (Oxford: Basil Blackwell, 1991.) Dolores Hayden, *The Power of Place: Urban Landscapes as Public History* (Cambridge, MA: MIT Press, 1997), 15–43. Mark Gottdiener, *The Social Production of Urban Space* (Austin: University of Texas Press, 1986), 110–156.

15. Eric Sandweiss, "Introduction," *Where We Live: A Guide to St. Louis Communities*, ed. Timothy Fox (St. Louis: Missouri Historical Society Press, 1995), 1.

16. Dorothee Brantz, "The Natural Space of Modernity: A Transatlantic Perspective on (Urban) Environmental History," *Historians and Nature*, eds. Ursula Lehmkuhl and Hermann Wellenreuther (Oxford: Berg, 2007), 195–225.

17. Rebecca Conard, "Spading Common Ground: Reconciling the Built and Natural Environments," *Public History and the Environment*, eds. Martin V. Melosi and Philip V. Scarpino (Malabar, FL: Krieger, 2004), 3–22. Genevieve P. Keller and Timothy J Keller, "Preserving Important Landscapes," *A Richer Heritage: Historic Preservation in the Twenty-First Century*, ed. Robert E. Stipe (Chapel Hill: University of North Carolina Press), 187-222.

18. Hayden, *The Power of Place*, 15.

19. Hayden, *The Power of Place*, 132–135, 171–172.

20. Hayden *The Power of Place*, 188–209.

21. Hayden *The Power of Place*, 138–187.

22. City Lore, "Place Matters Web Site: Creating Online Dialogues about Historical and Cultural Landscapes," National Endowment for the Humanities Planning Grant application, 1999, 1–2.

23. Marci Reaven, "Place Matters at the Creating Livable Communities New York Symposium," *Public History News* 26 (Winter 2006): 9.

24. City Lore, "Place Matters Web Site," 3–8. Reaven, "Place Matters at the Creating Livable Communities New York Symposium," 9.

25. Place Matters, *From Mambo to Hip Hop: Latin Music and Hip Hop Trail in Harlem and the Bronx*, brochure (New York: City Lore, 2002). City Lore, "Place Matters Web Site," 9. Reaven, "Place Matters at the Creating Livable Communities New York Symposium," 9.

26. Liz Ševčenko, Edgar W. Hopper, and Lisa Chice, *The Slave Galleries Restoration Project* (Washington, DC: Americans for the Arts, n.d.), 3–18. Edgar W. Hopper, Rev. Deacon, "The St. Augustine's Restoration and Preservation Project," paper presented at Activating the Past: An International Symposium on Historic Sites, University of Michigan, March 19, 2004, available at http:umich.edu/~ummsp/events/hsc_hopper.htm, accessed April 20, 2006, 1.

27. Old Town/Chinatown Neighborhood Association, "The Old Town History Project, Inc.," National Endowment for the Humanities Consultation Grant application, 2000, 1–3. Lynn Josse, "Final Report: 2004–2005 Public Policy Research Center Community Fellowship" (St. Louis: Public Policy Research Center, University of Missouri—St Louis, 2006), 10. Janet Christ, "Advocates Find Common Ground," *Oregonian* (February 4, 2000): Portland Zoner section, C03. Tim Sullivan, "Groups Promote Richness of Old Town Chinatown," *Oregonian* (May 20, 2005): C02. Janet Filips, "Chinatown Remade in Its Own Image," *Oregonian* (August 25, 2005): Portland Zoner section, 12. Joe Fitzgibbon, "Preserving Old Town Memories," *Oregonian* (July 1, 2004): EC7.

28. Margaret C. Wood, "Moving toward Transformative Democratic Action through Archaeology," *International Journal of Historical Archaeology* 6 (September 2002): 187–198.

29. Barbara Little, "Topical Convergence: Historical Archaeologists and Historians on Common Ground," *Historical Archaeology* 41 (Summer 2007): 10–12. Ivor Noel Hume, *Here Lies Virginia: An Archaeologist's View of Colonial Life and History*. (Charlottesville: University Press of Virginia, 1963).

30. Nick Merriman, "Introduction: Diversity and Dissonance in Public Archaeology," *Public Archaeology*, ed. Nick Merriman (London: Routledge, 2004), 3.

31. Cheryl J. LaRoche and Michael L. Blakely, "Seizing Intellectual Power: The Dialogue at the New York African Burial Ground," *Historical Archaeology* 31: 3 (1997): 84–106.

32. Kathleen Deagan, *Spanish St. Augustine: The Archaeology of a Colonial Creole Community* (New York: Academic, 1983), 3–4.

33. Thomas E. King, "Prehistory and Beyond: The Place of Archaeology," *The American Mosaic: Preserving the Nation's Heritage*, eds., Robert E. Stipe and Antoinette J. Lee (Washington, DC: United States Committee of the International Council on Monuments and Sites, 1997), 242.

34. Barbara Little, "Topical Convergence: Historical Archaeologists and Historians on Common Ground," 13.

35. Edward Staski, "Living in Cites: An Introduction," *Living in Cities: Current Research in Urban Archaeology*," Special Publication Series, no. 5, ed. E. Staski (Tucson: Society for Historical Archaeology, 1987), ix.

36. Parker B. Potter, Jr., *Public Archaeology in Annapolis: A Critical Approach to History in Maryland's Ancient City* (Washington, DC: Smithsonian Press, 1994.) Paul A. Shackel, Paul R. Mullins, and Mark S. Warner, eds., *Annapolis Pasts: Historical Archaeology in Annapolis, Maryland* (Knoxville: University of Tennessee Press, 1998.)

37. Mark Leone, Parker B. Potter, Jr., and Paul A. Shackel, "Toward a Critical Archaeology," *Current Anthropology* 28 (June 1987): 283–285. Potter, Jr., *Public Archaeology in Annapolis,* 213–214.

38. Leone, Potter, Jr., and Shackel, "Toward a Critical Archaeology," 285. Mark Leone and Parker B. Potter, Jr., *Archaeological Annapolis: A Guide to Seeing and Understanding Three Centuries of Change* (College Park: Historic Annapolis Foundation and the University of Maryland, College Park, 1984).

39. Potter, Jr., *Public Archaeology in Annapolis,* 175–192.

40. Larry McKee and Brian Thomas, "Starting a Conversation: The Public Style of Archaeology at the Hermitage," *Southeastern Archaeology* 17 (Winter 1998): 133.

41. Linda Derry, "Pre-Emancipation Archaeology: Does It Play in Selma, Alabama?" *Historical Archaeology* 31(Fall 1997): 24–25.

42. Pamela J. Cressey, *Approaches to Preserving a City's Past* (Alexandria, VA: Alexandria Archaeology), 1983. Pamela J. Cressey, "Community Archaeology in Alexandria, Virginia," *Conserve Neighborhoods* 69 (1987): 1–6. Pamela J. Cressey, *Landmarks: 30 Years of Archaeology in Alexandria,* Abstract No. 3 (Alexandria, VA: Alexandria Archaeology, Office of Historic Alexandria, 1991.)

43. Cressey, "Community Archaeology in Alexandria, Virginia," 1.

44. Cressey, "Community Archaeology in Alexandria, Virginia," 5.

45. Cressey, *Landmarks: 30 Years of Archaeology in Alexandria.* Pamela J. Cressey, *Walk and Bike the Alexandria Heritage Trail: Guide to Exploring a Virginia Town's Hidden Past.* (Dulles, VA: Capital Books, 2002.)

46. Preservation Alliance of Virginia, *Virginia's Economy and Historic Preservation: The Impact of Preservation on Jobs, Business, and Community* (Staunton: Preservation Alliance of Virginia, 1995), 4.

47. Pamela J. Cressey, "Community Archaeology in Alexandria, Virginia," in *Unlocking the Past: Celebrating Historical Archaeology in North America,* eds. Lu Ann De Cunzo and John H. Jameson, Jr. (Gainesville: University Press of Florida, 2005), 99.

48. Paul R. Mullins, "African-American Heritage in a Multicultural Community: An Archaeology of Race, Culture, and Consumption," *Places in Mind: Public Archaeology as Applied Anthropology*, eds. Paul A. Shackel and Erve J. Chambers (New York: Routledge, 2004), 59.

49. Mullins, "African-American Heritage in a Multicultural Community," 57–70.

50. Margaret C. Wood, "Moving Toward Transformative Democratic Action through Archaeolgy," 191. Barbara J. Little, "Archaeology and Civic Engagement," *Archaeology as a Tool for Civic Engagement*, eds. Barbara Little and Paul A. Shackel (Larham, MD: Rowman and Littlefield, 2007), 1–22.

51. Carol McDavid, "Beyond Strategy and Good Intention: Archaeology, Race, and White Privilege," *Archaeology as a Tool for Civic Engagement*, 67–88. David A Gadsby and Robert C. Chidester, "Heritage in Hampden: A Participatory Research Design for Public Archaeology in a Working-Class Neighborhood, Baltimore, Maryland," *Archaeology as a Tool for Civic Engagement*, 223–242. Anna S. Agbe-Davies, "Archaeology as Tool to Illuminate and Support Community Struggles in the Black Metropolis of the 20th and 21st Centuries." paper presented at the Society for Historical Archaeology meeting, Toronto, Canada, January 2009.

52. Leslie Allen, "Rally in the Alley," *Preservation* 52 (March/April 2000): 16–17.

53. Karolyn E. Smardz, "The Past through Tomorrow: Interpreting Toronto's Heritage to a Multicultural Public," *Presenting Archaeology to the Public: Digging for Truths*, ed. John H Jameson, Jr. (Walnut Creek, CA: Alta Mira Press, 1997), 101–113.

54 Laura Pabtie, "Photographers Put Past on Display," *Pittsburgh Post Gazette* (September 29, 2005): S-4.

55 Katie Zezima, "In Maine, Restoring History Long Hidden," *New York Times* (July 5 2005): B-5.

56 Hayden. *The Power of Place*, 95.

CHAPTER 3. AN EXPERIMENT IN NORTH ST. LOUIS

1. George Dorian Wendell, "Population Profile," *St. Louis Currents: A Guide to the Region and its Resources*, FOCUS, ed. (St. Louis: Missouri Historical Society Press, 1997), 15–17. James Neal Primm, *Lion of the Valley: St. Louis, Missouri*, second ed. (Boulder, CO: Pruett, 1990), 319–326, 479–504.

2. Eric Sandweiss, *St. Louis: The Evolution of an Urban Landscape* (Philadelphia: Temple University Press, 2001), 217–219. City Plan Commission of St. Louis, *Comprehensive City Plan* (St. Louis, MO: City Plan Commission of St. Louis, 1947), 35–40. Lana Stein, *St. Louis Politics: The Triumph of Tradition* (St. Louis: Missouri Historical Society Press, 2002), 85–97. Daniel J. Monti, *Race Redevelopment and the New Company Town* (Albany: State University of New York Press, 1990), 25–30, 42–44. Joseph Heathcott and Máire Agnes Murphy, "Corridors of Flight, Zones of Renewal: Industry, Planning, and Policy in the Making of Metropolitan St. Louis, 1940–1980," *Journal of Urban History* 6 (January 2005): 157–161. Primm, *Lion of the Valley*, 482.

3 Landmarks Association of St. Louis, *Newsletter* 34: 6 (1999): 1–4. Stein, *St. Louis Politics*, 114–115.

4 Primm, *Lion of the Valley*, 360–361. Carolyn Toft with Lynn Josse, *St. Louis: Landmarks and Historic Districts* (St. Louis, MO: Landmarks Association of St. Louis,

2002), 190–191. City Plan Commission of St. Louis, *Comprehensive City Plan*, 30–31. John A. Jakle and David Wilson, *Derelict Landscapes: The Wasting of America's Built Environment* (Lanham, MD: Rowman & Littlefield, 1992), 244–245.

5. Toft with Josse, *St. Louis: Landmarks and Historic Districts*, 190, 198–199. Patricia Degener, "Making Things Work in Soulard," *St. Louis Post Dispatch* (January 11, 1976): section J, 1.

6. Monti, *Race Redevelopment and the New Company Town*, 65–86.

7. Toft with Josse, *St. Louis: Landmarks and Historic*, 67–70. Roger H. Grant, Ron L. Hofsommer, and Osmund Overby, *St. Louis Union Station* (St. Louis, MO: St. Louis Mercantile Library, 1994), 59–90.

8. Tim Bryant, "Missouri Tax Credit is Spurring Development," *St. Louis Post Dispatch* (June 4, 1998), B1. "Missouri Historic Preservation Tax Credit Program," *St. Louis Post Dispatch* (November 5, 2001), Business Plus section, 8.

9. Missouri Department of Natural Resources, *Economic Impacts of Historic Preservation in Missouri* (Jefferson City: Missouri State Historic Preservation Office, 2001), 13.

10. Tavia Evans, "Developers Take Credits for Revival," *St. Louis Post Dispatch* (April 20, 2005): D1, D6.

11. Evans, "Developers Take Credits for Revival," D1, D6.

12. City Plan Commission of St. Louis, *Comprehensive City Plan*, Plate 13.

13. Miranda Rectenwald and Andrew Hurley, *From Village to Neighborhood: A History of Old North St. Louis* (St. Louis: Missouri Historical Society Press, 2004), 80–84.

14. Rectenwald and Hurley, *From Village to Neighborhood*, 85–91.

15. Rectenwald and Hurley, *From Village to Neighborhood*, 85–91.

16. Rectenwald and Hurley, *From Village to Neighborhood*, 91–92.

17. Laura Aldenfelder and Carolyn Toft, "SS. Cyril and Methodius Historic District," National Register of Historic Places Inventory-Nomination Form (St. Louis, MO: Landmarks Association of St. Louis, 1980). Jane M. Porter and Mary M. Stiritz, "Old North St. Louis Historic District," National Register of Historic Places Inventory-Nomination Form (St. Louis, MO: Landmarks Association of St. Louis, 1980). Mary M. Porter and Carolyn Toft, "Mullanphy Historic District," National Register of Historic Places Inventory-Nomination Form (St. Louis, MO: Landmarks Association of St. Louis, 1982).

18. Public Policy Research Center, University of Missouri–St. Louis, Application for Community Outreach Partnership Grant, Office of University Partnerships, U. S. Department of Housing and Urban Development, 2001, Factor 2, 1–4.

19. Public Policy Research Center, Application for Community Outreach Partnership Grant, Factor 3, 3. Public Policy Research Center, "UMSL Awarded $400,000 Grant for Old North St. Louis Project," *Interface* (Public Policy Research Center newsletter) 5 (Summer 2002): 1, 4.

20. Debbie Kiel, "Community Outreach Partnership Center Grant: Final Report. Environmental Health and Safety Activities," unpublished report on file at Public Policy Research Center, University of Missouri–St. Louis, 2004, 1–8. University of Missouri–St. Louis, "Final Progress Report, University of Missouri–St. Louis Community Outreach Partnership Center," on file in Public Policy Research Center, University of Missouri–St. Louis, 4–8.

21. University of Missouri–St. Louis, "Final Progress Report," 9–10.

22 Public Policy Research Center, Application for Community Outreach Partnership Grant, Factor 3, 8.

23 Public Policy Research Center, Application for Community Outreach Partnership Grant, Factor 3, 8–12. University of Missouri–St. Louis, "Final Progress Report." 10–11.

24. Old North St. Louis Restoration Group, "Strategic Plan, 2002–2005," unpublished report.

25. U.S. Department of Housing and Urban Development, Office of University Partnerships, available at http://www.oup.org/, accessed January 15, 2007.

26. Robert R. Weyeneth, "The Power of Apology and the Process of Historical Reconciliation," *Public Historian* 23 (Summer 2001): 27.

27. Aldenfelder and Toft, "SS. Cyril and Methodius Historic District." Porter and Stiritz, "Old North St. Louis Historic District." Porter and Toft, "Mullanphy Historic District."

28. Gloria Bratkowski, interviewed by Teresa Springer, November 19, 2002, 14–15, transcript on file in the Old North St. Louis Restoration Group office.

29. Rectenwald and Hurley, *From Village to Neighborhood*, 84–85.

30. Aldenfelder and Toft, "SS. Cyril and Methodius Historic District." Porter and Stiritz, "Old North St. Louis Historic District."

31. Zane Miller and Bruce Tucker, *Changing Plans for America's Inner Cities* (Columbus: Ohio State University Press, 1998), 89–91.

32. Rectenwald and Hurley, *From Village to Neighborhood*, 24–26, 29–31.

33. Carole Kammen, *On Doing Local History: Reflections on What Local Historians Do, Why, and What It Means* (Walnut Creek, CA: Alta Mira Press, 1995), 82.

34. James Neal Primm, "Missouri, St. Louis, and the Secession Crisis," *Germans for a Free Missouri: Translations from the St. Louis Radical Press, 1857–1862* , ed. and trans., Steven Rowan , (Columbia: University of Missouri Press, 1983), 3–22. Steven Rowan, "From 48er Radicalism to Working-Class Press: Franz Schmidt and the Freie Blätter of St. Louis, 1851–1853," *The German-American Radical Press: The Shaping of a Left Political Culture, 1850–1940*, eds. E. Shore, K. Fones-Wolf, and J. P. Danky (Urbana: University of Illinois Press, 1992), 31–48. Heinrich Boernstein, *Memoirs of a Nobody: The Missouri Years of an Austrian Radical 1849–1866*, ed. and trans. Steven Rowan (St. Louis: Missouri Historical Society Press, 1997), 292.

35. Perry Jaynes, "In Our Own Backyard: An Analysis of the Old North St. Louis Ceramic Assemblage," B.A. thesis, Department of Anthropology, University of Missouri, St. Louis, 2003.

36. Jeannette Lasansky, *Central Pennsylvania Redware Pottery, 1780–1904* (Lewisburg, PA: Union County Oral Traditions Project, 1979), 3–29. William C. Ketchum, Jr., *American Redware* (New York: Henry Holt, 1991), 81–93.

37. Mark D. Groover, *An Archaeological Study of Rural Capitalism and Material Life: The Gibbs Farmstead in Southern Appalachia, 1790–1920* (New York: Kluwer Academic/Plenum Publishing, 2003), 256–267.

38. William Hyde and Howard L. Conard, *Encyclopedia of the History of St. Louis: A Compendium of History and Biography for Ready Reference* (St. Louis, MO: Southern History Company, 1899), 142.

39. Catherine M. Barnes, "Broken Dishes: A Ceramic History of Old North St. Louis,' B.A. thesis, Department of Anthropology, University of Missouri, St. Louis, 2004.

40. Fred L. Israel, *1897 Sears Roebuck and Co. Catalogue* (Philadelphia: Chelsea House, 1993), 678.

41. Call-in comments of John Bratkowski, *St. Louis on the Air*, KWMU, May 10, 2005, available at http://www.kwmu.org/Programs/Slota/archivedetail.php?showid= 1703, accessed July 29, 2005.

42. Sean Thomas, executive director of the Old North Restoration Group, telephone interview with the author, March 12, 2008. In addition to the twenty town houses, thirty-two apartments in renovated buildings had been rented out to tenants and another eighty apartment units in rehabbed buildings were under construction. Also under way was the "Crown Square" development, offering 34,000 square feet of commercial space and two dozen historic loft apartments.

CHAPTER 4. HISTORY THAT MATTERS

1. Stephen G. Grable, "Applying Urban History to City Planning: A Case Study in Atlanta," *Public Historian* 1 (Summer 1979): 45–59.

2. Shelley Bookspan, "Liberating the Historian: The Promise of Public History," *Public Historian* 6 (Winter 1984): 62.

3. Paul S. Grogan and Tony Proscio, *Comeback Cities: A Blueprint for Urban Neighborhood Revival* (New York: Westview, 2000), 65–101. William Peterman, *Neighborhood Planning and Community-Based Development: The Potential and Limit of Grassroots Action* (Thousand Oaks, CA: Sage, 2000), 2–4. Leonard Pitt, "The 'Quiet Revolution': A History of Neighborhood Empowerment in Los Angeles," *Southern California Quarterly* 86:1 (2004): 65–82.

4. June Manning Thomas, "Neighborhood Planning: Uses of Oral History," *Journal of Planning History* 3 (February 2004), 58.

5. Thomas, "Neighborhood Planning: Uses of Oral History," 60–61.

6. Thomas, "Neighborhood Planning: Uses of Oral History," 55.

7. Elizabeth Pickard, "Opening the Gates: Segregation, Desegregation, and the Story of Lewis Place," *Gateway Heritage* 26 (Fall 2005): 16–27.

8. David T. Beito and Bruce Smith, "The Formation of Urban Infrastructure through Nongovernmental Planning: The Private Places of St. Louis, 1869–1920," *Journal of Urban History* 16 (May 1990): 264, 295.

9. Mary M. Stiritz and Carolyn Hewes Toft, "Lewis Place Historic District, National Register of Historic Places Inventory-Nomination Form," Landmarks Association of St. Louis, St. Louis, MO, 1979.

10. Pickard, "Opening the Gates," 23–26.

11. Beito and Smith, "The Formation of Urban Infrastructure through Nongovernmental Planning," 263–303.

12. James Buchanan, interview conducted by Elizabeth Pickard, May 13, 2005, transcript in author's possession.

13. Vernice Grace, interview conducted by Elizabeth Pickard, May 13, 2005, transcript in author's possession.

14. This information is based on informal conversations with members of the Lewis Place Improvement Association in 2007 and 2009.

15. Lewis Place Historical Preservation, "Opening the Gate," brochure, circa 2009, in possession of author.

16 Remarks of Pamela Talley, president of Lewis Place Historical Preservation, at the opening of "Point-of-View: Lewis Place," photography exhibit, Landmarks Association, St. Louis, MO, February 12, 2009.

17 Tim O'Neil, "Honoring a Struggle," *St. Louis Post Dispatch* (July 9, 2007): B1.

18. U.S. Bureau of the Census, *U.S. Censuses of Population and Housing: 1960. Census Tracts. Final Report PHC(1)-131* (Washington, DC: U.S. Government Printing Office 1962), 15, 23, 139, 147; U.S. Bureau of the Census, *Census of Population and Housing: 1970 Census Tracts. Final Report PHC(1)-181* (Washington, DC: U.S. Government Printing Office, 1972), P1, P3, P32, H1, H3, H32, P115, P117, P146; U.S. Bureau of the Census, *Census of Population and Housing: 1980. Census Tracts. Final Report PHC80-2-313* (Washington, DC: U.S. Government Printing Office, 1983), P1, P6, P66, H1, H6. H66, P328, P333, P393; City of St. Louis, U.S. Census 2000 Summary Files, St. Louis City Information Network, available at http://stlcin.missouri.org/census/sumtracts.cfm, summaries for Tracts 1181 and 1186, accessed June 12, 2006.

19. Forest Park Southeast Development Corporation, Forest Park Southeast Development Corporation, circa 2004, available at http://www.fpsedc.org, accessed March 18, 2007.

20. "Manchester Streetscape," Forest Park Southeast Development Corporation, 2009, available at http://www.fpsedc.org, accessed March 23, 2009.

21. "New Homes and Business Springing Up in Forest Park Southeast," *Community Journal* (Fall 2007): 6.

22. According to statistics from the 2000 Census, the district known as Jeff-Vander-Lou ranked among the lowest in the City of St. Louis in terms of household income and percentage of homeowners. One-quarter of all residential units lay vacant and over the previous decade the neighborhood had lost one-third of its population. City of St. Louis, U.S. Census 2000 Summary Files, St. Louis City Information Network, available at http://stlcin.missouri.org/census/sumtracts.cfm, summaries for Tracts 1211, 1212, accessed June 12, 2006,

23. D. D. Obika, "Scott Joplin Home Plans Resurrected," *St. Louis Post-Dispatch* (February 15, 1981), C2. "Macler Shepard: Founder and Chairman of Jeff-Vander-Lou Inc" (obituary), *St. Louis Post Dispatch* (October 25, 2005): B7.

24. Robert L. Koenig, "Plan for Restoring Scott Joplin Home on Upbeat," *St. Louis Post Dispatch* (April 25, 1983): 5A. Obika, "Scott Joplin Home Plans Resurrected," C2.

25. D. D. Obika, "Joplin Home Plan Studied," *St. Louis Post Dispatch* (March 15, 1981): B5. Tommy Robertson, "Joplin House Breaks Ground," *St. Louis Post Dispatch* (April 8, 1985): 3. Carlotta Lewis, Gary Walrath, and Delecia Huitt, "5 Year Operation Plan, Scott Joplin State Historic Site," Missouri Department of Natural Resources Report, 1999, 5–6, on file at Scott Joplin State Historic Site, St. Louis, MO

26. Lewis, Walrath, and Huitt, "5 Year Operation Plan," 3–4, 7, 44–45. Carolyn Hewes Toft with Lynn Josse, *St. Louis: Landmarks and Historic Districts* (St. Louis, MO: Landmarks Association of St. Louis, 2002), 91.

27. Benjamin S. Looker, *BAG: "Point at Which Creation Begins"* (St. Louis: Missouri Historical Society Press, 2004.)

28. Tim Woodcock, "Bill to Limit Unsavory Businesses in the Grove Causes Confusion," *West End Word* (February 5, 2008), available at http://www.westendword .com/NC/0/204.html, accessed December 17, 2009.

CHAPTER 5. MAKING A PLACE FOR NATURE

1. Laura A. Watt, Leigh Raymond, and Meryl L. Eschen, "Reflections on Preserving Ecological and Cultural Landscapes," *Environmental History* 9 (October, 2004): 622–625. William J. Murtagh, *Keeping Time: The History and Theory of Preservation in America* (Pittstown, NJ: Main Street Press, 1988), 23. Carol Shull and Dwight Pitcaithley, "Melding the Environment and Public History: The Evolution and Maturation of the National Park Service," *Public History and the Environment*, eds. Martin V. Melosi and Philip V. Scarpino (Malabar, FL: Krieger, 2004), 56–59. Rebecca Conard, "Spading Common Ground: Reconciling the Built and Natural Environments," *Public History and the Environment*, 7.

2. Conard, "Spading Common Ground," 8; Edward T. McMahon and Elizabeth A. Watson, "In Search of Collaboration: Historic Preservation and the Environmental Movement," *Information*, bulletin of the National Trust for Historic Preservation 71(1992), 4.

3. Dolores Hayden, *The Power of Place: Urban Landscapes as Public History* (Cambridge, MA: MIT Press, 1997), 20–21.

4. William Cronon, "The Trouble with Wilderness," *Uncommon Ground*, ed. William Cronon (New York: W.W. Norton, 1996), 69–90. Mark David Spence, *Dispossesing the Wilderness: Indian Removal and the Making of the National Parks* (New York: Oxford University Press, 1999). Anne Whiston Spirn, "Constructing Nature: The Legacy of Frederick Law Olmsted," *Uncommon Ground*, 91–113. David Glassberg, "Interpreting Landscapes," *Public History and the Environment*, 25. Stephen J. Pyne, *How the Grand Canyon Became Grand: A Short History* (New York: Penguin, 1998), 139–146.

5. Philip V. Scarpino, "The Creation of Place over Time: Interpreting Environmental Themes in Exhibit Format," *Public History and the Environment*, 139–153. Andrew Hurley, "Common Fields: An Introduction," *Common Fields: An Environmental History of St. Louis*, ed. Andrew Hurley (St. Louis: Missouri Historical Society Press, 1997), 1–11.

6. Charles E. Roe, "The Natural Environment," *A Richer Heritage: Historic Preservation in the Twenty-First Century*, ed. Robert E. Stipe (Chapel Hill: University of North Carolina Press, 2003), 247.

7. Watt, Raymond, and Eschen, "Reflections on Preserving Ecological and Cultural Landscapes," 621, 629–637. McMahon and Watson, "In Search of Collaboration," 4–5.

8. Roe, "The Natural Environment," 243. Michael J. Devine, "For the Preservationist," *History News* 45 (September/October, 1990): 34–35. James Park Sloan, "Watercourse of History," *Preservation* 48 (September/October 1996): 86–91.

9. Roe, "The Natural Environment," 238–239. Genevieve P. Keller and Timothy J. Keller, "Preserving Important Landscapes," *A Richer Heritage: Historic Preservation in the Twenty-First Century*, 196–197.

10. Roe. "The Natural Environment," 223–234.

11. Scarpinc, "Creation of Place over Time," 139–146. Glassberg, "Interpreting Landscapes," 23–29.

12 For an example of earlier variants of environmental protest among racial minorities, see Robert Gioielli, "Hard Asphalt and Heavy Metals: Urban Environmentalism n Postwar America" (Ph.D. dissertation, University of Cincinnati, 2008); Andrew Hurley, *Environmental Inequalties: Class, Race, and Industrial Pollution in Gary, Indiana, 1940–1980* (Chapel Hill: University of North Carolina Press, 1995); Matthew Candy, *Concrete and Clay: Reworking Nature in New York City* (Cambridge, MA: MIT Press, 2002), 153–186.

13 Robert D. Bullard, ed., *Unequal Protection: Environmental Justice and Communities of Color* (San Francisco: Sierra Club Books, 1994). Marianne Lavalle and Marcia Coyle, "Unequal Protection: The Racial Divide in Environmental Law," *National Law Journal* 15 (September 21, 1992): S1–S6. Christopher Foreman and Martin V. Melosi, "Environmental Justice: Policy Challenges and Public History," *Public History and the Environment*, 227–232.

14. Dawn Nothwehr and Sylvia Hood Washington, *Struggles for Environmental Justice and Health in Chicago: An African American and Catholic Perspective* (Chicago: John J. Egan Center, DePaul University, 2004). Ines Sommer, producer, *Struggles for Environmental Justice and Health in Chicago: African American and Catholic Perspectives*, video documentary (Chicago: Knights of Peter Claver, 2006). Sylvia Hood Washngton, "History by the People and for the People: Using Oral History/Memory for Environmental Justice," unpublished paper presented at the American Society for Environmental History meeting, Victoria, Canada, 2004.

15. River des Peres Watershed Coalition, available at http://www.thegreencenter .org/rdp/, accessed June 15, 2006.

16. Green Center, University City, MO. Untitled brochure, n.d.

17. Hugh Gorman, "Urban Areas, Environmental Decision Making, and Uses of History to Inform Public Choices," *Public History and the Environment*, 208–209.

18. Martin V. Melosi, "The Fresno Sanitary Landfill in an American Cultural Context," *Public Historian* 24 (Summer 2002): 17–35.

19. Gary L. Hightshoe, *Native Trees, Shrubs, and Vines for Urban and Rural America: A Planting Design Manual for Environmental Designers* (Reinhold, NY: Van Nostrand, 1988), 5–7. Andy Wasowski and Sally Wasowski, *The Landscaping Revolution: Garden with Mother Nature, not against Her* (Lincolnwood, IL: Contemporary Books, 2000), 1–64.

20. Robert Bittner, "Forest City: Detroit Works to Recover Its Historic Green Canopy," *Preservation* 54 (January/February 2002), 18–19. The Greening of Detroit, information available at http://www.greeningofdetroit.com, 2004–2006, accessed June 11, 2006.

21. Ann Breen and Dick Rigby, *The New Waterfront: A Worldwide Urban Success Story* (New York: McGraw Hill, 1996). Barry Shaw, "History at the Water's Edge," *Waterfronts in Post-Industrial Cities*, ed. Richard Marshall (London: Spon, 2001), 160–172. Bruce Ehrlich and Peter Dreier, "The New Boston Discovers the Old Tourism and the Struggle for a Livable City," *The Tourist City*, eds. Dennis R. Judd and Susan S. Fainstein (New Haven, CT: Yale University Press, 1999), 155–178. G. J.

Ashworth and J. E. Tunbridge, *The Tourist-Historic City: Retrospect and Prospect of Managing the Heritage City* (Amsterdam: Pergamon, 2000), 87–91. Larry R. Ford, *Cities and Buildings: Skyscrapers, Skid Rows, and Suburbs* (Baltimore, MD: Johns Hopkins University Press, 1994), 83–84, 115–119. Kent A. Robertson, "Downtown Redevelopment Strategies in the United States: An End-of-the-Century Assessment," *Journal of the American Planning Association* 61 (Autumn 1995), 429–437. Michael Fagence, "City Waterfront Redevelopment for Leisure, Recreation, and Tourism: Some Common Themes," *Recreation and Tourism as a Catalyst for Urban Waterfront Development: An International Survey*, eds. Stephen J. Craig-Smith and Michael Fagence (Westport, CT: Praeger, 1995), 135–156.

22. R. Timothy Sieber, "Waterfront Revitalization in Postindustrial Port Cities of North America," *City and Society* 5:2 (1991): 120–136. J. Goss, "Disquiet on the Waterfront: Reflections on Nostalgia and Utopia in the Urban Archetypes of Festival Marketplaces," *Urban Geography* 17 (1996): 221–247. Andrew Merrifield, "The Struggle over Place: Redeveloping American Can in Southeast Baltimore," *Transactions of the Institute of British Geographers* 18 (1993): 115–117. Christine M. Boyer, *The City of Collective Memory: Its Historical Imagery and Architectural Entertainments* (Cambridge, MA: MIT Press, 1994), 421–476. Michael Brill, "Transformation, Nostalgia, and Illusion in Public Life and Public Place," *Public Places and Spaces*, eds. Irwin Altman and Ervin H. Zube (New York: Plenum, 1989), 7–30. Robert Campbell, "The Lure of the Marketplace: Real-Life Theater," *Historic Preservation* 32 (January/February 1980): 46–49. Sharon Zukin, *Landscapes of Power: From Detroit to Disney World* (Berkeley: University of California Press, 1991), 25, 50.

23. See, especially, Dennis R. Judd, "Constructing the Tourist Bubble," *The Tourist City*, 35–53.

24. American Rivers, "South St. Paul Riverfront Design Workshop, April 18, 2001, Executive Summary," available at http://www.amrivers.org/docs/SSP.pdf, accessed September 7, 2003. Nebraska Department of Environmental Quality, "Environmental Update," Spring 2002, available at http://www.deq.state.ne.us/Newslett.nsf. Cooper, Robinson, and Partners, "The New Memphis Waterfront, Executive Summary," circa 2003, available at www.memphisriverfront.com/master_plan/masterplan_printable.cfm, accessed September 5, 2003. *Rivers of Steel*, available at http://www.riversofsteel.com, September 20, 2004. Gregory Korte, "City Plans Oasis on Riverfront," *Cincinnati Enquirer* (May 12, 2005): A1, A12. City of Pittsburgh, *The Riverfront Development Plan: A Comprehensive Plan for the Three Rivers* (Pittsburgh, PA, 1998).

25. Jennifer Price, "Paradise Reclaimed: A Field Guide to the LA River," *LA Weekly* (August 10–16, 2001): 23–29. Urban and Environmental Policy Institute at Occidental College, "Re-Envisioning the L.A. River and Los Angeles' Urban Environment," September 14, 2000, available at http://www.lariver.oxy.edu/events/brief/htm, accessed October 2002. Blake Gumprecht, *The Los Angeles River: Its Life, Death, and Possible Rebirth* (Baltimore, MD: Johns Hopkins University, 1999), 131–233. Jared Orsi, *Hazardous Metropolis: Flooding and Urban Ecology in Los Angeles* (Berkeley: University of California Press, 2004), 50–52, 102, 111–12.

26. "Newtown Creek Initiative," available at http://www.placeinhistory.org/Projects/NewtownCreek/NewtownCreekMainPage.htm, n.d., accessed, December 28, 2005.

27. City of Pittsburgh, *Riverfront Development Plan*. Lawrence R. Hajna, "Steeltown's Renaissance," *South Jersey Courier Post Online* (August 11, 2005), available at http://www.southjerseynews.com, accessed June 30, 2006.

28 Susan Hall and Connie Tomasula, *St. Louis Riverfront Trail Enhancements Plan* (St. Louis Planning and Urban Design Agency, 2001). Confluence Greenway brochure, circa 2001, in author's possession. Confluence Greenway, "The Confluence Greenway," background information sheet, circa 2001, in author's possession.

29. Kris Zapalac, Missouri Department of Natural Resources, State Historic Preservation Office, "A Heroine for Us All," handout for Mary Meachum Freedom Crossing publicity, June 2004, in author's possesssion. "Slaves Captured," *Missouri Republican*, May 22, 1855.

30. Grace Hill Settlement House, available at http://www.gracehill.org, n.d., accessed July 23, 2004.

31. Mary Meachum Freedom Crossing Design Team, "Community Design Workshop," March 2004, notes of meeting in author's possession.

32. Mary Meachum Freedom Crossing Design Team, "Community Design Workshop."

33. Colleen M. Hamilton, Cheryl A. Markham, and Joseph M. Nixon, *Report of Phase I Level Cultural Resource Survey of Proposed Bissell Point Treatment Plant Expansion Area, City of St. Louis, St. Louis County, Missouri* (St. Louis, MO: Havens & Emerson, Sverdrup Parcel and Metropolitan Sewer District of St. Louis, 1985).

34. F. Terry Norris, "Where Did the Villages Go? Steamboats, Deforestation, and Archaeological Loss in the Mississippi Valley," *Common Fields: An Environmental History of St. Louis*, 73–89.

35. John Vignali, interviewed by Holly Hughes, November 8, 2002, 7, transcript on file at the Old North St. Louis Restoration Group office, St. Louis, MO.

36. Ruth Gannaway, interviewed by Tom Harland, November 13, 2002, 4, transcript on file at the Old North St. Louis Restoration Group office.

37. Mike Genovese, interviewed by Miranda Rabus, November 19, 2002, 7, transcript on file at the Old North St. Louis Restoration Group office.

38. Anna Garamella, interviewed by Andrew Hurley, March 19, 2003, not transcribed, videotape in author's possession.

39. James Reid, interviewed by Andrew Hurley, May 16, 2003, 9, transcript on file at the Old North St. Louis Restoration Group office.

40. City Plan Commission of St. Louis, *St. Louis Riverfront* (St. Louis, MO, 1915), 21–30. A. S. Werrenmeyer, "The Municipal Docks," *Who's Who in North St. Loui.*, ed. North St. Louis Businessmen's Association (St. Louis:, MO: North St. Louis Businessmens Association, 1925), 148–150.

41. Andrew Hurley, "Floods, Rats, and Toxic Waste: Allocating Environmental Hazards since World War II," *Common Fields: An Environmental History of St. Louis*, 242–262.

42. Louise Thompson, interviewed by Teresa Springer, May 3, 2003, 5, transcript on file at the Old North St. Louis Restoration Group office. Vignali, interview, 7.

43. "City Authorizes Negotiations with Squatters," *St. Louis Post Dispatch* (April 16, 1959), A12.

44. Telephone conversation with Nicole Blumner, Project Director, St. Louis Development Corporation, October 5, 2004. Al Stamborski, "City Attempts to Retain, Grow Number of Businesses Along Riverfront Corridor," *St. Louis Post Dispatch* (October 29, 1999): C1. Doug Moore, "Slay, Green Now Squabble over Landing Land Swap, City Wants Gambling Center," *St. Louis Post Dispatch* (December 19, 2002): C1. Heather Cole, "City Planning Industrial Parks for North Riverfront," *St. Louis Business Journal* (October 13, 2003), available at http://stlouis.bizjournals.com/stlouis/stories/2003/10/13/story1.html, accessed December 22, 2009.

45 Telephone conversation with Douglas Eller, Family Support and Neighborhood Projects Director, Grace Hill Settlement House, and Project Director, Mary Meachum Freedom Crossing, July 30, 2004.

46 Gorman, "Urban Areas, Environmental Decision Making, and Uses of History to Inform Public Choices," 215.

47. McMahon and Watson, "In Search of Collaboration," 2–3.

48. Watt, Raymond, and Eschen, "Reflections on Preserving Ecological and Cultural Landscapes," 637–641. Glassberg, "Interpreting Landscapes," 30. Nora J. Mitchell and Katherine T. Lacy, "Reading Stories Written on the Land," *History News* 52 (Summer 1997): 26.

49. Portland Parks and Recreation, *South Waterfront Greenway Development Plan Design Component-Phase 1* (Portland, 2004). Randy Gragg, "Sight Lines: An Artful Integration," *Oregonian* (April 18, 2004): E1. "Portland Deserves Something Spectacular," *Oregonian* (November 28, 2007): B6.

CHAPTER 6. SCHOLARS IN THE ASPHALT JUNGLE

1. Dolores Hayden, *The Power of Place: Urban Landscapes as Public History* (Cambridge, MA: MIT Press, 1997), 76–77.

2. American Association of Museums, "Museums and Community Initiative," available at http://www.aam-us.org/sp/m-and-c.cfm, 1999, accessed September 28, 2007.

3. Robert Archibald, *The New Town Square: Museums and Communities in Transition* (Walnut Creek, CA: Alta Mira Press, 2004), 207.

4. Mariam C. Noland and Katie M. Goatley, "How Community Organizations Can Help Museums Fulfill Their Civic Missions," *Mastering Civic Engagement: A Challenge to Museums*, ed. American Association of Museums (Washington, DC: American Association of Museums, 2002), 49–56.

5. Judith Larsen, "Putting the Present into History: A Museum Challenges the Community to Listen to Today's Voices and Learn from its Past," *History News* 57 (Winter 2002): 22–25.

6. Irene Hirano, "A Public Service Responsibility," *Mastering Civic Engagement*, 77–78.

7. Jennifer Scott, "The Relevancy-Driven Museum," *Heritage365* 35 (2008): 8–25.

8. Rosann Guggino Garcia, "A Visible Community Center," *Mastering Civic Engagement* 65–67.

9. Marsha C. Jordan, "Building a Sense of Place through Exploring the 'Hood,'" *History News* 54 (Autumn 1999): 22–25.

10   Philip Nyden, "The Challenges and Opportunities of Engaged Research," *Scholarship in Action: Applied Research and Community Change*, ed. Linda Silka (Washington DC: U.S. Department of Housing and Urban Development, Office of University Partnerships 2006), 11–26.

11   Barbara Holland, "New Views of Research for the 21st Century: The Role of Engaged Scholarship," *Scholarship in Action*, 1–10.

12   Kenneth M. Reardon, "Participatory Action Research as Service Learning," *Academic Service Learning: A Pedagogy of Action and Reflection*, eds. Robert A. Rhoads and Jeffrey P. F. Howard (San Francisco: Jossey-Bass, 1998), 57–64.

13   Susan Dicklitch, "Human Rights-Human Wrongs: Making Political Science Real Through Service-Learning," *Service Learning in Higher Education*, ed. Dan W. Butin (New York: Palgrave Macmillan, 2005), 127–138.

14.   Robert A. Rhoads, "Critical Multiculturalism and Service Learning," *Academic Service Learning*, 42.

15.   Florence Fay Pritchard and George I. Whitehead, III, *Serve and Learn: Implementing and Evaluating Service-Learning in Middle and High Schools* (Mahwah, NJ: Lawrence Erlbaum Associates, 2004), 1–15.

16.   Dan W. Butin, "Preface: Disturbing Normalizations of Service-Learning," *Service Learning in Higher Education*, vii. Reardon, "Participatory Action Research as Service Learning," 57.

17.   Ira Harkavy and Bill M. Donovan, "Introduction," *Connecting Past and Present: Concepts and Models for Service-Learning in History,"* eds. Ira Harkavy and Bill M. Donovan (Washington, DC: American Association for Higher Education, 2000), 1.

18.   Albert Camarillo, "Reflections of a Historian on Teaching a Service-Learning Course about Poverty and Homelessness in America," *Connecting Past and Present*, 103–116. Michael Zuckerman, "The Turnerian Frontier: A New Approach to the Study of the American Character," *Connecting Past and Present*, 83–102.

19.   Linda Shopes, "Oral History and the Study of Communities: Problems, Paradoxes, and Possibilities," *Journal of American History* 89 (September 2002): 588–598.

20.   Shelley Bookspan, "Liberating the Historian: The Promise of Public History," *Public Historian* 6 (Winter 1984): 59–60.

21.   David Lowenthal, *Possessed by the Past: The Heritage Crusade and the Spoils of History* (New York: Free Press, 1996).

22.   Frans F. J. Schouten, "Heritage as Historical Reality," *Heritage, Tourism, and Society*, ed. David T. Hebert (London: Mansell, 1995), 21.

23.   Lowenthal, *Possessed by the Past*, 2–3. Also see, Paul A. Shackel, "Introduction: The Making of the American Landscape," *Myth, Memory and the Making of the American Landscape*, ed. Paul. A. Shackel (Gainesville: University of Florida, 2001), 1–16.

24.   Lowenthal, *Possessed by the Past*, 119.

25.   David Hamer, *History in Urban Places: The Historic Districts of the United States* (Columbus Ohio State Press, 1998), 83, 86–87, 101, 134.

26.   Robert Weible, "Lowell: Building a New Appreciation for Historical Place," *Public Historian* 6 (Summer 1984): 27–38. Hamer, *History in Urban Places*, 115–120.

27.   Cathy Stanton, *The Lowell Experiment: Public History in a Postindustrial City* (Amherst: University of Massachusetts Press, 2006), 112.

28. Paul R. Mullins, "African American Heritage in a Multicultural Community: An Archaeology of Race, Culture, and Consumption," *Places in Mind: Public Archaeology as Applied Anthropology*, eds. Paul A. Shackel and Erve J. Chambers (New York: Routledge, 2004), 57–69.

29. Robert Weyeneth, "History, He Wrote: Murder, Politics, and the Challenges of Public History in a Community with a Secret," *Public Historian* 16 (Spring 1994): 51–73.

30. "Robert Riggins, Business Owner, Church Volunteer," *St. Louis Post Dispatch* (April 19, 2006): D7.

31. Alan Downer, "Native Americans and Preservation," *A Richer Heritage: Historic Preservation in the Twenty-First Century*, ed. Robert E. Stipe (Chapel Hill: University of North Carolina Press, 2003), 405–422.

32. Angela Cavender Wilson, "Educating America: The Historian's Responsibility to Native Americans and the Public," *Perspectives: American Historical Association Newsletter* 38 (May 2000): 46–47. David Hurst Thomas, *Skull Wars: Kennewick Man, Archaeology, and the Battle for Native American Identity* (New York: Basic Books, 2000), 239–253.

33. Douglas W. Owsley and Richard L. Jantz, "Archaeological Politics and Public Interest in Paleoamerican Studies: Lessons from Gordon Creek Woman and Kennewick Man," *American Antiquity* 66 (October 2001): 565–575.

34. James H. Jones, *Bad Blood: The Tuskegee Syphilis Experiment* (New York: Free Press, 1981).

35. James Oliver Horton, "Slavery in American History: An Uncomfortable National Dialogue," *Slavery and Public History: The Tough Stuff of American Memory*, ed. James Oliver Horton and Lois E. Horton (New York: New Press, 2006), 50–53.

36. Mabel O. Wilson, "Between Room 307: Spaces of Memory at the National Civil Rights Museum," *Sites of Memory: Perspectives on Architecture and Race*, ed. Craig Evan Barton (Princeton, NJ: Princeton Architectural Press, 2001), 12.

37. Liz Ševčenko, Edgar W. Hopper, and Lisa Chice, *The Slave Galleries Restoration Project* (Washington DC: Americans for the Arts, n.d.), 7–8.

38. Helen Baldwin, et al., *Heritage of St. Louis* (St. Louis, MO: St. Louis Public Schools, 1964), 59.

39. Carol Kammen, "The Underground Railroad and Local History," *History News* 54 (Spring 1999): 3–4.

40. June Manning Thomas, "Neighborhood Planning: Uses of Oral History," *Journal of Planning History* 2 (February 2004): 67. Antoinette J. Lee, "The Social and Ethnic Dimensions of Historic Preservation," *A Richer Heritage*, 385–404.

41. Carol Shull and Dwight T. Pitchaithley, "Melding the Environment and Public History: The Evolution and Maturation of the National Park Service," *Public History and the Environment*, eds. Martin V. Melosi and Philip Scarpino (Malabar, FL: Krieger, 2004), 64.

42. Warren Lehrer and Judith Sloan, "Crossing the Boulevard," 2003, available at http://www.crossingtheboulevard.org, accessed December 21, 2007. Alyssa Wilson, "A Public History Evaluation of Crossing the BLVD: Strangers, Neighbors, Aliens in a New America," student paper for History 6012, University of Missouri–St. Louis, November 2007, 6.

43 Marie Tyler-McGraw, "Southern Comfort Levels: Race, Heritage Tourism, and the Civil War in Richmond," *Slavery and Public History*, 151–168. Jonathan I. Leib, "Robert E. Lee: 'Race,' Representation and Redevelopment along Richmond, Virginia's Canal Walk," *Southeastern Geographer* 44 (2004): 236–262.

44 Colin Bundy, "New Nation, New History? Constructing the Past in Post-Apartheid South Africa," ed. Hans Erik Stolten, *History Making and Present Day Politics: The Meaning of Collective Memory in South Africa* (Uppsala: Nordiska Afrikainstitutet, 2007), 79–81.

45 Truth and Reconciliation Commission, *Truth and Reconciliation Commission of South Africa Report*, vol. 1 (Cape Town Truth and Reconciliation Commission, 1998), 55. Desmond Mpilo Tutu, *No Future without Forgiveness* (New York: Doubleday, 1999), 26, 56, 218.

46. Truth and Reconciliation Commission, *Truth and Reconciliation Commission of South Africa Report*, vol. 1, 15–18. Richard A. Wilson, *The Politics of Truth and Reconciliation in South Africa: Legitimizing the Post-Apartheid State* (Cambridge, UK: Cambridge University Press, 2001), 51–54. Deborah Posel, "The TRC Report: What Kind of History? What Kind of Truth?" *Commissioning the Past: Understanding South Africa's Truth and Reconciliation Commission*, eds. Deborah Posel and Graeme Simpson (Johannesburg: Witwatersrand University Press, 2001), 147–172.

47. Willie Henderson, "Metaphors, Narrative, and 'Truth': South Africa's TRC," *African Affairs* 99 (July 2000): 457–465.

48. Mahmood Mamdani, "The Truth according to the TRC," *The Politics of Memory: Truth, Healing and Social Justice*, eds. Ifi Amadiume and Abdullahi an-Na'im (London: Zed Books, 2000), 176–183.

49. Elizabeth Stanley, "Evaluating the Truth and Reconciliation Commission," *Journal of Modern African Studies* 39:3 (2001): 525–546. Also, Elaine Unterhalter, "Truth Rather than Justice? Historical Narratives, Gender, and Public Education in South Africa," *History Making and Present Day Politics*, 100–102.

50. Ciraj Rassool, "The Rise of Heritage and the Reconstitution of History in South Africa," *Kronos* 26 (2000): 6.

51. Rassool, "The Rise of Heritage and the Reconstitution of History in South Africa," 14–15.

52. Anne E. Coombes, *History after Apartheid: Visual Culture and Public Memory in a Democratic South Africa* (Durham, NC: Duke University Press, 2003), 8. Also see the essays in Wilmot James and Linda Van de Vijver, eds. *After the TRC: Reflections on Truth and Reconciliation in South Africa* (Athens: Ohio University Press, 2001), especially Colin Bundy, "The Beast of the Past: History and the TRC," 9–20; and Posel and Simpson, *Commissioning the Past*.

53. Truth and Reconciliation Commission, *Truth and Reconciliation Commission of South Africa Report*, vols. 1, 2.

54. Stanley, "Evaluating the Truth and Reconciliation Commission," 530, 537.

55. Truth and Reconciliation Commission, *Truth and Reconciliation Commission of South Africa Report*, vol. 1, 110–114. Tutu, *No Future without Forgiveness*, 26.

56. Annette Bridges, public presentation, Scott Joplin State Historic Site, January 11, 2007 transcript in author's possession.

57. Matt Hall, "Home to Have Harmony Again," *St. Louis Post Dispatch* (August 26, 1986): 9A.

58. Parker Potter, Jr., *Archaeology in Annapolis: A Critical Approach to History in Maryland's Ancient City* (Washington, DC: Smithsonian Press, 1994), 40–42.

59. David Hurst Thomas, *Skull Wars*, 239–253.

60. For a more generalized advocacy of this position, see Michael P. Lynch, *True to Life: Why Truth Matters* (Cambridge, MA: MIT Press, 2005), 34.

CHAPTER 7. CONCLUSION

1. Stewart Brand, *How Buildings Learn: What Happens after They're Built* (New York: Viking, 1994).

2. Tom Graves, "An Exchange with Stewart Brand," *Preservation* 55 (May/June 2003): 24.

3. Carol Shull and Dwight T. Pithcaithley, "Melding the Environment and Public History: The Evolution and Maturation of the National Park Service," *Public History and the Environment*, eds. Martin V. Melosi and Philip Scarpino (Malabar, FL: Krieger, 2004), 64. Harry R. Rubenstein, "Good History Is Not Enough," *Perspectives: American Historical Association Newsletter* 38 (May 2000): 39–41.

4. Rebecca Yamin, "Alternative Narratives: Respectability at New York's Five Points," *The Archaeology of Urban Landscapes: Explorations in Slumland*, eds. Alan Mayne and Tim Murray (Cambridge, UK: Cambridge University Press, 2001), 166.

5. Robin Elisabeth Datel, "Preservation and a Sense of Orientation for American Cities," *Geographical Review* 75 (April 1985): 129.

6. Alan Mayne and Tim Murray, "The Archaeology of Urban Landscapes: Explorations in Slumland," *Archaeology of Urban Landscapes*, 1–7.

7. Yamin, "Alternative Narratives," 154–170.

8. Donald A. Ritchie, *Doing Oral History: A Practical Guide* (Oxford: Oxford University Press, 2003); Valerie Raleigh Yow, *Recording Oral History: A Practical Guide for the Humanities and Social Scientists* (Walnut Creek, CA: Alta Mira Press, 2003); Southern Oral History Progam, *Oral History: A Practical Guide* (Chapel Hill: University of North Carolina at Chapel Hill, Department of History, 2000); Linda Shopes, "Making Sense of Oral History," *History Matters: The U.S. Survey Course on the Web*, available at http://historymatters.gmu.edu/mse/oral/, February 2002.

9. Michael Frisch, *A Shared Authority: Essays on the Craft and Meaning of Oral and Public History* (Albany: State University of New York Press, 1990), 159.

10. Linda Shopes, "Oral History and the Study of Communities: Problems, Paradoxes, and Possibilities," *Journal of American History* 89 (September 2002): 588–598.

11. Paul R. Mullins, "African American Heritage in a Multicultural Community: An Archaeology of Race, Culture, and Consumption," *Places in Mind: Public Archaeology as Applied Anthropology*, eds. Paul A. Shackel and Erve J. Chambers (New York: Routledge, 2004), 64.

12. Parker B. Potter, Jr., *Public Archaeology in Annapolis: A Critical Approach to History in Maryland's Ancient City* (Washington, DC: Smithsonian Press, 1994), 194.

13. Tom Daykin, "Making Brewer's Hill More Affordable: Apartments Will Rent at Below Market Rates," *Milwaukee Journal Sentinel* (April 25, 2004): F1. Gina

Piccalo, "At the Corner of Have and Have Not: The Developers Meet the Downtrodden at Downtown's Alexandria Hotel," *Los Angeles Times* (May 22, 2005): E1. Bill Dries, "Life Downtown Gets Pricier—Some Ask: What about Average Wage Earners?" *Memphis Commercial Appeal* (May 13, 2005): A1.

14   National Park Service, U.S. Department of the Interior, "Affordable Housing through Historic Preservation," available at http://www.cr.nps.gov/hps/tps/Affordable/index.htm, accessed September 23, 2005.

15   Roy Lubove, *Twentieth Century Pittsburgh: The Post-Steel Era* (Pittsburgh, PA: University of Pittsburgh Press, 1996), 208–254. Richard Moe and Carter Wilkie, *Changing Places: Rebuilding Community in the Age of Sprawl* (New York: Henry Holt, 1997), 119–138. Nathan Weinberg, *Preservation in American Towns and Cities* (Boulder, CO: Westview, 1979), 107–119.

16.   Roberta Brandes Gratz, *The Living City: How Urban Residents Are Revitalizing America's Neighborhoods and Downtown Shopping Districts by Thinking Small in a Big Way* (New York: Simon and Schuster, 1989), 46–73. Richard Ernie Reed, *Return to the City: How to Restore Old Buildings and Ourselves in America's Historic Urban Neighborhoods* (Garden City, NJ: Doubleday, 1979), 72–83. Weinberg, *Preservation in American Towns and Cities*, 95–107.

17.   Arthur P. Ziegler, Jr., Leopold Adler III, and Walter C. Kidney, *Revolving Funds for Historic Preservation: A Manual of Practice* (Pittsburgh, PA: Ober, 1975). National Trust for Historic Preservation, "Revolving Funds," 2007, available at http://www.nationaltrust.org/revolving_funds/index.html, accessed June 7, 2007.

18.   Paul S Grogan and Tony Proscio, *Comeback Cities: A Blueprint for Urban Neighborhood Renewal* (Boulder, CO: Westview, 2000), 106–126. Debbie Howlett, "Home Is where the Hardhat Is," *Preservation* 51 (May-June 1999): 16–9. Jeff Horseman, "Development Does Not Have to Destroy," *The Capital* (March 8, 2005): A1.

Index

Andrew Hurley is Professor of History at the University of Missouri–St. Louis. He is the author of *Diners, Bowling Alleys, and Trailer Parks: Chasing the American Dream in Postwar Consumer Culture* and *Environmental Inequalities: Class, Race, and Industrial Pollution in Gary, Indiana, 1945–1980.*